Not Called

Not Called

Recovering the Biblical Framework
of Divine Guidance

Richard Kronk

Foreword by Tim Crouch

WIPF & STOCK · Eugene, Oregon

NOT CALLED
Recovering the Biblical Framework of Divine Guidance

Copyright © 2022 Richard Kronk. All rights reserved. Except for brief quotations in critical publications or reviews, no part of this book may be reproduced in any manner without prior written permission from the publisher. Write: Permissions, Wipf and Stock Publishers, 199 W. 8th Ave., Suite 3, Eugene, OR 97401.

Wipf & Stock
An Imprint of Wipf and Stock Publishers
199 W. 8th Ave., Suite 3
Eugene, OR 97401

www.wipfandstock.com

PAPERBACK ISBN: 978-1-6667-1871-3
HARDCOVER ISBN: 978-1-6667-1872-0
EBOOK ISBN: 978-1-6667-1873-7

01/17/22

Unless otherwise indicated, all Scripture quotations are taken from the Holy Bible: New American Standard Version® (NASB®), copyright © 1971, 1977, 1995 by The Lockman Foundation. Used by permission of Thomas Nelson, Inc. All rights reserved.

Scripture quotations are from the Holy Bible: New International Version® (NIV®) are copyright © 1973 by The New York Bible Society International and 1978 by the New York International Bible Society. Used by permission of The Zondervan Corporation, Inc. All rights reserved.

To Denise, my long-term partner in this journey. Apart from God, no one understands better the questions and experiences that compelled me to write this book. Eternally grateful that God called us both to himself and continues to lead us in this journey we share together.

If you don't have a definite call to stay here, you are called to go.
—KEITH GREEN

Contents

List of Tables | ix
Foreword by Tim Crouch | xi
Preface | xv
Acknowledgments | xxi
Introduction | xxiii
Endnotes | xxvii

Section 1: Where We Are and How We Got Here: A Contemporary Understanding of the Call of God | 1

1 Collin's Story | 3
2 The Call of God: A Historical Survey | 9
3 The Call of God: A Contemporary Understanding | 32

Section 2: Biblical, Cultural, and Practical Challenges to the Contemporary Understanding of the Call of God | 71

4 What Does the Bible Say? | 73
5 Cultural Challenges | 107
6 Practical Challenges | 149

Section 3: A Proposed Reimagining of What It Means to Be Called of God | 177

7 The Call of God: A New Proposal | 179
  Endnotes | 207

Bibliography | 225

List of Tables

Table 1: Call of God Survey Demographics | 47

Table 2: Calling Distribution | 48

Table 3: Two Views of Calling | 61

Table 4: Calling in the Old Testament | 79

Table 5: Common Elements in the Call Narratives of Old Testament Prophets | 82

Table 6: Calling in the Gospels | 85

Table 7: Paul's Statement on the Divine Origin of His Apostleship | 94

Table 8: Types of Biblical Guidance | 199

Foreword

> "Prepare the way for the Lord, make straight paths for him.
> Every valley shall be filled in, every mountain and hill made
> low. The crooked roads shall become straight, the rough
> ways smooth. And all people will see God's salvation"
>
> (LUKE 3:4-6 NIV).

THE GOD WHO CREATED this world is up to something amazing on its behalf. John the Baptist, in the days before Jesus began to minister, drew on ancient words of the prophet Isaiah to make it clear that God's plan to save the world would be his own doing. A straight and level path out of the wilderness were something that God would have to make, himself. It's his doing.

The New Testament good news that John began declaring was that God would do this through His Son, Jesus. And Jesus, when he'd conquered the barriers of sin and flaws, told his disciples that, when the Holy Spirit fell upon them, they'd be the witnesses that would assure all flesh would indeed see the salvation of God. This Triune God—it's his doing.

I love Luke's rendering of the Isaiah-and-Baptist words because they remind us that God's plan for all humans of all nations is in his hands. God does not need us—or any particular ones of us—to bring this about. Nor has he asked any one of us to run out and do something for him. His call is not a divine "get 'er done." Rather, he announces what he's up to and asks us all to "prepare the way"—to bring our hearts on board with the wonder of what he's doing, to live in the light of it.

God's call to his people to live their lives in tune with his salvation purposes, to be witnesses of them, has been understood variously through the centuries. For generations, followers of Christ have struggled to understand the notion of being called by God. Often, we gravitate toward an understanding that we, or at least a special some of us, are called out of normal life (whatever that is) to do something more specific or more special delegated to us by God. And we'd better get it right.

For one, this might be separation from the world to a life of ascetic devotion and solitude, while for another, it is a call to activism, heroism, or even the dangerous idea of God-ordained authority. Wondering or fretting or even presuming about that type of calling, searching for it and convincing our children they must search for it, has too much shaped the lives and experience of many believers in Jesus. Whether monks of medieval days or nervous teenagers navigating educational and vocational decisions today, Jesus's people can work themselves into quite a tizzy when the notion of calling gets twisted away from the basic fact that God is the one on the move. God is solidly in control of a good plan that he's moving forward to a conclusion worthy of his goodness. He's not desperate to get us to assume a role he needs us to play but that we might miss. He's calling us to join in the reality of who he is and what he's doing.

In the volume in your hands, Rick Kronk helps us to step back and see that our understanding of the call of God can be driven by our own assumptions about it. It can become time-twisted or culture-twisted—reshaped into an idea more of our making than of God's good revelation. "What am I here to do?" can rise like an idol, towering above "Whose am I?" We can wander far afield, searching for the game plan of God's rather than for God. We can label life choices as holy and not, as God's best and runners-up, in ways God never intended.

More than this, dominating but questionable notions can also exclude many who hope in Jesus but live without the kind of privilege that makes it easy for some of us to believe we are able, and required, to chart out life's journey in advance. A view of calling as a me-centered reality that God has prepared for each, individual one of us to find as we study, plan, marry (or not), start families (or not), and climb life's ladders is likely too narrowly bound to our own time and cultural setting to be what the God of salvation-for-all-peoples is likely intending for all his own.

Make no mistake, the sweeping plan of God that all peoples of the world will see his salvation can have life-altering implications for any of us. God is up to something in this world: it is about his intention to restore the life-in-him he intends for all peoples of the world, and he wants those who've received it to share it with others who've not heard. Mission organizations like the one I lead and schools like the one where Rick Kronk teaches will continue to need to prepare and field those who know God has led them to go to those still least-impacted by his good plans. God will speak to our hearts, stir our values, direct our paths, and move us by his Spirit.

But Rick Kronk is right that God's calling is more about the recognition that we are to live in relationship with a God-on-the-move, discovering often what it will mean, than it is about capturing, once and for all, some full script we believe he's written out just for us. These chapters show us that God's purposes move steadily toward their ends as God orchestrates goodness. He's not desperate that we guess it all right and not frustrated by our failure to figure it out or obey it. He's asking us to "come, follow me," to "seek first my kingdom and righteousness," and to see how all the other pieces come together as our very real and different lives are lived out in trust, obedience, and readiness. This is how we "prepare the way for the Lord" in our own lives. And it is a good journey, because it is more his than mine. As I live my life in light of his good purposes, understand they are purposes for all peoples of our planet, and submit myself to him and this story, I can trust that I'll hear his voice and be ready to help me give my yes. In fact, may this read be one that draws many to say yes daily to the way-maker God.

Dr. Timothy Crouch
Vice President for Alliance Missions, C&MA US
December 27, 2021

Preface

SO WHY ANOTHER BOOK dealing with the question of the call of God? As a former missionary and mission agency administrator and a current missions professor, I have interacted both personally and professionally with this concept for over thirty years. My efforts to come to grips with this question have given rise to the following concerns:

Despite the familiarity with the general concept of what it means to receive a call from God to vocational Christian service, surveys of mostly college students reveal a striking level of uncertainty with regards to how one receives such a call and how it is to be interpreted. Students often describe their perceived call in terms of a mystical experience that often becomes (at least part of) the basis for selecting a college major, a spouse, and a career. Given the magnitude of the importance of these decisions in an increasingly complex world, is an appeal to a highly mystical, loosely defined experience sufficient?

With regards to religious organizations such as missions agencies or local churches, assessing a prospective candidate's suitability for employment often includes an attempt to validate a candidate's call to ministry. There is a deep significance associated with such a perceived call both for the candidate who (for reasons we will explore later) has correlated the idea of a divine call with that of ministry vocation as well as for the agency/organization that is concerned not just about getting the "right people on the bus" but keeping them there as well. Results from the ReMAP II[1] research confirm both of these points by noting that "we have yet to meet a long-term missionary who has not felt that a personal sense of call was utterly vital to their own missionary journey" and that the notion of "calling" received an extremely high rating for missionary significance and performance from mission agencies, resulting in improved rates of retention of missionaries. Overall, the research indicated that a clear sense of calling was of even greater consequence for retention than pre-field ministry experience in a local church.

Nevertheless, despite the importance attached to the notion of a call for the ministry candidate, the research team also acknowledged that "knowing what a 'call' is proves a much harder question to answer."[2] But this begs the question, if having an experience of a divine call is of such importance for both the missionary candidate and the prospective agency, should there not be more clarity as to what a divine call is? Furthermore, does it make sense for both sides to place such importance on something that remains so loosely defined and personally interpreted? Is it not possible that potential ministry candidates who come with the expectation of a divine call first appropriate life circumstances, feelings, and encounters and then borrow the vocabulary of the expected reality in order to satisfy the perceived criteria of the interviewing agency? In response to this possibility, agencies commit themselves to confirming the reality of the call via references, ministry experience, and various assessments. And yet, if it is already admitted that the definition of a divine call is unclear, then what exactly are the efforts to validate such a call actually validating?

The challenge in all of this is, in part, at least, due to the fact that the criteria used to validate a divine call are based (as will be shown) on varying definitions of the concept, despite the agreement over the difference between a primary call to salvation and a subsequent call to vocational ministry. But even here, theological, philosophical, and cultural influences have given rise to further considerations that seek to distinguish between what are referred to as the internal (or secret) call and its external confirmation. In addition, some distinguish different kinds of vocational calls: one that applies strictly to men as a qualifying criterion for pastoral ministry and another that applies to both men and women who feel directed toward cross-cultural missionary service. Given this range of prospective meaning, it is evident that there is no common understanding of the experience of a divine call, neither what it means nor how one receives it. In light of this, to what extent is it meaningful for a religious organization to attempt to measure something that is described in largely personal and mystical terms against a definition and set of criteria that are so open to debate?

Preface

Beyond the philosophical and practical concerns associated with the expectation of a call of God as an essential criterion for religious vocation, the world in which we live is increasingly complex and demands an increasingly complex blend of skills and resources needed to respond to the ever-changing nature of ministry opportunities. In light of this global complexity, is a call to ministry sufficient? How does such a call fit with the additional experience and skills that are essential to a particular ministry role? Relatedly, is a call so essential to the ministry role, such that those who cannot give sufficient evidence of such should be considered ill-equipped and therefore unqualified?

As will be shown later, much of the confusion surrounding the meaning and implication of a call to vocational ministry is related to the historical evolution of the concept. The current understanding of the call of God (at least as it is processed in the West) has its roots in medieval Catholic theology and the distinction between clergy who received a "vocation" (call) and the laity who did not. With the advent of the Protestant Reformation, theological shifts in ecclesiology and the identity of the believer and his/her relationship to society affected this issue of calling by removing the hard clergy/laity distinction and enlarging and, eventually, all but equating vocation (call) with work. But the evolution of the concept did not end there. The rise of individualism in the wake of the Enlightenment and the emergence of career choice in democratized societies that profited fully from the Industrial Revolution have also influenced how we understand the call of God, such that now, calling is no longer necessarily associated with a religious experience whatsoever.[3] But the question remains, can we honestly say that Paul's understanding of his call as an apostle received while on the road to Damascus is at all similar to a twenty-something college student's good feeling about helping poor people, when she then decides to study social work so she can maybe work with a local foodbank when she graduates?

Finally, the Bible makes it clear that God's salvific interest and involvement in our lives as his children are both intentional—God speaks (Heb 1:1–2), God loves (John 3:16), God saves (Eph 2:8–10)—and also comprehendable—his divine power has granted to us everything pertaining to life and godliness, through the true knowledge of him who called us (2 Pet 1:3). In other words, what God has accomplished for us in Christ is both purposeful and knowable (even if only partially).

Furthermore, this active salvific engagement between God and mankind is necessarily transhistorical as well as transcultural. The argument throughout the New Testament is that there is (no longer) any distinction between the Jew and the Greek (Rom 10:12, Gal 3:28, among others). All, regardless of race, ethnicity, social status, or gender, may receive the fullness of salvation through Christ (Rom 1:16). And though this became explicitly clear in Paul's writings—especially Romans and Galatians—the inclusion of the nations in the salvific blessing of God is present throughout the Old Testament, as revealed through the Abrahamic covenant (Gen 12), in which God promised to bless all nations.

If the experience of salvation that reconciles us to God is inherently transcultural and transhistorical, is this not also the case for the divine intent for mankind, as noted in the cultural mandate (Gen 1:27–28)? In other words, if the primary call of God is equally applied to all, does not the secondary call of God, by necessity, also require a transcultural and transhistorical application, such that no one is excluded on the basis of race, ethnicity, social class, or gender? Are we in agreement with Luther then when he argues that the clergy-laity distinction that elevates those who pursue a religious vocation above those who do not is simply a denial of the spiritual equality of all believers?

> It is pure invention that pope, bishop, priests, and monks are called the spiritual estate while princes, lords, artisans, and farmers are called the temporal state. This is indeed a piece of deceit and hypocrisy. Yet no one need be intimidated by it, and for this reason: all Christians are truly of the spiritual estate and there is no difference among them except that of office. Paul says in 1 Corinthians 12 that we are all one body, yet every member has its own work by which it serves the others. This is because we are all Christians alike; for baptism, gospel, and faith alone make us spiritual and a Christian people.[4]

If this is so, then given our current understanding and use of the call of God as a vocational/career indicator, what about those for whom career choice is not possible? Can the Dalit[5] who is subject to caste considerations actually pursue a call as a cross-cultural missionary or a school teacher or a doctor? Can a Chinese believer bound by filial piety exercise his or her divine call at the expense of parental obligation? Our expectation that this is possible without consideration for the cultural and societal influences in India or China suggests that we may have appropriated Western, individualistic, career-choice philosophy into the meaning and use of the call of God and made it into a largely religious means of answering the arguably First World question "What do you want to be when you grow up?" This result raises the question of just how far modern, Western Christianity has deviated from the biblical meaning and application of the concept.

In light of the above concerns, this book seeks to accomplish several things:

1. Give voice to hundreds of mostly college students as they describe their understanding of the call of God: what they think it means and how they think they may have received one or not.
2. Compare differing definitions and understandings of the call that are advocated by various denominations and organizations as a factor associated with religious vocation.
3. Evaluate current (broad) understandings and uses of the call of God in light of historical influences.
4. Appeal to a fresh look at the biblical data with regards to the notion of a vocational call as distinct from a soteriological call.
5. Offer a way forward that draws meaning primarily from the Bible, seeks to clarify how a vocational call can be understood and referenced, and reduces the confusion and uncertainty often associated with validating a call of God.

To do so, this book is organized into three sections. Section 1 deals with a review of contemporary understandings of the call of God and offers a historical summary of how the concept has evolved in the Western tradition. Section 2 discusses a range of challenges to contemporary understandings and uses of the call of God in light of biblical, cultural, and practical challenges to these understandings. And finally, in section 3, an attempt is made to offer a reimagining of what it means to be called of God that serves believers across the scope of national, cultural, and social strata now and into the future.

Acknowledgments

Like a fine wine or a good cheese, the best things in life are often a long time in the making. It would be inappropriate to suggest that what is found between the covers of this book could in any way be considered one of the finer things of life, but it has been a long time in the making.

Like wine and cheese, books are not made alone in a corner. The thoughts and questions posed across these pages are ones that I have asked myself, yes, but, more frequently, have asked of others. And so it is to them that I give thanks—to all those colleagues, students, and friends who have been courageous enough to join me in asking hard questions and pursuing answers that satisfy. So thanks to Steve and Beth, Keith and Karen, Alice, Cindy, Dan, William and Joanie, Marianne, Roy and Jennifer, Dan and Lois, James and Polly, and Jim who, in their unknown and often invisible way, helped me articulate the questions that eventually led me to the answers.

The challenge of writing is only matched by the challenge of research. And when it is done at the same time as the demands of a full-time teaching schedule, other assets are needed. And so, a special shout-out to Torri who kept the articles and books flowing my way nearly as fast as I could request them and to Abigail whose eye for detail helped bring the manuscript into its final form.

A special thanks to those who were gracious to give time and effort to reading the early manuscript and offering great comments and provoking questions, all in an effort to make this final product both coherent and edifying. To Ken, Phil, Herb, and Margaret I am deeply grateful. The strengths of this work are a credit to their insightful and loving critique. Whatever weaknesses that remain are on me.

Finally, I want to express my deep love and affection for my wife of nearly four decades who has had a front-row seat in this journey of mine and ours as I/we try to follow through on the call of God. I can't say enough to thank her for her unflagging support and encouragement, especially when answers to the questions I was asking were not forthcoming. Little did she know that when she said yes all those years ago, this is what it would mean.

Introduction

IN JULY OF 2013, my wife and I packed up our things and returned to the US after nearly eighteen years of missionary activity in France and Germany that ranged from evangelism and discipleship to administration. Our high expectations of church planting success among Muslims had been worn down over time as the complexity of the task, mixed with personnel challenges and opposition from other missionaries, played out in almost daily battles. Yes, we had seen Muslims come to faith. Some had been baptized. A few were continuing in their walk with Christ, though it seemed as though they were never very far from being overwhelmed by the pressure from unconverted family members and the never-ending challenges of social and economic instability as immigrants.

Our decision to leave the field after all those years was not due to some major falling-out with other team members or our mission administration. Neither our kids nor our marriage were in crisis. Our roles in the organization had not been taken from us. But we were leaving, and it was probably for good; we wouldn't be coming back. Despite our years of service, as we packed our container and boarded the plane that would fly us back to the US, we were taking part in the process of attrition—leaving our assignment before fulfilling its ultimate goal.

Looking back over those many years, it could be said that we had accomplished what we had committed to doing when we, along with hundreds of others, said yes to pursuing a missionary career on a December evening in 1981 at the Urbana Missions Conference—even though we had not realized the outcome of a sustainable, reproducing church among North African Muslim converts. And yet, there is a certain feeling of dissatisfaction in the back of my mind when I think about and talk about our missionary years. This barely perceptible disappointment is not so much related to the going where we went or the doing what we did but to the leaving of the missionary field and the transition to a new life and ministry reality in the US. In reflecting back on our missionary years, which came to an end some eighteen years after they began, I couldn't help but ask the obvious question, "Was I, were we, called to this work?" If so, what does that mean if we leave our missionary assignment—for whatever reason? Have we somehow failed God? Is a call to missionary service (or other ministry, for that matter) irrevocable? Can it change? If so, what legitimizes a change in ministry or a departure from it?

The journey that took us to our missionary assignment began in 1981 when Denise and I, along with some 17,000 others, attended the Urbana Missions Conference at the Urbana-Champaign University campus. The theme of the gathering was "Let Every Tongue Confess That Jesus Christ Is Lord." Over the course of the four-day conference, we were both overwhelmed by the information concerning the state of the Great Commission relative to the remaining task at hand, as well as moved by the possibility of becoming an active part of the missionary enterprise. I still remember comments like "There are more missionaries to Eskimos than to the entire Muslim world" (nearly 800,000 Muslims at that time) and "Muslims, it's their turn!"

On the last evening of the conference, Denise and I both filled out and signed the World Evangelism Decision Card on which we acknowledged that we believed it was God's will for us to serve him abroad and that we would pray and make inquiry to that end. Furthermore, we pledged to begin a systematic study about world missions, make plans to participate in a summer missions program, and seek further training for preparation to become missionaries.

Following the Urbana '81 conference, I returned to Michigan State University where, two years later, I finished my bachelor of science degree in civil engineering. In 1983, I married Denise Edwards, a graduate, like me, from MSU's engineering program (electrical) and a fellow attendee of the '81 Urbana Missions Conference.

It is worth noting that Denise and I had begun dating in the fall of 1981, just a few months before the conference kicked off during Christmas break of that same year. We were both active in our respective campus ministries, she with InterVarsity, me with Campus Crusade for Christ. Our dating life included prayer and Bible reading/discussion from the beginning, and our participation in the Urbana Conference later that year was a logical attempt to answer the questions "What is God's will for our lives?" and, relatedly, "What has God 'called' us to do?"

Over the course of the fifteen years following the Urbana gathering, Denise and I made plans to follow through on what we believed to be God's will for us: to serve in an overseas, cross-cultural missionary context. Our preparations included working several years as engineers in industry while we built relationships with international students, completion of four-year master's of theology degrees from Dallas Theological Seminary, and successful application to serve under Christar (formerly, International Missions, Inc.) in a church-planting capacity in France among North African Muslim immigrants. In December of 1995, Denise and I, along with our two children, boarded a plane from Minneapolis to Lyon, France. As mentioned earlier, we spent the next eighteen years in missionary service and returned permanently to the US in 2013.

Our return to the US was precipitated by a number of things that commonly recur in the stories of missionaries who return to their places of origin following international service: a growing sense of disconnect from effective ministry (we had moved to Germany when France continued to deny a renewal to our visa), declining finances and increasing costs (resulting in cashing in retirement funds to pay our annual tax bill), major life changes for our young adult children (weddings and new college enrollment), and increased opportunity to contribute differently to the missionary endeavor (as a theology/missions educator).

Studies of missionary attrition commonly acknowledge the challenges related to raising children, health and medical concerns, finances, and, famously, inter-missionary conflict as leading reasons why people leave their place of missionary service. What is remarkable in these studies is not so much the causes of conflict (we are human, after all) or the existence of life-challenging circumstances that missionaries face, but the fact that these complications lead to rates of attrition on the order of 5 percent per year. Furthermore, of those who do leave ministry service, 71 percent do so for what are considered to be preventable reasons![6] In short, our departure, though part of our personal story, was not unique.

A 5 percent annual attrition rate translates into a loss of nearly 20 percent (or more) of the missionary workforce over the course of a traditional four-year term of service. Research into the reasons for attrition attempt to distinguish between preventable and non-preventable causes. The so-called non-preventable side of the ledger includes such things as retirement, unforeseen health concerns, unstable economic and/or political environments of host countries, and natural disasters that oblige non-citizens to repatriate for at least some time as long as conditions are unfavorable to the missionary endeavor. On the preventable side are such things as lack of home support, problems with peers, inadequate pre-field preparation, and lack of "call."[7]

So if, as noted by mission-related attrition studies, the lack of call is considered to be a factor in premature departure from missionary service, then what actually constitutes a call of God? How is a call received? Is it limited to what we consider to be vocational ministry (missionary or pastoral) service, and is it necessary for such service? If so, how is it validated? Can a call be changed or revised? If so, how? What happens if a call isn't realized, due to health or finances or other issues? And what does one do about his or her call when in a relationship (dating or marriage) in which the other person does not seem to share the same call? In addition to these questions, the understanding of calling historically and culturally must also be raised, for if a "call of God" is indeed necessary for ministry service, then it must be historically and transculturally realizable. Finally, what are the biblical parameters that define this call, and how do they apply to individual members of the church?

Endnotes

1. The ReMAP II (Reducing Missionary Attrition Project) was undertaken by the Mission Commission of the World Evangelical Alliance. Results were published in book form in 2007, edited by Hay et al., under the title of *Worth Keeping: Global Perspectives on Best Practices in Missionary Retention*. The project was a multi-national collaborative effort by a team of researchers who conducted a survey of active missionaries in twenty-two countries on six continents (23). The data base collected by these surveys represents nearly 40 percent of the global missionary force today (3).
2. Hay et al., *Worth Keeping*, 95.
3. See Duffy and Sedlacek, "Presence of and Search for Calling," 592.
4. Froehlich, "Luther on Vocation," 201.
5. Dalits are one of many lower castes in India that are also referred to as "Untouchables." Rules of caste dictate everything from social standing and relationships to employment. With regards to the Dalits, their place in Indian society has been relegated to some of the lowest of the low, which has obliged them to take employment oriented to such things as sewer cleaning, animal carcass disposal, and garbage collecting.
6. Taylor, *Too Valuable to Lose*, 13.
7. Taylor, *Too Valuable to Lose*, 10.

―――― *Section 1* ――――

Where We Are and How We Got Here
A Contemporary Understanding of the Call of God

1

Collin's Story

COLLIN IS A RECENT graduate of a Christian college that is located in the American South. While a student, Collin pursued a degree in outdoor leadership and communication. In addition to his studies, Collin played basketball on the college team and served in various volunteer ministry roles. When asked about his future following college, this is what he said:

> OK, yeah, so I feel called to work with Muslim youth, and it is kind of an interesting way that it came about. So, during the summer between my sophomore and junior year of college I worked at a camp in North Carolina. During staff training, our leader said to go be out in nature and creation in order to connect with the Lord and spend time listening to him through creation. So, I went over to a river and was praying and contemplating the stream and was drawing different connections to God in our lives as believers with the river, which was really cool. I went back to where our main camp was and pulled out the only little Scripture that I had, which was a little booklet of John and I was like, "I wonder if there's something about water in here."
>
> And so I thumbed through John at the campground where we were camping and came to the spot in John 7 where Jesus was talking about streams of living water. I got really excited because of the connection in Scripture to the stream I was just at. From there I was intrigued and wanting to keep thinking and learning about that.

From there, I came back to our main staff housing area and was thumbing through the bookshelf, which I've done before. But I just happened to look at it again and I'm going through, I'm going through, I'm going through, and then I see a book that I never saw before called *Streams of Living Water*. I was surprised and excited because I had just been thinking about that. So I decided that I was going to read this.

So, I read the whole book. And there were two things I took away. One of them was that the Holy Spirit is a very key element in walking with Christ. And the second one was when I came across a spot where Brother Yun was talking about how you can serve and follow Christ wherever you are. He then mentioned Muslims, and I couldn't move past and was drawn into that word. And I was thinking that it was the Lord kind of like stopping me there.

And I then was thinking, "OK, so you're wanting me to reach Muslims, Jesus?" I was then thinking, how in the world would I reach Muslims? And I was thinking back over my life and I was like, "Well, I've worked with youth my whole life. So I guess I could work with Muslim youth."

And kind of since then, that's kind of been what I feel I've been called to. And I've seen things that seem to line up with that conclusion like various books and classes I've had while also meeting more Islamic people. And I just see my own heart for Muslim people growing, like eating up classes on Islamic related things. And so, yeah, that's kind it's kind of how I came to consider that I think I am called to work with Muslims, especially Muslim youth.[1]

Collin's story exhibits several common ideas related to the concept of calling. First is the idea that calling is something that comes from God. As Collin processed the various pieces of discovery which seemed to center around water, he was convinced that if what he was experiencing was some kind of message, that the message was indeed from God. His question, "OK, so you're wanting me to reach Muslims, Jesus?" reflects his understanding that if there was any sort of life-direction in what he was experiencing, it was from God.

Secondly, Collin seems to be convinced that the purpose of calling is to give direction to one's life. Despite his educational pursuits in outdoor leadership, the importance of a divine call is such that he believes he is inclined to follow it, even if it means making a change in perceived career-direction.

Thirdly, calling can be the summation of a number of otherwise unrelated and otherwise unremarkable circumstances. For Collin, it begins with his summer employment at a camp. During his time there, his team leader instructs him to take some time in nature to "connect with the Lord and spend time listening to him through creation." In so doing, Collin spends time by the stream, which intrigues and stimulates his recollection of how God related to his children via the river. Upon returning to the main camp, Collin thumbs through the book of John and is struck by the reference to "streams of living water" that Jesus discusses in John 7. Later that same day, he picks a book from one of the bookshelves in the staff area whose title corresponds with the theme of water with which he has now interacted a couple of times that day. In that book, the author speaks of the importance of the Holy Spirit to the life of the believer. Sometime later, that same author mentions Muslims. In this moment, Collin feels as if the water, the Holy Spirit, Muslims, and his life converge, and he asks, "OK, so you're wanting me to reach Muslims, Jesus?" Despite the fluid connection of the water to the Holy Spirit to Muslims, Collin feels the weight of something special. Looking back on this moment, Collin describes this as the time when he felt called—called to reach Muslims.

Collin's experience and his unquestioned understanding that this "message" or calling was from God is a common theme among men and women who aspire to ministry-related careers. Calling is, at least among Christians, universally understood as something that originates in the divine will and that is communicated in some way to believers. Interestingly, the notion of calling is increasingly popular in corporate strategies for retention of employees—especially in white-collar sectors such as business, education, and medicine—and is described as an important aspect of degree and career choice for secular occupations and nonreligious individuals.

As observed in Collin's story, calling is also understood to be direction-giving. Those who describe having received a call from God look to this experience as that which gave them the information and impetus to pursue a particular career path, even if that direction differed widely from their prior career objective.

Lastly, Collin's call-experience is unique. It emerges out of a series of otherwise unrelated events that add up to something he interprets as a message from God. The experience of the call, as will be discussed later, is highly individual and shaped both by the individual's expectation of the experience and by the community to which the individual belongs. This aspect of uniqueness makes calling a tremendously powerful motivator but also famously difficult to validate by others, such as credentialing bodies, for whom a call-experience is all but essential.

As we will see later, these aspects of the call—its divine source, its life-directing impact, and its unique expression—are common elements that regularly recur in the testimonies of those who acknowledge having perceived a call-experience. Perhaps not surprisingly, the notion that calling is important and expected—especially by students who attend Christian colleges in the US—is considerable. But this is not only a Christian-related phenomenon. Surveys of US college students at public universities who represent a range of religious and nonreligious affiliations also describe calling as an important factor in their degree choice and later career pursuits.

For Collin and for countless others, the call-experience as described above has played an important role in sending individuals across the globe on missionary-related assignments. It has served to compel people to serve in difficult domestic contexts among the poor and the sick. It has convinced some to relocate, to change jobs, to sell or give away their possessions for the sake of serving others. In many cases, it has been the "voice" that has helped people persevere in the midst of difficult conditions so that they did not give up and did not turn back. Calling, as it is understood by Collin and others in the Christian community, is a widely-held, essential aspect that validates someone's participation in Christian ministry. For many the question is not "Is a call necessary?" but "Have I been called?" As Thomas Hale points out, "Being a missionary begins with being called. You don't choose to be a missionary; you're called to be one. The only choice is whether to obey."[2] He later goes on to argue that whereas all Christians receive a "general" call to obey the Great Commission, some receive a "special" call that sets them apart for ministry-related and, often, missionary service, precisely because the nature of the task demands "a special anointing, a special empowerment, in order to carry out their duties. [They need a divine call because] their vocations demand more than the ordinary perseverance and spiritual maturity."[3] But is the experience that Collin attributes to calling and that Hale argues is essential for missionary service actually necessary, biblically so? Is a special, or separate, or extraordinary experience in which God sets someone apart for ministry-related service a biblical norm, or has it become so over the course of (primarily) Western church history and the evolution of Western culture?

This really is the question that this book is attempting to evaluate. In so doing, the point is not to exclude the possibility that God has revealed his will nor to minimize the personal experience of those who are convinced that a particular experience has given direction and meaning to their lives. That God speaks to people is a fundamental aspect of the Christian faith throughout the ages. But how does that encounter—which is referred to as the call of God—relate to the biblical framework that it purports to represent? Simply put, does the type of experience illustrated by Collin's story reflect the biblical notion of calling? If so, then what are the boundaries that make a call-experience "biblical" and how then should the recipient respond? If not, then what do we make of these experiences that have become an expectation and condition of ministry service—especially of vocational ministry?

The following chapters will explore this question and associated themes by first addressing the historical development of the concept of calling. Next the contemporary setting will be explored, which will summarize how the call of God is understood in the current Western context. In chapter 4, a review of the biblical data on calling from both Old and New Testaments will be discussed. Chapter 5 will highlight some of the cultural challenges to the contemporary understanding of the call of God. Chapter 6 will discuss a number of practical challenges to the application of the call of God as it is understood today. Finally, chapter 7 will offer a proposed reimagining of the concept of the call of God and lay out implications for the individual and for credentialing bodies.

After the fourth century, "to convert" meant to leave the world and embrace the monastic "vocation"; the term "vocation" itself now referred exclusively to the divine call to the monastic "profession," and "profession" was now the word for the solemn act of taking the monastic vows.

—KARLFRIED FROELICH

We owe it to Guillaume Farel to have presented to Calvin the call of God to the public ministry of teaching and preaching the Gospel, when Farel summoned Calvin to help in the restoration of the church in Geneva, under the threat of God's wrath were he to refuse this call.

—RANDALL ZACHMANN

Slowly (over time) such words as work, trade, employment, and occupation came to be used interchangeably with calling and vocation. As this happened, the guidelines for callings shifted; instead of being directed by commands of God, they were seen as directed by duties and roles in society. Eventually the day came when faith and calling were separated completely. The original demand that each Christian should have a calling was boiled down to the demand that each citizen should have a job.

—OS GUINNESS

2

The Call of God
A Historical Survey

Introduction

A REVIEW OF THE increasing volume of literature regarding God's calling seems to confirm that most who consider the question of calling do so in light of two separate but related experiences referred to as a primary and secondary call of God. Os Guinness, in his book *The Call*, says it like this:

> Our primary calling as followers of Christ is by him, to him and for him. First and foremost, we are called to Someone (God), not to something (such as motherhood, politics, or teaching) or to somewhere (such as the inner city or Outer Mongolia). Our secondary calling, considering who God is as sovereign, is that everyone, everywhere, and in everything should think, speak, live and act entirely for him. We can therefore properly say as a matter of secondary calling that we are called to homemaking or to the practice of law or to art history. But these things are always the secondary, never the primary calling. They are "callings" rather than the "calling." They are our personal answer to God's address, our response to God's summons. Secondary callings matter, but only because the primary calling matters most.[4]

In highlighting the distinction between primary and secondary calling, Guinness and others[5] make a distinction between the call to salvation and the call to Christian service. In so doing, they appeal to the separate but related experiences of the soteriological call as found in 1 Peter 1:14–15; 2 Peter 1:3; Hebrews 3:1; Galatians 1:6; and 1 Thessalonians

2:11–12 and the so-called "vocational" call to service that is often associated with Abraham (Gen 12), Moses (Exod 2–3), and Paul (Acts 9). In the soteriological (and primary) call, God invites, summons, and urges men and women to repent and trust in Christ's finished work on the cross. The response to this call, enabled by grace through faith, results in salvation. The primary call represents God's efforts to redeem creation through the response of faith to the offer of salvation made possible through the death and resurrection of Jesus Christ. The call of God to salvation (which includes the soteriological package of justification, reconciliation, adoption, and new birth) can be found in the words of Jesus as recorded in Matthew 11:28–30, where he says, "Come to Me, all who are weary and heavy-laden, and I will give you rest. Take My yoke upon you and learn from Me, for I am gentle and humble in heart, and you will find rest for your souls. For My yoke is easy and My burden is light." And again, in John 7:37, "Now on the last day, the great day of the feast, Jesus stood and cried out, saying, 'If anyone is thirsty, let him come to Me and drink.'" Admittedly, the terms of the invitation to salvation in both of these instances are carried by the particular metaphor that may have both intrigued some and put off others, but the invitation to "come" to him and the summons to respond to an exceptional offer are nevertheless real.

In the vocational (and secondary) call, God selects, assigns, equips, and sends men and women to participate in the fulfillment of the *missio Dei* in accordance with his divine prerogative. Just as in the distribution of the gifts of the Spirit (1 Cor 12:4–11), the believer has no say as to the nature or timing of this call. It could be argued that those who are considered to have received a particular vocational call of God (e.g., Abraham, Moses, or Paul) neither sought nor expected it. The call of God was extended to these individuals as an expression of the sovereign outworking of God's plan for the world. Finally, though this secondary call is considered distinct from the primary call and unique to the individual, it is understood that in every case it flows out from, and is subsequent to, the primary call.

The agreement over the meaning of the call of God, beyond maintaining the distinction between the soteriological use and the vocational use of the concept, seems to end there. Some authors, such as Jason Allen[6] and Albert Mohler,[7] break down this secondary call into three parts or possibilities that reflect an increasingly narrow ministry focus: a call to minister, which is implied for every believer; a call to ministry for some who possess the gifts, opportunities, and inner compulsion to serve in a particular role for a period of time; and finally, a call to *the* ministry for those whom God has particularly set apart for his church. In making this distinction, they argue that, though all believers have some obligation that is tied to their identity as followers of Christ, God reserves an additional or extraordinary call for some[8] that sets them apart for a particular church or mission-related role.

Similarly, yet distinctly, Gordon Smith argues that the secondary call, though also reflective of multiple domains of application, is somewhat less church-focused and allows for a seemingly wider range of application, even beyond that which one would normally consider to be related to ministry. He notes that

> for each individual there is a specific call—a defining purpose or mission, a reason for being. Every individual is called of God to respond through service in the World. Each person has a unique calling in this second sense . . . [in addition,] there is the call that we face each day in response to the multiple demands on our lives—our immediate duties and responsibilities.[9]

In summarizing the secondary call in this way, Smith appears to equate the call of God with the fulfilment of one's daily obligations, religious or not.

These differing conceptions of the call are further complicated by other voices, both Protestant and Catholic, in the growing body of literature on the topic, which, instead of bringing added clarity, serve to further muddy the waters. In a recent book on this topic, David Sills writes, "The New Testament records instances of God's calling as well, especially to salvation and service. A call from God can be to salvation, to the ministry, to missions, or to some specific service, to holiness, to live in peace with all men, etc."[10] Here, the author lists the apparent possibilities of a call of God without distinguishing between the primary and secondary call and then adds a few additional categories to the mix without biblical validation. In a decidedly Catholic contribution to this discussion, Meredith Ann Secomb notes that "more recently, Vatican II and papal statements have pointed to the Christian vocation as being a call to a life of holiness and to a life lived in truth and love."[11]

It is clear from these few comments on the concept that the call of God lacks a consistent definition. This thought is echoed by Ryan Duffy[12] when he argues that there are "no universally agreed upon definitions of vocation or calling," and yet, the terms are used frequently as if their meaning were universally understood. Though agreement is apparent with regard to the primary call of God as soteriological, the nature and effect of a so-called secondary or vocational call of God continues to evolve. Additionally, the relationship of this secondary or vocational call to the domain of work is assumed without taking into account the historical and cultural influences that continue to shape its meaning.

The Biblical Framework

The notion of work as a dimension of the human experience is introduced early in the creation narrative. Once God had completed his creative sequence, establishing the flora and fauna of the pre-fall era, he put humans to work cultivating the garden and naming the beasts (Gen 2:15–20a). Work, for however long it was undertaken before it was cursed, was a satisfying, fruitful, and God-pleasing activity. Interestingly, some commentators suggest that the Hebrew word used here for work, *avodah* (עֲבוֹדָה), can also be used to refer to the act of worship.[13] In Exodus 8:1 (NIV), we read, "This is what the Lord says: Let my people go, so that they may worship (*avodah*) me." And again, in Joshua 24:15 (NIV), "But as for me and my household, we will serve (*avodah*) the Lord." It could be argued that Adam in his pre-fall condition worshipped God in the execution of his work. His very presence in the garden was the context for a life of worship and obedience. It is with this in mind that Austin Burkhart concludes, "The Ancient Hebrews had a deep understanding of how faith and work came together in their lives. It shouldn't be surprising, then, that they used the same word for work and worship."[14]

With the advent of the fall (though no one knows how long Adam and Eve actually enjoyed their paradise beforehand), work took on a decidedly onerous condition. No longer would the ground cooperate freely. From then on, it was considered cursed. The work that heretofore had provided Adam and Eve with sustenance and plenty is now described as sorrowful labor[15] through which they would do battle against thorns and thistles. Subsequent to the fall, humankind make and eat bread "by the sweat of [their] brow" (Gen 3:19 NIV) until their strength is spent and "[they] return to the ground."

In this picture of creation, we note the presence of work as a part of the human condition given by God as an assignment associated with Adam's role as vice-regent. Prior to the fall, the narrative makes it clear that work, and all that surrounded it, was included in what God had declared to be "good" (Gen 1:31)—signifying at the least that what he had made was fulfilling its divine intent.

It may be tempting to read the concept of a divine call back into this creation account in an effort to find an original precedent, perhaps a vocational type by which we can understand work and vocation today. But does the creation account of Adam's work provide for such a connection? Some may argue that the larger aspect of what is referred to as the cultural mandate, found in Genesis 1:28, serves this purpose by laying out for Adam and Eve a grand vision of their role as the first couple on the earth. From this perspective, the charge to "be fruitful and multiply and fill the earth and subdue it; and rule over . . . every living thing," serves as the overarching divine mandate—a comprehensive life-orienting directive or, for lack of a better word, a divine call. As Andy Crouch argues, "Culture is what we make of the world. Culture is, first of all, the name for our relentless, restless human effort to take the world as it's given to us and make something else."[16] And this task of culture-making is what God, in his creational grand plan, gave to humankind as their purpose.

> This truth is embedded in the Genesis story of beginnings. Not only does God himself function as both Creator and Ruler, breather of possibilities and setter of limits, he intends the same for those who are made in his image. Without the task of gardening—cultivating, tending, ruling and creating using the bountiful raw material of nature—the woman and the man would have had nothing to do, nothing to be . . . . The beginning of culture and the beginning of humanity are one and the same because culture is what we were made to do.[17]

This idea that humankind was given the task of cultural development echoes the thoughts of Abraham Kuyper in his insistence on the positive impact of the Christian on society through his or her participation in common grace.[18] In Kuyper's thought, God's intent that humankind would have dominion over his creation via the cultivation of resources and rule over all that he had made unfolds over time as a progressive expression of the *imago Dei*. Though Kuyper does not make use of the term vocation or call to define this overarching task, the scope and alignment of the task with divine prerogatives suggest its rapprochement with the concept. But again, the question remains, is this idea of culture making and/or the micro-tasks associated with various aspects of such (like cultivating, breadmaking, or creature-naming), what is meant by the concept of a call of God?

With the advent of the effects of the fall now visited upon Adam and Eve, work that now has become sorrowful labor no longer automatically serves the dual purpose of satisfying fruitful activity and God-glorifying worship. Sin has invaded this domain and what was once life-giving has become life-taking, backbreaking, and a constant reminder of the broken state of affairs. It is in this light that Jacques Ellul comments:

> It is not necessary to undertake a lengthy study to realize that nothing in the Bible allows us to identify work with calling.... [Work,] in any case ... does not represent a service to God. It is an imperative for survival, and the Bible remains realistic enough not to superimpose upon this necessity a superfluous spiritual decoration. Moreover, the Bible is not essentially concerned with this situation of work. It is the common and distressing lot of everyone, but it is not particularly important.[19]

Ellul observes that work takes a back seat to the rest of the unfolding drama of God's redemptive story, and he argues that if God had intended to associate work with the divine call at any point in history, He would have done so in such a way that the point would not have been lost. Rather than work being given an elevated status as a key element of humanity's part in the divine drama, it resides in the background of the redemptive story. Yes, according to Ellul, humans work, but work—in and of itself—does not bring particular satisfaction nor serve as an obvious reflection of the spiritual life of an individual or community.

Furthermore, with regard to the people of Israel, at one point, their experience of work takes on a particularly nasty dimension. For it is following the death of Joseph, son of Jacob and great-grandson of Abraham, that the Hebrews reside as slaves in Egypt. During the approximately four hundred years that they served as slaves under Pharaoh, life as defined by slave labor was anything but restorative, honorable, or satisfying. Moses records the following in the first chapter of Exodus:

> So they [the Egyptians] appointed taskmasters over them [the Hebrews] to afflict them with hard labor.... [And] the Egyptians compelled the sons of Israel to labor rigorously; and they made their lives bitter with hard labor in mortar and brocks and all kinds of labor in the field, all their labors which they rigorously imposed on them. (Exod 1: 11, 13–14)

Work, relegated here to the destructive by-product of slavery, becomes detestable and associated with depravation and death.

Following their deliverance from slavery, Moses led the people of Israel into a new chapter in their relationship to God that was consummated in the giving of the law. Under the administration of the law of Moses, work was subject to a particular regimen and was considered activity that was incompatible with observance of the Sabbath. In fact, those who are found working in violation of the Sabbath conditions were to be stoned to death (Exod 31:15). In this context, God seemed to be making a distinction between work and rest. Not because work was inherently evil—after all, God had assigned the work of keeping the garden to Adam before the fall—but the obligation to rest from work on the Sabbath was intended as an expression of trust that God would provide for the physical needs of his children, even on days of nonwork. In effect, the Sabbath was a reminder that whereas God had given work to humankind as the mechanism of exercising dominion over the creation as God's co-regent, it was God who caused the work to yield its fruit.

Though the role of work does not get much additional attention in the remainder of the Old Testament, Solomon provides a couple of important messages that apply to work in the book of Proverbs[20] and then again in the book of Ecclesiastes. In Proverbs, Solomon uses the backdrop of wisdom (arguably, the theme of the book) to contend that honor attends the one who does one's work with diligence and purpose, in contrast to the lazy person who avoids work (Prov 10:4–5; 12:11; 28:19). The book closes with a masterful picture of the honorable woman who displays her virtue through her hard work (Prov 31).

In the book of Ecclesiastes, Solomon makes an interesting case for the folly of trusting in work in place of trusting in God. In several places, he notes that work cannot guarantee satisfaction or success or even long life because of the frailty of life and the inherent fickleness of riches (cf. Eccl 1:3, 14; 2:11, 17–23). As he ponders these realities, he ends by urging his audience to be content with the work and outcome that God gives to each person. Work is a means, not an end, according to Solomon. One finds contentment not in the extent of his riches but in what God gives one to do (cf. Eccl 3:23–24; 5:18–19). Despite the value Solomon assigns to the value of hard work as a realignment with a divine good (and means for blessing), the notion of a divine calling being associated with work at this juncture is not evident.

With the advent of the New Testament story, the notion of work is still regulated by the Mosaic law—necessary for life but not permitted on the Sabbath. However, as the first-century church emerges, with its increasingly Jewish-Gentile mix, the conditions of the law governing religious life are progressively replaced by what Paul refers to as the law of Christ (Gal 6:2). This new "law" of the new covenant is primarily focused on the morality of relationships over against the ceremonial aspects of the Mosaic law of the old covenant. In the wake of these new conventions, which speak to Jew and gentile alike (in Christ), laws governing work (i.e., Sabbath restrictions) are reimagined. Work through its material rewards takes on a communal service aspect as a means of demonstrating love to those in the church (Acts 2:42–47; 1 Cor 16:1–4; 2 Cor 8:1–5). Additionally, and perhaps because of the necessity to maintain the unity and integrity of the emerging community of faith in the midst of a hostile social context, Paul warns the church in Thessalonica that "if anyone is not willing to work, then he is not to eat, either" (2 Thess 3:10). He goes on to note, "For we hear that some among you are leading an undisciplined life, doing no work at all, but acting like busybodies. Now such persons we command and exhort in the Lord Jesus Christ to work in quiet fashion and eat their own bread" (vv. 11–12). Work, for Paul, at least, is integral to the normal Christian life. It serves as an expression of a life of discipline and can provide means for others (widows, in case of famine or loss of social standing, etc.) as a demonstration of service to the community. But even at this juncture, the clear association of work with a divine call is left wanting.

The association of calling with some type of work, even if that work is spiritual in nature, seems to lack biblical support. For whereas God made humans in his image and in so doing gave them the capacity to work, in the wake of the fall, work became painful and the fruits of one's labor subject to the effects of sin. As slaves under Pharoah, the people of Israel endured four hundred years of servitude in which labor lacked all notion of satisfaction. Under the law of Moses, work becomes subject to religious laws, making it secondary in importance to obedience to the law. Though Solomon theorizes on the place of work in the life of men, he concludes that work is worth doing well but utilitarian, at best. Work remains subject to the law until the emergence of the church peopled by both Jew and gentile for whom the law did not apply. The apostle Paul in his role of spiritual statesman and advocate for the inclusion of gentiles in the newly constituted church describes work as a responsibility for all and a vehicle for serving others less fortunate. In all of this, however, the Bible provides no clear discussion of the association of calling with work.

Greek Unity and Christian Privilege

Sociologically speaking, Jewish and Christian voices were not the only ones in the first century that gave shape to human experience. Also at work were Greek philosophical currents[21] that not only influenced the lives of those who lived during the first couple of centuries on either side of Christ but also shaped what we refer to as Western thought and culture up to the present era.

For the Greeks, the highest, most satisfying life was one lived in unity. In such a life, all that one experienced was considered to be contributory to the union of life and purpose, cause and existence. Ellul, in his comments on this idea of a unified life, states, "Man should be all of God and for God—in all that he does and in all his works. His life is not made up of incoherent and successive moments but is one in the recapitulation of Christ. Likewise, man's diverse works are not thrown to chance; they form a whole with respect to the grace which has been given by God."[22] Therefore, because life is one and undivided, material and physical, sacred and secular are brought together in a particular calling that fits with the particular station occupied by the individual. Ellul continues by noting,

> There will be a calling, a vocation addressed by God, not only in His service and in accordance with the proclamation of the Gospel, but also for the "states" we adopt: a vocation for marriage or celibacy, for example. Therefore, there will be a vocation for work and even for a particular work. This is what is required for our lives to be One in God.[23]

Secondarily, Ellul observes that there also reemerges in medieval thought this notion that God had purposefully assigned humankind the responsibility for the care and maintenance of the created order. Thus, work that could be shown to contribute to the welfare of creation and, by extension, of society could be understood also as a type of God-ordained vocation or calling. And yet, despite its nod to a divine source, the notion of calling in this era did not reside completely within the realm of the religious, for even "military service in the fourth century could become a calling because it was part of the maintenance of the worldly order willed by God."[24]

The notion of calling here, under the influence of Greek thought, begins to emerge as a unifying sense of purpose, enabling life to be lived in satisfaction because of its contribution to the sense of unity—oneness—with God.

Over the next several centuries, the place of the Roman Church in Western Europe moved from a persecuted minority to a privileged majority. The most dramatic aspects of this shift in public perception are the conversion of the Emperor Constantine in AD 312 and the establishment of Catholic Christianity as the religion of the empire under Theodosius in AD 380.[25] Though pagan life continued under Constantine, the legal declaration of Catholic Christianity as the religion of the empire by Theodosius sparked a rapid Christianization of the populace. Among other benefits, the Church entered an era of freedom from state-sponsored persecution and enjoyed, for a change, legal, political, and social favor.

But by the end of the fourth century or early in the fifth, the preference for Christianity and shift in social perception of the faith began to call into question what it meant to be a disciple of Christ as well as the relative social cost of identifying with the church—a cost that had been associated with the faith since its inception in the first century. For, according to Karlfried Froehlich, "everyone was (or was supposed to be) a Christian by imperial decree and was baptized as an infant. [So,] how did you become a Christian when you and everyone else around you already is one—never mind that most people's Christianity did not go very deep because it was just the civil religion of the realm?"[26]

The Christianization of the empire led to a particular sense of introspection in some who concluded that true faith was marked by discipline, sacrifice, and suffering in keeping with the example of Jesus. Thus, though Christ commanded his church to love each other, he also issued "special" counsels for those who wished to follow him more deeply—away from the trappings of Christian society, away from the casual Christianity of the masses and into a realm of personal devotion (obedience to the words of Christ) marked by deprivation of such things as relationships (isolation), intimacy (chastity), and material property (poverty). Those who took up this life of identity with Christ by trading a life in medieval society for a life of solitude were called monks (from the Greek word *monos* = alone, forsaken, solitary). It wasn't long before this single-minded devotion to Christ became associated with a divine calling or vocation.[27] And subsequently, "'to convert' meant to leave the world and embrace the monastic 'vocation'; the term *vocation* itself now referred exclusively to the divine call to the monastic 'profession', and 'profession' was now the word for the solemn act of taking the monastic vows."[28]

It is really here, in this particular strand of Christian devotion, that the notion of a divine calling or vocation begins to take root as a reference to a uniquely religious occupation. As history unfolds, it is evident that the notion emerges out of Catholic medieval theology in response to a unique sociopolitical context. For the next twelve hundred years or so, the concept of a divine call or vocation is closely associated with the religious orders and marks an increasingly rigid separation of the religious class or clergy (who were recipients of a call or who had taken a vocation) from the laity (who had not).

Martin Luther and the Reimagining of Calling

Historians disagree over the relative influence of factors that led to the massive upheavals in Western society from the end of the Crusades (thirteenth century) to the Age of the Enlightenment (seventeenth and eighteenth centuries). Among the factors that must be considered are such things as the progressive collapse of the feudal state (thirteenth through fifteenth centuries), the scourge of the bubonic plague (fourteenth century), and invasion from the East (Mongols, thirteenth century; Ottoman Turks fourteenth through fifteenth centuries). Though these events were independent of each other, they nevertheless contributed to a decline in confidence in the Roman Church, which claimed to speak for and represent the divine prerogative while serving as a priest for a fallen world. To a people whose worldview argued that prosperity and peace were signs of blessing from God and that poverty and conflict were signs of cursing, what were they to make of several hundred years of death and destruction? Clearly, God was unhappy. But why? Had they not done what God through the pope and cardinal and priest had insisted on? Had they not attended Mass and pledged allegiance to the Virgin Mary? Had they not given generously out of their meager means to finance the Church and given their sons to the Church (or to the king who served in the Church's name) for the sake of the greater good?

In that the lay person turned to the Church in these times in an effort to find relief—both physical and spiritual—the continued downward spiral of societal conditions led many to surrender their confidence in the Church. For what good was it to trust in God and his spokesman on earth (the Roman Church), if one's cries for help yielded no relief? McLaurine Zentner sums it up well in stating:

> A major reason why the plague had such a damaging effect on the Church was due to the deterioration of its hierarchical bureaucracy before the onset of the plague had even begun.... The Church had gradually become more secular as its focus turned toward wealth and political power. Thus, the Church already found itself at a disadvantage during this time because of its weakened state.... When the Black Death struck Europe in 1347, the increasingly secular Church was forced to respond when its religious, spiritual, and instructive capabilities were found wanting.[29]

Unable to deliver the people from their plight, the Church's excesses increasingly became reasons for society's distress and provoked a search for alternatives to the Church that gave rise to such things as the flagellation movement,[30] mysticism, extra-ecclesiastical experiences (such as dreams and visions), and scapegoating.[31]

Though Martin Luther arrived on the scene nearly 150 years after the plague had first left its mark on Western Europe,[32] the Church by this time had not fully recovered from its decline in the eyes of its constituents. And Luther, despite his role as monk, priest, and educator within the Catholic Church,[33] found himself increasingly at odds with its position on a number of theological points. One issue that provoked Luther was the concept of vocation or calling. By Luther's day, this term had come to define and distinguish the Catholic clergy, and especially the monastic orders, from the non-clergy or laity.

But in addition to theological issues that Luther proved capable of challenging, he was also increasingly chafed by the lifestyle of many in the monastic orders, though he himself had been a monk of the Augustinian order for a year at Erfurt. He was especially troubled by what he observed as the perception of the perceived value of their work. In short, the clergy had come to perceive their state as elevated, privileged, with access to divine graces that put them spiritually above their non-clergy countrymen. Furthermore, the monastic orders had become a place of excess, marked by gluttony, immorality, and riches. Against such reckless abuse of grace Luther railed. In his treatise entitled *Against the Spiritual Estate of the Pope*, Luther notes,

> For everyone wants to become a bishop, a priest, or a monk, especially the best young boys. They are encouraged in this, not for God's sake but rather so that they can live well with the property of others and revel in good days, without having to live on

the basis of their own efforts and to eat the bread in the sweat of their own face, as all men ought to do, Genesis 3. But everyone knows very well that they have hearts trained in greed. For they invent endless ruses to grab the properties of the whole world. To do so they even use God, the sacraments, the mass, and all spiritual things—this is apart from what they bring together through false usury, lying, and cheating.[34]

His assessment of the Catholic clergy, and especially of the monastic orders, ranged from his critique of their theology, which he concluded was compromised by extra-biblical inventions driven by papal decree, to an excoriation of a wanton, even blasphemous, lifestyle, which Luther noted was an affront not just to the reputation of the Church but to Christ himself. Additionally, and in the interest of our present theme, Luther also challenged the Catholic understanding of vocation or calling, which, he argued, had become the currency of the Church by which it granted a life of fabricated spirituality to all to whom it was applied.

For, as noted earlier, the stark clergy-laity distinction was founded on this notion of vocation. And since the fourth century, the term had come to be associated all but exclusively with the "divine call" to the monastic profession. But in that Luther saw clearly that those who considered themselves holy shepherds of the flock of God by appropriation of this so-called divine vocation were nothing more than pretenders at best and liars, cheaters, and murderers at worst. It was also clear that these self-proclaimed religious agents of the gospel had not received any sort of divine commendation. Their immoral lifestyle and biblical and theological ignorance were rather a testament to their unregenerate nature and showed that they were in fact no better than anyone else. In his "Open Letter to the Christian Nobility Concerning the Reform of the Christian Estate," which was published in 1520, Luther makes the following argument:

> Therefore, just as those who are now called "spiritual"—priests, bishops, or popes—are neither different from other Christians nor superior to them, except that they are charged with the administration of the Word of God and the sacraments, which is their work and office, so it is with the temporal authorities,—they bear sword and rod with which to punish the evil and to protect the good. A cobbler, a smith, a farmer, each has the work and office of his trade, and yet they are all alike consecrated priests and bishops, and everyone by means of his own work or

office must benefit and serve every other, that in this way many kinds of work may be done for the bodily and spiritual welfare of the community, even as all the members of the body serve one another.[35]

In other words, there are no differences between the lay person and the priest or monk. Luther would repeat this argument often and elsewhere appeal to the words of St. Peter, that all believers are "a chosen race, a royal priesthood, a holy nation, a people for his own possession" (1 Pet 2:9) in order to make his case.[36] In God's eyes, according to Luther, each has been assigned a particular role to play (which Luther will subsequently describe in terms of a life "station"), but none are more precious or meritorious than another.

It should be understood that Luther's emerging understanding of vocation (or call) was born largely out of a reaction to the monastic orders and an appeal to the value of all work—religious or secular. This revaluing of work was itself drawn from his conclusion that works have (or work has) nothing to do with salvation but rather belong(s) to the human experience. Work, for Luther, was an expression of service to humanity. Or, as Max Weber argues, in that all work was (potentially, at least) that which had been assigned to humans by God himself, it was therefore innately "good."[37] And this particular work—of whatever nature it might be—constituted the scope of one's life station (social position). Fulfilling one's calling then meant fulfilling the obligations associated with one's assigned life station in the context of, and in service to, the community.

What is of particular interest within the scope of how Luther derived his revised understanding of calling was its connection to his understanding of society at large. For Luther, social structure and its related economic expression was effectively a fixed, closed-box paradigm imposed upon humankind by the providence of God. From the eleventh century onward, European social structure was under pressure from a number of forces that would in the end render irrevocable changes to both political and economic institutions. Luther nevertheless recognized and upheld the legitimacy of the socioeconomic order that prevailed in his day, which was composed of the aristocracy, the artisan/business class, and the peasant. And though once the proverbial cat was out of the bag with regard to his initial public challenge to certain practices of the Church, and his critique became more pointed and vociferous, Luther never intended to call into question the legitimacy of the Church itself nor of the social order in which he lived. As evidence of this, one has only to refer to Luther's forceful response to the fomenters of the Peasant Rebellion that erupted in 1524–1525 across Germany, fomenters who made use of his writings to fuel their cause.[38]

For Luther, then, resignation to one's station in life, marked by a commitment to meet the obligations derived therefrom, was an expression of submission to the divine will. According to Luther, a man "should remain once and for all in the station and calling in which God has placed him . . . . [A man's] calling is something which man has to accept as a divine ordinance to which he must adapt himself."[39] For Luther, it is clear that the idea of calling is not so much a matter of "What does God want me to do with my life?" as much as it is a resignation to that which God has given me to do based upon my station/place in society. The obligations associated with my station in life constitute the calling that I must fulfill as the expression of my divine duty. This idea seems to be what Paul was getting at when he commended the Corinthians to, each one, "remain in the calling in which he was called" (1 Cor 7:20).

Martin Luther: Called to be a Lawyer-Priest

But what of Luther's own story? According to historians, he was born into a well-to-do family in the town of Mansfield, a smallish town located about 150 miles southwest of Berlin. At some point in Luther's youth, his father, Hans, had launched a copper-smelting business, thanks to a sizeable loan from relatives. With the intent of including him in the future workings of the enterprise, Hans Luther secured for his son an excellent education in the run-up to an eventual legal career. Luther applied himself to his studies and dutifully entered the university in Erfurt, where over the course of three years, he completed his master's degree in liberal arts and entered law school. In so doing, Luther had become the first in the line of his family to attend university and complete a degree of any kind. To many, especially to Luther's father, the future of this young man from Mansfield seemed bright indeed. But one evening during the summer following his first year of law school, something happened to Luther that changed not only his future but that of Christendom, forever. Caught in a wild thunderstorm that frightened him to his core and conjured up in him the fiercest of all possible condemnations, it is said that he cried out in a panicked oath, "I will become a monk!" Within the month, Luther abandoned his legal studies and presented himself to the Augustinian Monastery in Erfurt to take holy orders.[40]

It appears from all accounts that Luther did not consider his move from the legal profession to the Church as a contradiction to his understanding of one's station in life, despite his stated conviction that the social order was fixed and that one should content oneself with his or her station as an expression of submission to the divine will. But by abandoning his law studies for a career in the Church, was he not in effect violating his own principles? Does he not suggest by abandoning his legal career that the social order is not as fixed as he maintained? Despite the torrent of words that he would unleash in the decades to come in taking on the Church and other opponents, Luther does not seem to have pondered this apparent "fly in the ointment" of his own worldview. Perhaps this lack of reflection is simply an attestation to the reality that not even the best of men can fully and consistently live within their own worldview. Perhaps Luther saw his departure from the secular to the sacred domain as part of the permitted reordering of life. It was, for Luther, after all, the taking of holy orders, by which he assumed a vocation, or calling.

But what of work itself? How is it connected, if at all, to calling? Under Luther and across the evolution of Protestantism in general (and Calvinism in particular), over the next couple hundred years, the relationship of work to calling follows a certain sinuous path that at times seems to double back on itself. For on the one hand, Luther appeals to the union of the sacred and secular domains by insisting that all is from God (including work). In so doing, he argues that the cobbler who fixes shoes is fulfilling his divine call in his work as much as the preacher does in his—no more and certainly no less. For Luther, it seems, any and all work is therefore innately satisfying of the divine obligation upon humankind. And yet on the other hand, Luther, in his equating common labor with so-called "spiritual work," did not suggest that the Church or the ministry of the clergy were unnecessary or that, somehow, those who served the Church in such capacity were not called. Rather, by arguing that the work of the shepherd and cobbler was equal in God's eyes to the work of the priest, he "eliminated" the laity.[41] And yet, those who serve the Church indeed have been called to do so, not only by God but also by the Church itself who extends an invitation or "calling" to the approved candidate.[42]

But there is another take on the nature and value of work that bubbles up at this time in history as a commentary on the reality of the hardship of life. Work in many cases was hard, painful, and sometimes deadly.

The curse that Adam received, rendering to him the lot that he would have to eat his bread by the sweat of his brow (Gen 3: 17–19), was evident to all. Because of the relationship of one's station in life to the divine will, Luther maintained that despite the reality of the cost of one's toil, it must be received with an acquiescence to providence. Work, even that which is hard, painful, and poorly recompensed, comes from God. In this, one again hears the echo of the appeal to the divine will that has assigned to each his lot. One's life purpose is subsumed then in the faithful submission to this task that comes to one from God, even in all its toil (1 Cor 7).

The Puritan Contribution

As the Reformation matured in its thought over the next hundred years or so, an emphasis on the moral state of humans as individuals before God grew in importance. This was perhaps most clearly seen in Luther's articulation of the priesthood of all believers (1 Pet 2:9), which, among other things, fueled the rise of the independent local assembly and challenged the claim of the Catholic clergy that they alone controlled access to heaven. But this new focus on individuals and their place in the world led to what Weber refers to as the "moral emphasis on, and the religious sanction of, organized worldly labour in a calling."[43] In other words, the equating of calling to so-called secular pursuits led to an elevated respect for all sorts of "nonreligious" work. And in this conceptualization of the individual who stands before God, one finds increasingly the idea that God has indeed "called" each person to a particular profession. This focus on the individual replaces the idea of a general calling for work and replaces it with a unique calling that comes to men and women alike and orients them as individuals to particular work.

The evolution of the concept of an individualized calling is more fully embraced with the rise of the Puritans who, as an English derivative of the continental variations of Protestantism in general and Calvinism in particular, becomes particularly important for the eventual American religious context. For the Puritans, the relationship of work to calling becomes that much more direct.

> For everyone without exception God's Providence has prepared a calling which he should profess and in which he should labour. And this calling is not, as it was for the Lutheran, a fate to which

he must submit and which he must make the best of, but God's commandment to the individual to work for the divine glory.[44]

Here, in this remodeling of the concept, work becomes a calling, or rather is experienced as such, as it serves to bring God glory. But what kinds of work then bring God glory? It is that work that serves the common good and improves the moral condition (the ascetic purity of the soul) of the one who works. Interestingly, the measure of the moral condition of labor and, by association, one's calling continues to evolve under Puritan thought and eventually renders the following conclusion:

> It is true that the usefulness of a calling and thus its favour in the sight of God, is measured primarily in moral terms, and thus in terms of the goods produced in it for the community.[45]

With this understanding of work and calling so intertwined, it is a rather short leap to begin to consider certain kinds of work as valid, God-honoring "callings," while other work that does not meet these conditions as simple, unadorned labor.

The Modern Era

Despite the influence of Puritanism on the understanding of work and calling, it must not be forgotten that the religious understanding of the concepts was also profoundly affected by political and economic upheavals that contributed to the social context of the day. The Enlightenment, the rise of the nation-state, and, somewhat later, the Industrial Revolution all contributed to the meaning of the terms. The French sociologist Jacques Ellul suggests that it is with the emergence of the Modern Era (approximately AD 1500–1800) that the social forces of secularization and radically changed commerce coalesce to shape the concepts of work and calling into the concepts we understand today.

The first of the social forces to make its impact, he argues, is capitalism, which emerges somewhere between the end of the Middle Ages and the nineteenth century. Capitalism, according to Weber, reflects the organization of "labour in the service of a rational organization for the provision of humanity with material goods."[46] What makes it important for the discussion of work and calling is that, under capitalism, labor becomes a commodity. The worker "sells" himself for a price—a wage. Under this paradigm, work has meaning only as it enables the worker (now the employee) to satisfy his survival needs. And if conditions arise such that the employer is no longer able to pay his workers what they think they need or deserve, the workers are "free agents," able to pursue employment elsewhere. For Ellul, capitalism once and for all severs the relationship of work and calling. For though he argues that God can indeed redeem any context such that the work contracted and recompensed could "be lived by man as a gift and a calling,"[47] the fundamental rapport is dissolved.

Secondly, Ellul describes the impact of the "mechanization of work," by which he means the deconstruction of labor into its component parts. By so doing, labor—at least in terms of its outcomes—displays increased efficiencies and, hence, increased profits. What took the artisan days or weeks to produce is now done in a matter of hours and days. But such increased efficiencies lead inevitably to a devaluation of the laborer. No longer is the worker an integral component of the work, who brings individual thought, inventiveness, and industry to the task. All that matters now is the rapid output of indiscriminate widgets that are assembled later and by others to comprise a unit that is later and by others installed into some final assemblage. Such mechanization dehumanizes the worker and sounds an additional blow to the relationship of work to calling.

Finally, Ellul calls out the third destructive force to the relationship of work to calling as "technization." By this he means the superspecialization of the worker who is capable of contributing only specialized knowledge (cognitive or kinetic) to the ever-increasing complexity of the business enterprise. For the "technician," the scope of the task and the disconnection of the labor from the final product is such that the worker maintains no sense of his contribution to himself or society. As a technician, he has truly become a cog in a much larger, impersonal machine—a machine driven by profit (capitalism) and perhaps only marginally able to contribute to the common good (e.g., Coca-Cola [with cocaine], hydrogen-enabled dirigibles, Pet Rocks, etc.).[48] This result leaves no room for work to even approximate vocation or calling as it was conceived. And as Ellul notes, the globalization and acceleration of capitalistic, mechanized, technicized industry only exacerbates the dehumanization of the worker and the further separation of work from calling.

It would appear at this juncture that the functional meaning of calling and its relationship to work would have disappeared and been relegated to the social reality of bygone eras. However, the idea that somehow God still intervenes in the lives of his people in such a way so as to order or direct or lead them into some sort of particular occupation was never quite extinguished. And in this conception of the influence of the divine will, there continue to be certain occupations that retain the spark of a divine call, occupations that some Christians (but not only Christians) consider as those that unite the concepts of work and calling. Occupations to which people are considered called to today include (but are not limited to):

- Medical professionals (nurses, doctors, psychologists) who heal and preserve life
- Educators who aid in the formation of character
- Lawyers who defend the poor
- Social workers who assist in life adjustment

If we were to explore the commonalities in these occupations that distinguish them (perhaps) from others not in this list, we could identify the following characteristics:

- Each offers a clear contribution to the common good.
- Each requires particular credentials.
- Each can find referential biblical support.

Ellul, in the end, is nevertheless unsatisfied with even this concession to the work-calling conception. For him, even those occupations that meet the above criteria and seem to derive their validity from God are "bourgeois professions" that imply that Christians who serve in such capacity are "part of an elite." Furthermore, "they have become as technical as any other profession, and professional exigencies rapidly efface the sense of calling."[49]

So where does this leave us? With what conception of the meaning of calling are we left? It is clear that the world in which we live is vastly different from that of the patriarchs, Jesus, or Martin Luther. But does this admission suggest that there can be no work-calling connection?

Recent studies dealing with the nature of work in modern society have seemed to settle on a varied conception of work, viewing it through four interrelated, overlapping terms: job, occupation, career and vocation.[50] In this fourfold understanding, Elizabeth Brewer articulates a spectrum of modern-day economic reality present in the West and other First World societies, in which the "job" refers to a purely financially driven opportunity that requires low skills and may even be temporary or seasonal. The person taking a job does so primarily for the income and may have little or no interest in the actual contribution of the employer to society (e.g., "burger flipper"). At the other end of the spectrum lies vocation or calling. Brewer conceives of vocation as that which "transcends [a] personally significant path of career into a numinous one. Here, [in vocation,] one transcends the immediate and mortal to serve the highest nature of work: creation."[51] This vocation is something that people are called to do by "a supernatural Source which could be God, Divine, Transcendent, Eternal, or Infinite. [In any case,] the concept of vocations recognizes something greater than humanity, beyond, larger," with a focus on the expression of one's true self rather than on earning fame or money.[52] Finally, Brewer acknowledges that because the pursuit of a vocation is motivated by something other than economic or social status, it may in fact involve work outside of an income-producing arrangement.

Despite the hyper-capitalistic, mechanized, technicized economic context of contemporary Western society, the notion of calling in relationship to work has not completely disappeared. The notion of calling, as we understand it today, clearly emerges from the biblical narrative in which God seemingly called upon certain individuals to play a larger-than-life role in the outworking of divine history. Over time this notion of calling was given over entirely to those who were engaged in the direct ministry of the church such that the clergy, as they became known as, were those who were called, and the laity, those with all manner of secular occupations, were not. In the wake of the Protestant Reformation which highlighted the notion of the priesthood of all believers, secular occupations came to be viewed as callings in the same way as sacred offices. And though this equalizing of occupation leveled the sacred-secular divide, as Western society continued to evolve, the notion that some occupations (e.g., church-related ministry, teaching, medicine, and law) nevertheless retained a certain mystique that demanded a particular calling, candidates for such roles, together with credentialing bodies, all but established the necessity of a call-experience as a prerequisite for employment.

Calling: A Historical Summary

Social and religious evolution over the centuries has not only shifted the meaning and relationship of humankind to work in each era and social context, it has also influenced how humankind understands the purpose of life lived out in relationship to God himself. Looking back over history through the dual lenses of our contemporary setting and understanding, it is not uncommon for us to assign calling to the likes of Abraham, Moses, or Paul, though it is unlikely that such people understood their life work in a similar way. Furthermore, the Bible seems not to offer a clear and compelling argument that equates calling with work at all, secular or sacred.

In our contemporary Western context, though a comprehensive, standardized definition is lacking, calling continues to be used as a reference to a particular type of activity. The activity that qualifies as a calling seems to derive its legitimacy from some "Other" (who may be God, but not necessarily) who impresses upon individuals a particular compulsion that drives them to participate. This compulsion, motivated as it is by a numinous, mystical appeal, may play itself out as the primary, remunerated occupation or as a secondary, voluntary pursuit. For those who equate calling with an occupation or profession, those that contribute to the common good (e.g., medical professionals, educators, religious workers, etc.) stand apart from those that do not. And finally, calling, in the contemporary Western context, is made possible by First World economic and social conditions that allow the individual to pursue an actual answer to the question "God, what do you want me to do with my life?"

But how are these descriptions of calling understood by those whose role in life is still before them? Does a sense of calling affect student choice of college major, for example? How does calling serve to orient someone towards a future occupation? How are church denominations and ministry-related organizations making use of calling as part of their vetting of candidates? Does it matter to ministry executives if a potential candidate can articulate a clear sense of calling? Is a clear sense of calling a viable predictor of ministry fit and success? It is to these and other related questions that we will now turn.

Can a calling be entirely secular? Yes. That answer rests on the evidence of fact. Among America's well-educated elites especially, many people do think in nonreligious terms. . . . As far as they can see, there is no one or nothing calling them. . . . In addition, religious language may make some of them uncomfortable; it feels false.

—MICHAEL NOVAK

Individuals whose career decisions are strongly influenced by religion or spirituality may refer to their careers as a calling or a vocation. In addition to a focus on purpose and meaning in life, which characterizes a vocation . . ., the calling emerges as a summons from an "external source" which may be God or another source as defined by the individual.

—ESPERENZA HERNANDEZ

Although some people may pursue a calling out of religious beliefs, such a set of beliefs is neither a necessary nor a sufficient condition for having a calling.

—DOUGLASS HALL

3

The Call of God
A Contemporary Understanding

Introduction

FROM THE HISTORICAL OVERVIEW provided in chapter 1, it is clear that the understanding that we assign to the notion of the call of God has undergone a long and sinuous evolutionary journey. Though ultimately rooted in biblical theology, the notion of the call has appropriated cultural, and particularly Western, elements across the centuries. It is also evident that despite the widespread use of the concept, especially with regard to vetting potential candidates in faith-based organizations, a common agreed-upon definition is lacking, as are the means by which the experience of the call of God is validated. Though attempts have been proposed (many of which we will explore over the course of this chapter) to bring an objective aspect to the affirmation of one's call, the mystical nature of the experience is nonetheless considered fundamental, even if the capacity to describe it is limited. This mix of religious, historical, and cultural factors have all influenced how we understand and apply the call of God to life and work today.

The Catholic Conception

From the inception of the church in the first century until the Protestant Reformation of the sixteenth, the dogma of the Roman Catholic Church dominated the domains of theology and philosophy in the Western tradition. As noted in the previous chapter, the concept of the call of God as taken up by the Roman tradition in the first several centuries following Christ reflected a strange blend of biblical theology (marked by the sovereignty of God and the *missio Dei*) and Greek philosophy that upheld a unifying sense of purpose as the life ideal—whatever that unifying sense of purpose might be.

With the advent of Christendom under Theodosius I, the Catholic faith assumed a role of religious majority. In reaction to the Christianization of the empire, some rejected the cultural Christianity of the general populace and adopted a life of particular consecration marked by ascetic practices and deprivations. The rise in popularity of this consecrated lifestyle resulted in the association of the monastic life with the notion of a divine calling. And following a certain logic, the association was justified. Why else would a man or woman leave the comforts of home, abandon his or her circle of relationships, and sacrifice his or her economic future to spend his or her days in single-minded, isolated, poverty? In this context, "to convert" became associated with the choice to leave the world and assume a monastic life or "vocation." And thus, the notion of "calling" became identified with the religious "professional" life. Those Christians who followed this path as a member of a religious order (and the offices of the church are included here) were understood to have responded to a "call of God" that gave them access to their vocation. All those who had not received and responded to such a call understood their role in life in terms of a non-vocation.

Society has changed drastically since the era of the early monastic orders, and Catholic doxis and praxis has as well. One of the most significant shifts in contemporary Catholic thought emerged from Vatican II (Oct. 1962–Dec. 1965). The thrust of the changes that were subsequently adopted by the Church were more than just a matter of culturally updating or adapting to the modern era, but a "fresh breath of the Holy Spirit on the Church."[53] In addition to certain outcomes that sought to simplify access to the Catholic faith (Mass no longer needed to be conducted in Latin, for example), Vatican II acknowledged that the future of the Catholic Church was contingent on an increased involvement by the laity, not just in terms of passive attendance at the Sunday worship (or Saturday or Friday) but in carrying out the mission of the Church every day of the week as the hands and feet of Jesus. Such a revived view of participation in the ministry of the Church by the laity naturally raised questions as to the nature of the call of God to ministry.

In updating its conception of the divine call of God in the wake of Vatican II, Catholic theology maintained its commitment to a holistic view of man and woman in light of his or her identity, purpose, and relationship to the divine order. In short, Catholic theology maintained that God was the Creator who rightly demanded obedience through faith. Humankind, as one created in the image of God, was obliged then to obey God through faith. At the heart of Catholic theology is the idea that all of life is to be understood in terms of this relationship between the Creator and the created (humankind) and it is in this notion of relationship that the fundamental framework for calling is found.

With regard to the concept of calling, then, Catholic theology proposed that all Christians are recipients of two separate but interrelated callings. The first, or primary, call is to holiness—to be and become one who exhibits both faith and obedience to Christ.[54] The secondary calling relates more specifically to one's vocation and is realized in one of three domains:

- A religious professional or clergy member
- Marriage
- Consecrated singleness

For the first domain of religious professional, the Christian's primary relationship is oriented to the Church, both local and universal. For the domain of marriage, the Christian's primary relationship is with his or her spouse and children. For the domain of consecrated singleness, the Christian's primary relationship is with Christ.[55]

Under the Catholic understanding of calling, then, the Christian is made aware of his or her calling through the agency of these primary relationships—first, of course, with Christ; and then, depending on the direction of the call, with a potential spouse or the Church. Fundamentally, Christians should expect that God will not hide his will but rather desires to reveal his will through prayer and reflection, a process of "sifting of the heart and mind to look at what is in the individual in terms of joys, pains, gifts, patterns, desires, opportunities, etc.," which serve to inform individuals of the calling that God has for them.[56] This process of discernment can be understood as a kind of "internal call" that stands in wait for validation that is expressed as the "external call" provided by the corresponding relational partner (e.g., the Church, a spouse, or Christ himself).

When it comes to the call of God to ministry in the Catholic Church, the validation of the external call is perceived through an extended process of evaluation of the candidate that looks at the personal, spiritual, and emotional make-up in order to affirm the internal call.[57] Following this evaluation, the candidate may be invited to take the next steps for candidature, or the outcome may be that a definitive determination of one's sense of an inward call cannot be made. In this case, the candidate is encouraged to continue to grow in his or her faith and to continue to prayerfully seek to discern the will of God for his or her life, which may involve a season of waiting and maturing or even a shift in vocational outcome.

It is worth noting that the Catholic conception of the call of God understands God's call to be permanent and intimately tied to identity, such that, given a failure to faithfully carry out the role and function of the calling that results in dismissal from a clerical position, the individual nevertheless retains the calling. The consequence of one's failure (whether moral or professional) is in the prohibition to exercise one's call to its fullness in an official, public capacity. One example of this kind of indelible mark left by the call of God on an individual is that of King David.

It is clear from the narrative that describes David's selection as the successor to Saul that David had not accidentally fallen into his position as king, nor did he depose Saul through some well-designed plot. Rather, the chronicler makes it clear that David was chosen by God to lead the people of Israel. Under David's reign, Israel finally enjoyed a measure of peace and divine blessing under the rule of a righteous king. In addition to all but removing the threat of the Philistines, David established Jerusalem as the new capital, which would eventually become home to the temple constructed by David's son, Solomon.

This example of the divine hand of God on someone who would not otherwise have been considered for such a role exemplifies the extraordinary nature of Old Testament calling. The pattern seems to be that God intervenes to set aside an individual for a larger-than-life task in order to advance the divine drama. Apart from the intervention of God, however, the individual would never have been considered. In this case, David was the youngest of eight sons and both unskilled and unequipped to serve as a king. Even Samuel, who had been given the task of identifying and anointing the successor to Saul, was surprised when the eldest brother was found to have not been chosen by God for the task (see 1 Sam 16: 6–13).

For much of David's reign, the outcome of his participation in the role to which he was called validated the divine nature of its origin. God had called David to be king. Nevertheless, David proved that, despite his divine call, he was not immune to sin. At one point about halfway through his forty-year reign, David conspired to take for himself the wife of one of his officers. Through the intervention of the prophet Nathan, it finally came out that David had not only illegitimately taken Bathsheba, the wife of Uriah, in violation of the sacrament of marriage but also arranged to have Uriah killed in battle. Confronted with his sin, David confessed. The fallout from this sin affected his family (the son born to Bathsheba died [2 Sam 12:15–17]) and eventually the nation of Israel, as violence in David's family line periodically erupted and at times threatened to overturn David's rightful rule. Nevertheless, despite the erosion of David's righteous persona and a weakened hold on the throne, David never ceased being king.[58] In fact, later biblical writers hold up David as an example by which other leaders in Israel should be judged (cf. 1 Kgs 9:4–5; 11:4–6).

And so, according to the Catholic understanding, someone who receives a religious calling may undergo dismissal from the public exercise of vocation but remain—indelibly so—called as a king, or priest or sister or deacon. The Catholic conception of calling can be summarized as divine, inclusive, and indelible, thus enrolling every Christian in the work of God, through the Church, in the context of essential relationships.

The Protestant Revision

In the wake of the Reformation, a number of doctrines and practices of the Christian faith underwent changes that enabled Protestantism to eventually establish itself as a separate body of faith. With the challenge to the priesthood that men like Martin Luther (and others) brought, a new understanding of clergy inevitably emerged. And with that change came a shift in the understanding of calling.

Some of the most familiar of Luther's critiques of the Roman Catholic Church center around his discussion and defense of the priesthood of all believers. Luther's personal grasp of this concept grew out of a growing conflict he felt between what he read in Scripture—in particular, passages like 1 Peter 2:9—and ecclesiastical behavior that seemed to him to be self-serving and abusive.

One example of this spiritualized abuse eventually takes center stage, beginning with one of Luther's early public acts of challenge to the

Roman Church with the posting of the ninety-five theses on the door of the Castle Church in Wittenburg. It was in Luther's day that Pope Leo X promulgated the scheme of selling indulgences in order to raise money for the construction of St. Peter's Basilica in Rome. Though the conception of such an odious, manipulation of the common churchgoer was of particular offence to Luther's conscience, Luther was personally provoked when Johann Tetzel brought this message to the region where Luther was serving as local pastor/priest and profited from a number of those who were members of Luther's own congregation.[59] If the notion that the laity could purchase forgiveness in advance and receive written certificates of "proof" of forgiveness were not bad enough, a more diabolical conjuring of the scheme promised the possibility of delivering loved ones from purgatorial suffering in exchange for money. In his work on Luther, Metaxes recounts an appeal for the sale of indulgences attributed to Tetzel.

> Listen now, God and St Peter call you. Consider the salvation of your souls and those of your loved ones departed. You priest, you noble, you merchant, you virgin, you matron, you youth, you old man, enter now into your church, which is the Church of St Peter. Visit the most holy cross erected before you and ever imploring you. Have you considered that you are lashed in a furious tempest amid the temptations and dangers of the world, and that you do not know whether you can reach the haven, not of your mortal body, but of your immortal soul?
>   Consider that all who are contrite and have confessed and made contribution will receive complete remission of all their sins. Listen to the voice of your dear dead relatives and friends, beseeching you and saying, "Pity us, pity us. We are in dire torment from which you can redeem us for a pittance." Do you not wish to? Open your ears. Hear the father saying to his son, the mother to her daughter, "We bore you, nourished you, brought you up, left you our fortunes, and you are so cruel and hard that now you are not willing for so little to set us free. Will you let us lie here in flames? Will you delay our promised glory?"[60]

In addition to doctrinal manipulation, Luther was equally troubled by the seeming disregard for what he considered to be the essential spiritual character and maturity of those who presented themselves for ecclesiastical office. Over the centuries the Roman Catholic Church had found itself to be in control of vast swaths of land that they managed for income, in many cases through a network of tenant farmers. This, together with their ability to raise funds at the simple injunction of spiritual obligation (e.g., a tithe) on the faithful congregant eager to acquire as much merit as possible for the hope of an afterlife in Peter's bosom, made the Roman Catholic Church extremely wealthy and the life of its clergy a privileged and desirable one—especially when compared to the hardships and bitterness of life experienced by the majority of the peasant population. To get a handle on the degree of spiritual rot that had begun to weaken the very structure of the Roman Church, Metaxes offers a particularly graphic summary of clerical ambition[61] by noting,

> The scramble for ecclesiastical office was exceptionally great in the fifteenth century. Persons of every age, condition, and degree of education wanted benefices and, since offices were for sale, they had no difficulty in obtaining them provided they had the cash. Simony, nepotism, and favoritism brought into the Church a most undesirable class of clergy, for many of them were indifferent to their spiritual duties. Not a few there were who could not read the ritual, hence many literary aids and cheap cross-cuts were compiled to aid them. Others were unacquainted with their duties as confessors. As a rule, the clergy cared little for books. Many of them were not true to their vows. Most of the canons led an easy life; caroused, joked, and drank; were indifferent about worship and never punctual; did the minimum of religious service; and enjoyed their benefices without the thought of their duties.[62]

Though not all who held priestly office (or who joined the ranks of the various monastic orders, such as the Benedictines, Franciscans, or Dominicans) were incompetent nor corrupt, the odious behavior of some of the more prominent office holders significantly affected public perception of the Church as a whole. One such example of papal corruption worth citing at length is the damning portrayal of Alexander VI, who served as pope from 1492–1503, provided by historian Alexander Flick.

> [The election of Alexander VI] to the Papal office was secured through the use of larger sums of money to purchase votes than had ever been employed for a similar purpose previously or subsequently. His reign began with a strict administration of justice, orderly government and an outward show of splendor, which pleased his friends and hushed his enemies. But it was not long before his unbridled passion for enriching his relatives at the expense of the Church and his neighbors began to appear. To gain this purpose he was ready to commit any crime, to rob the Church and the Italian nobility, and to plunge all Italy into

bloody wars. A long series of infamous scandals resulted such as the city of Popes had never before witnessed, riotous immorality, cruel despotism, frauds and faithlessness, murder and unmentionable crimes, and barefaced nepotism. The city swarmed with Spanish assassins, poisoners, informers and prostitutes. Heretics and Jews were admitted to Rome on the payment of bribes. The Pope himself cast aside all show of decorum as the spiritual guide of Christendom, lived a purely secular life, and indulged in the chase, dancing, stage plays and indecent orgies.[63]

Though Pope Alexander VI may have been exceptional in the scope of his corruption, he was not alone in using and abusing the authority and privilege of the Church to serve his own ends. Such abuses and wholesale disregard for the people of God led Luther to observe that the "Roman Catholics regard their priests as special; ordination creates the priest as an *alter christus* (another Christ). Priests then (mis)use their office to lord it over the laity, excommunicating lay believers and enforcing assent to doctrine."[64] Furthermore, in the exercise of their self-ascribed spiritual authority, "rather than representing the spirit of Christ as a ministerium, priests exercise dominion over the laity. They withhold the sacraments, read the canonical hours to themselves, hold private masses, and promote their self-interest. They do not preach the gospel of freedom in Christ. Where then, Luther asks, is the true priest?"[65]

Despite the perception that Luther's critique of the Catholic clergy suggested that he would have preferred to efface the entire structure for some more egalitarian or democratic-inspired form, Luther is clear to argue that it is not the system that is rotten per se but the abuse of a system that no longer serves the people of God as it should. As Christine Helmer notes,

> Luther's argument was not to rid the church of a sacerdotal priesthood by replacing it with a common priesthood, but rather [to] call for reform of the sacerdotal understanding whereby spiritual authority lay within the congregation which the clergy serve as their representative. Luther's polemic against the clergy exposes its failure to do justice to Christ's mandate of ruling the church through its benefits. Clerical arrogance is the object of Luther's sarcasm. Yet, Luther does not abrogate the sacerdotal priesthood.[66]

Luther understood that spiritual authority lay not in the external priesthood but rather in the collective body of the local church, which informed his insistence on the priesthood of all believers. For he argues, on more than one occasion, that a congregation of believers is denoted as the place where the word is preached. And it is the preaching of the word from which all other priestly functions are derived. Furthermore, because this task is given to all Christians, it follows then that the tasks associated with the priestly office are therefore those of all Christians, without distinction.[67]

In addition, it is by virtue of baptism—the outward sign of the inward act of grace alone, through faith alone, in Christ alone—that the individual becomes a spiritual priestly member of a congregation. Thus, Luther concludes,

> It is faith which believes the testament, receives the sign and offers the believer to God. This is the true priestly office. Thus, all believers are spiritual priests before God through faith in Jesus Christ. Therefore, all Christian men are priests, all women priestesses, be they young or old, master or servant, mistress or maid, learned or unlearned.[68]

Because of this spiritual office that is given to all Christians, they, as members of Christ's body spiritually and the local congregation temporally, retain the authority to carry out the functions of the priest, including "teaching, preaching, baptizing, consecrating the Eucharist, binding and loosing sins, praying, sacrificing, and judging doctrines and spirits."[69]

Having established the nature of the Christian with regard to their priestly functions, Luther takes the next step and argues for the autonomy of the local church with regard to those who serve them through ecclesiastical office. For, he argues, if the spiritual function of the priest resides in the believer apart from some external (human) authority, then it follows that the body of believers also has the authority to choose from among their membership those who are skilled and able to lead them.

> Those who occupy a public office (of the church), what the Romans inappropriately referred to as the external priesthood, hold office for the sake of good order. They should not be called priests; but are more appropriately called ministers, deacons, bishops, stewards, or presbyters. Additionally, because they serve the needs of the community on behalf of the community, the community should have the right to choose a minister (i.e., call a minister) from within the community to serve in this office. And when the community is not being served, it has the right to recall a minister.[70]

Here, finally, in this description of the basic organization of the local assembly, Luther reveals his perception of the call to ministry. In contrast to the mystical nature of the Roman Catholic process of comprehending the mantle of suitability for a religious vocation, for Luther, the call to assume an office of ministry in a local church as a minister, deacon, bishop, etc. was a function of the selection by the members of the local assembly. It was then not the role of other priests (or bishops) to choose but that of the local body of believers to deem a person capable of exercising the functions of the spiritual priesthood, not in some elevated position of spiritual authority or privileged insight but as a fellow-servant of the Christ who exemplified what it meant to serve others through self-sacrificial love. As Cyril Eastwood argues, in Luther's view,

> The Christian is a member of the universal priesthood by baptism, but he is given a special task within that priesthood by the call of God which is confirmed by the congregation. This is what Luther means when he says, "We are all priests, but we are all not vicars. The minister's call is mediated through the congregation."[71]

For Luther, what mattered most with regard to the necessity of church leadership was humility, simplicity, and order. For, he argued, "the ministry of the ordained must be controlled and limited for the sake of good order. The person who serves as a minister must be a servant of all and when that person is no longer able to be a servant another is chosen to take over the office. This is the way to distinguish between the office of preaching, or the ministry, and the general priesthood of all baptized Christians."[72] And finally, "we are all priests, as it is written in 1 Peter 2:9; so that all of us should proclaim God's word and works at every time and in every place, and persons from all ranks, races and stations may be specially called to the ministry, if they have the grace and understanding of the Scriptures to teach others."[73]

For Luther, the spiritual authority of the priesthood of all believers as exercised in the life of the local congregation was more than just theoretical. In 1522, the community of Leisnig, Germany, began the process of moving from a Catholic structure to the new Protestant one. To facilitate this process of reimagining the structure and functions of the congregation, the local church members called upon Luther for assistance. In the wake of this effort, Luther composed a tract entitled "That a Christian Assembly or Congregation Has the Right and Power to Judge All Teaching and to Call, Appoint, and Dismiss Teachers, Established and Proven by Scripture." In this treatise, Luther plainly asserts that local church ministry should be exercised by a minister who is chosen (called) by the church congregation from among their own members as a direct application of the notion of the priesthood of all believers.[74] For Luther, this priesthood is a divine declaration applicable to all who follow Christ, without consideration of ethnicity, race, gender, or social status of any kind. This visioning of the priesthood "takes away from the Roman Church authorities the right to impose pastors on congregations because, in his estimation, 'bishops, religious foundations, monasteries and all who are associated with them have long ceased to be Christians or Christian congregations . . .'[75] because of their reliance on human ordinances rather than God's word."[76]

With regard to this notion of the divine call to ministry, one aspect that is conspicuously absent in the writings or sermons of Luther on the subject is the idea that the "call" is perceived by the believer separately or prior to the call from the local congregation to serve them in an official capacity. For Luther, in that each believer is charged with the ministry of the word, every Christian is therefore potentially able to serve the congregation as its minister as a preacher and teacher of the word.[77] That all members of a local congregation did not exercise their teaching and preaching prerogative was more a matter of order and common sense as well as a reflection that some would be more apt to teach and preach and so therefore more suited to do so.[78] But nowhere in his commentaries on related passages nor in the previously mentioned tract composed for the assembly in Leisnig does Luther suggest that one individual would be more suited for the pastoral role because of an anterior mystical experience which somehow set him apart.[79] Luther never suggests that the local congregation seek to validate such an experience, nor does he recommend that individuals seek for nor wait for such an experience before being considered to lead the congregation.[80]

Finally, in this discussion of calling, Luther acknowledges that believers have a life outside the church by which they earn their living. In contrast to the Roman Catholic vision of the separation between the clergy and the laity, Luther raises the specter of the equality of humanity. Furthermore, Luther argues that it is this equalizing of humanity as prescribed by the priesthood of all believers that renders every man (and woman) capable of such. Again, Eastwood comments,

> All believers share this high dignity whatever their calling might be; a shoemaker, a smith, a farmer each has his manual occupation and work; and yet, at the same time, all are eligible to act as priests and bishops. Every one of them in his occupation or handicraft ought to be useful to his fellows and serve them in such a way that the various trades are all directed to the best advantage of the community, and promote the well-being of body and soul, just as the organs of the body serve each other.[81]

In this, Luther does not associate the notion of calling to any role outside the church. The non-church functions that Christians exercise in order to earn their living are considered to be the station in life to which they have been providentially assigned so as to be useful to the community. In the exercise of their station Luther nevertheless argues for the capacity of each and any Christian—regardless of station—to exercise the divine obligation, the calling to serve.

With the rise of Protestant thought energized by Luther's public challenge to the Roman Catholic Church, the notion of the call of God to ministry becomes directly tied to the believer's faith in Christ that renders every Christian a minister of the word. For Luther, all believers share a common calling—the call to service. It is this service—rendered through the word as a minister of a local congregation—that was made possible by a divine call mediated through the members of the local assembly.

The next most prominent voice in the development of Protestant doctrine with regard to the church and its relationship to believers is that of John Calvin. Calvin (1509–1564) was born and raised in France and left his mark on sixteenth-century Protestantism as a teacher, pastor, and theologian. Calvin is best known, perhaps, for his monumental treatise *The Institutes of the Christian Religion*, which he initially published in 1536 and subsequently revised and expanded in several additional editions until the final version in 1559. This text, which became a foundational document for the eventual emergence of Calvinist doctrine, was designed as an instructional work to be used for the preparation of men for pastoral roles in Protestant churches.

In addition to his *Institutes*, Calvin was a fairly prolific writer and speaker who left behind volumes of commentaries, tracts, and other material that chronicle both his theological and personal development with regard to the place of the church in society. In that Calvin recognized that he was living in a liminal age between a dominant church-state symbiosis in which spiritual and civil authority were all but merged and that of a stateless church, it is not surprising that Calvin comments on the ministerial profession and the means by which one assumes the role.

If nothing else, Calvin makes himself clear on several issues related to the nature of the call of God to ministry, by virtue of the wealth of repeated thoughts that he has left us, much of which is found in his commentaries on the books of the Bible. A brief survey of his thoughts can be subdivided into several categories. Firstly, Calvin argues for the necessity of a divine call that precedes and legitimizes a ministerial candidate. In his commentary on Acts 13:2, he says, "No man is to be counted a lawful pastor of the Church save he which is called of God."[82] Additionally, in his words on Ephesians 4:11, he says, "True pastors do not rashly thrust themselves forward by their own judgment but are raised up by the Lord."[83]

Secondly, Calvin understands that the call is comprised of two distinct pieces: an internal call by which the Holy Spirit prepares, convinces, and urges the candidate to consider the ministry, and an external call by which the local congregation validates the character and capacities of the candidate and extends the invitation to serve them as pastor. In his thoughts on Jeremiah 23:21, he says, "There is a twofold call; one is internal and the other belongs to order, and may, therefore, be called external or ecclesiastical."[84] And again, later in his comments on the same verse, he adds, "But the external call is never legitimate, except it be preceded by the internal; for it does not belong to us to create prophets, or apostles, or pastors, as this is the special work of the Holy Spirit."[85]

This idea that the external call is necessarily part of the process of placing an individual in pastoral ministry is also echoed in the *Institutes* when he says, "We therefore hold, that this call of a minister is lawful according to the Word of God, when those who seemed fit are created by the consent and approval of the people."[86] In emphasizing the role of the congregation in confirming this divine call in accordance with the word of God, Calvin is clearly distinguishing the Protestant approach from that of the Catholic tradition, which did not involve the congregation in any part of the process. In so doing, not only does Calvin elevate the word of God above tradition, he also ascribes authority to the church as a collective priesthood over and against the Catholic understanding of the clergy-laity divide.

Furthermore, with regard to the fit of the candidate to the office of pastor, Calvin argues that the individual in question is divinely endowed with the means to carry out the task. In his thoughts on 1 Timothy 3:2, he says, "They who have the charge of governing the people [as their pastor], ought to be qualified for teaching in applying the Word of God judiciously to the advantage of the people."[87] Lest anyone think that such qualifications are merely natural endowments or acquired through academic means, Calvin argues in his comments on John 20:22, "Those whom Christ calls to the pastoral office he likewise adorns with the necessary gifts, that they may be qualified for discharging the office."[88] And again from his thoughts on Ephesians 4:11–14, he says, "When men are called by God, God endows them with gifts."[89]

Despite Calvin's clear treatment of the nature and necessity of the divine call that involves both internal and external forms, his own story of ministerial calling involves a number of irregular features, which, though defining for his own ministry scope, are conspicuously absent from his teaching and instructions to those under his pastoral care.

Calvin's professional career was early on shaped by his role as a lawyer. His academic pursuits brought him into contact with the religious quarrel of his day—primarily that of Catholicism versus Protestantism, a struggle that was particularly vehement in Paris, France, where he was living and working. His retreat from Paris in 1533 to Basel (due to Catholic disapproval of the growing Protestant reform movement of which Calvin had become part) gave him a sense of increased urgency to complete his written defense of the Protestant faith (the *Institutes*), which found its final form in 1559.

But it was while Calvin was residing in Basel that another Protestant Reformer, William Farel, convinced him to remain in Switzerland and assist him in planting Protestantism in the region. Interestingly, whereas Calvin would eventually argue that a divine call to ministry is the evidenced fruit of an internal, secret call that is validated by the local church, Calvin describes his own call to help in the restoration of the Protestant Church as an appeal from Farel who threatened God's wrath if he were to refuse![90] Following his departure from Basel in 1536, Calvin again sought to return to a quiet life of reflection and writing when he was once again pursued and cajoled to return to his so-called calling of teaching.

> Then loosed from my vocation and free [to follow my own desire], I decided to live quietly as a private individual. But that most distinguished minister of Christ, Martin Bucer, dragged me back again to a new post with the same curse which Farel had used against me. Terrified by the example of Jonah, which he had set before me, I continued the work of teaching.[91]

And so, it appears that Calvin does not find himself in the ministry of the word as a result of the formula he employs later and for others: namely, an inner divine call that is matched and evidenced by particular gifts associated with teaching and preaching the word of God and is recognized and confirmed by the local congregation who extends an external call. Was this because he considered himself an exception to his own rule, or did prevailing circumstances (the state of the church, the appeals from other godly men, a timely opportunity) seem to override the pattern he prescribed to others? We may never know, however, the legacy of this pattern; an internal supernatural call matched by an external call from a local church (or now, parachurch ministry) has become the pattern by which individuals have sought to discern their place in ministry to the present time.

A Contemporary Assessment

With regard to the question of the nature and necessity of a divine call, Catholic tradition has arguably retained a more coherent and consistent pattern of thought than has Protestantism. This consistency in doctrine and practice is primarily due to the nature of the Protestant tradition that allows for freedom of biblical interpretation and application, unfettered (often) by a common ecclesiastical authority. And so, Baptists understand and practice their Christian faith in ways that differ from Methodists, Lutherans do so in contrast to Nazarenes, and Pentecostals from Anglicans. History also tells us that Protestantism has not only been affected by its internal theological differences, which resulted in the creation of various denominations, but also by political and social changes, all of which have been influenced by the cultural and pre-Protestant religious context of the society in which they took root, such that Baptists in France differ from Baptists in the US, Methodists in Switzerland differ from Methodists in South Korea, and Anglicans in England differ from Anglicans in Africa.

But what of the question of the call of God? What is the common understanding among those who are, by virtue of their age demographic, most concerned about finding their place in life (i.e., college students)? How do major Protestant denominations understand and make use of the call of God to determine suitable candidates for ministerial roles? How does this understanding compare with the practice of parachurch

The Call of God: A Contemporary Understanding 47

ministries and religiously-oriented NGOs who often provide nonreligious services (medical, academic, or community development)?

Christian College Students

In an effort to understand how current college students comprehend and interact with the notion of the call of God, more than 350 anonymous surveys of students attending Christian colleges in the US were compiled and analyzed.[92] The surveys collected data concerning the students' own perceptions of having received what they consider to be a divine call of God, how this call was received, if it had changed over time, and how it affected their particular choice of college major. Table 1 depicts the overall demographics of the student participants.

Table 1: Call of God Survey Demographics[93]

Total Male	Total Female	Total Surveys	Called (Yes)	% Called	Avg Age When Call Received
121	233	354	295	83%	16.4 years

As noted in table 1, for those who had received a call of God, the average age of when this calling occurred was just over sixteen years of age. For the student in the US educational system (in which the vast majority of these students were), a sixteen-year-old is most likely in the sophomore or junior year of high school. Secondly, the overall percentage of those surveyed who indicated that they had received a divine call is over 80 percent. Both of these outcomes correspond with evidence compiled by the Research Consortium on Career Pathways and Twenty-First Century Skills. The consortium's research notes that 74 percent of sophomores and 78 percent of high school juniors (who would be sixteen or seventeen years old) are thinking about career options.[94] It is in these last couple of years of high school that students' thoughts and plans turn more seriously towards the future as the questions of next steps and future occupations compete for attention amidst college entrance exams, after-school and summer jobs, and the specter of leaving home. Though the data do not support any sort of cause-and-effect relationship, it seems plausible that as students consider the various factors that go into making a career choice, the perception of a call of God—however it is defined—may contribute to helping students sort out their particular place amongst the host of possibilities for future work.[95]

Table 2 provides a summary of perceived calling distribution among male and female students in light of their college majors.

Table 2: Calling Distribution

	Male (No)	Female (No)	Male (Yes)	Female (Yes)	Totals
Ministry Majors	9	15	62	127	213
Non-Ministry Majors	12	20	38	71	141
Totals	21	35	100	198	354

With regard to calling, it is worth noting that two-thirds of those who indicated that they had received a call of God were also pursuing a typical ministry-related major.[96] Furthermore, a greater percentage of both male and female students indicated that they had received a call of God, regardless of their college major, than those that had not. Nearly 90 percent of female students and 87 percent of male students pursuing a ministry-related major indicated that they had received a call of God. This contrasts with 78 percent of female students and 76 percent of male students who were not pursuing a ministry-related major but who also indicated that they had received a call of God. If nothing else, the fact that calling seems to factor into the experience of both male and female students at such a level suggests that calling is not only common but also perhaps an expected element of Christian college students' life experience. The vast majority of college students describe calling as part of the run-up to their college experience; those without a calling experience are in the decided minority.

The survey data recorded above reflects a self-understanding of the meaning of the call of God. In other words, the survey was designed to record self-ascribed understandings of the concept and not a response to a preformulated definition of calling. In this case, it is possible that some who indicated that they had received a divine call may never have really had one and likewise some who did not perceive such a call may have indeed been called—at least as far as this survey instrument is concerned. Which leads us to the question, how do students describe their understanding of call of God? What common themes, experiences, descriptions, and, if evident, biblical references or patterns can be observed?

When it comes to the understanding of calling, student descriptions can be grouped together under several categories that include mystical vs. rational, process vs. immediate, and specific vs. vague. One additional category that stands by itself for lack of a common theme is simply referred to as "outlier." This category includes descriptions of the call that land outside the themes and descriptors that, across the data pool, appear to be common or familiar.

Those students who described their calling in terms that seem to fit a mystical or, at least, a nonrational or suprarational experience refer to calling as a gut feeling or a "tug" at their heart. One female student described her call-experience like this: "While in prayer I felt the presence of God and suddenly it felt like my whole life would make sense." Another female student described her call-experience as "an impression in my spirit through multiple people and [life] experiences." A third student, male, described his experience of the call as "the Holy Spirit spoke through someone [about my future] during prayer and anointing." The common elements in this type of call are references to feelings, divine communication, and mystical experiences that seem to imprint on the individuals some understanding of a purpose or direction for their lives.

Other students describe their call-experience in terms that could be understood as rational or independent of a mystical element. In these instances, students identify their calling with skills and ministry-related giftings, opportunities that present themselves, or ministry-related experiences that seem to confirm a related future. One female student described her coming to understand her calling "through a personal trial [in which] I learned that I have gifts to help others in the same way." Another female student perceived her calling when "I realized that I work well with younger children. I believe God gave me the patience and energy to do so." Finally, one male student said that his call came as a result of "follow[ing] through on an opportunity to train in missions." In these instances, calling is associated with skills and opportunities to serve that appear to confirm a future direction for the individuals.

For some students, the call of God seemed to be understood in very specific terms. For some, their calling related most directly to the role of missionary. For others, the specificity included such things as crisis pregnancy ministry or a specific location like China or Russia or even, as noted by one female student, the call "to disciple and teach young girls in a 3rd world country." For these students, specific details related to locations or ministry roles seem to be a type of divine stamp of approval that gives them the freedom and clarity to pursue a particular direction in life.

For most students, however, the nature of calling seems much less specific, even vague. Many students refer to their calling in terms that arguably apply generally to all Christians. One male student described his call as "to serve His people in order to expand the Kingdom of Heaven." One female student described calling as to "devote my life to furthering the Kingdom." And another female student said calling was best described as "restoration for the lost, broken, hurting and those [whom] people have forgotten."

In addition to having students describe their personal account related to their calling, the survey also asked if students had undergone a change in how they understood their call: had God brought someone or something into their world subsequent to their initial calling experience that seemed to clarify their perceived call or even redirect them somewhere else? The vast majority of students indicated that they had not perceived a shift in their calling. This may be, in part, perhaps, due to the relatively brief amount of time that had transpired for most since the time of their perceived call. However, those who did speak of a change or shift in their calling noted that, for the most part, the shift had largely been in terms of confirming or intensifying the call received years earlier as a result of additional information or experiences that had served to confirm their perceived directive.

In light of this student data, a number of conclusions can be drawn. Firstly, students attending Christian colleges in the US seem to correlate calling of God with pursuit of ministry as a career. Well over 80 percent of students who pursued a ministry-related major in college described themselves as having received a call of God to do so.

Secondly, both male and female students recount very similar experiences when describing their calling, both in terms of overall percentage but also with regard to the categories of mystical vs. rational, process vs. immediate, and specific vs. vague.

Thirdly, whereas ministry roles were almost exclusively reserved for male candidates in the past (though this has shifted in many parachurch organizations and NGOs, some church-related roles are still limited to men), contemporary egalitarianism values in the US with regard to career choice have apparently shifted both the expectation and experience of women such that female students report a calling experience as frequently as male students.

Fourthly, when students describe their calling experience as a process that involves multiple factors, several elements are commonly cited: Scripture and its role in informing biblical priorities, prayer and the effort to hear from God, and input from significant others who challenge and give counsel. Many students described their call in this multifaceted way. One male student said his call was the result of "godly people, prayer and the Bible." Another student, female, said that her calling came as a result of the "influence of a community of people engaged in missions, plus the confirmation [of my call] through active ministry." Again, one female student put it this way: my call came as a result of "Bible [reading] plus preaching plus time spent in the Middle East."

Fifthly, even for those students who are not pursuing a ministry-related major, the experience of a call of God is nearly as present as for those who are. This correspondence suggests that Christian students expect to receive a call of God as part of their Christian experience to help them understand where they fit in the world. Even though they are not pursuing a ministry-related career path, these students describe their future work in spiritual terms with intentional spiritual outcomes that are perhaps more commonly associated with ministry-related career pursuits. One male student who is pursuing a degree in sports management said that his calling is "to not necessarily evangelize per se, but to disciple others," ostensibly through the vehicle of sports management. Another student, female, is pursuing nursing. With regard to her nursing career, she said, "God is calling me to be a nurse and to give love to others as Jesus gave to us." One other female student who is studying education described her calling in these terms: "When God puts the vision in you. It's a goal or a purpose that he gives you. This is the way you'll be able to serve him and share his name."

Finally, a number of students described their experience of a divine call in terms that fall outside of the collective norms expressed in the survey data. One female student described her call as "a good, flexible career [in which] I would be able to do the most good." Another female student noted that calling was "a career path set ahead, and something that works out, even though it feels like it shouldn't somehow." Lastly, one male student stated that his calling was "to be able to work and provide for my family." For reasons that go beyond the scope of this research, these responses beg the question as to the perceived necessity of a divine experience as part of the normal Christian life. In other words, is the perceived expectation of a divine call so pervasive in the world of Christian college students that students feel they must identify some experience that can then be considered a divine call in order to legitimately find their place in life?

Interestingly, this notion of the importance of a divine call as part of the expected Christian experience is supported by research conducted by Ryan Duffy and William Sedlacek (2007) on incoming, first-year students at a large mid-Atlantic public university. Among other things, they note that the perceived experience of a call strongly affects college student choice of major and subsequent career pursuits. They surmise that

> when students have a calling to a certain career, they are likely to heed this call and decide on the career path which they are called to. It may be that when a student has a career calling, this accelerates the career process and allows even for first year college students to feel decided about their future. The strong relationship between the presence of a calling and self-clarity may also elucidate the process by which a calling affects career behavior.[97]

Research on spiritual experiences that are later described in personal testimonials, such as conversion (from one religious identity to another), highlights a phenomenon referred to as "reconstructed biography." According to Lewis Rambo, the testimony (whether delivered as a performance or in casual conversation) involves two elements: one is language transformation, in which the new convert adapts vocabulary and ideas of the new religious community; the second is biographical reconstruction, in which the new convert reviews and re-narrates his or her personal history through the perspective of the new vocabulary and religious concepts in such a way so as to align his or her previous life experience with the collective experience of the new religious community. The "testimony [then] is the adaptation of this modified rhetoric to explain one's conversion experience, to tell one's story."[98] Again Rambo notes,

> Although all of ordinary human life can be seen as a subtle process of reorganizing one's biography, in religious conversion there is often an implicit or explicit requirement to reinterpret one's life, to gain a new vision of its meaning, with new metaphors, new images, new stories .... The convert learns what is expected by listening to other testimonies and gradually begins

to see his or her life within the common perspective. The individual appropriates a new frame of reference, which helps him or her to be a new person.[99]

The prevalence of student reference to a divine call could be evidence of this kind of appropriation in an effort to align with expected spiritual norms. Because, as we shall see later, faith-based organizations make use of the call as a criterion in the hiring process, successful candidates are careful to articulate a coherent experience of a divine call that satisfies the expectations—both in terms of vocabulary as well as themes described—of the faith-based employer.

Calling among college students is a leading factor in both choice of college major and subsequent career pursuits. For those who indicate a call to some role or path, calling seems to fit one of three motifs: general vs. specific, process vs. immediate, and mystical vs. rational. Because of the importance of a perceived call in the Christian community, students may assign call-level importance to past experiences, which helps them fit the perceived norm.

Protestant Denominations

It is not surprising to note that as European society (if it can be summed up as such) evolved since the days of the Reformation, so has the nature of the local church. What was previously monolithic in structure, purpose, and function under the Catholic Church became increasingly diverse as Protestantism emerged and developed under varying and sometimes competing theological positions. Whereas Luther and Calvin advocated for a new understanding of the relationship of the believer to God and the church (summed up by the priesthood of all believers) when it came to applying the notion of the call of God to ministry, it was ministry associated with the local church only, for there was no such thing as a parachurch organization at the time.

Today, most Protestant denominations operate under the conviction that those who aspire to leadership within the church must give evidence of some notion of a call to ministry. In keeping with the understanding of this concept from Calvin, the individual must first experience an inner-subjective call which is perceived to originate in God and compel the individual to pursue a ministry role. But with regard to church ministry, an inner call is not sufficient in and of itself. The fully realized call of God is complete only after the local church extends an invitation (call) to the individual to take on the ministry role in the church. Furthermore, as noted earlier, Calvin (and others) firmly believed that a legitimate call of God not only predisposed the individual to aspire to a ministry role but also was accompanied by the necessary giftings to successfully fulfil the responsibilities of the calling.[100]

As Richard Pitt points out, the divine call to ministry is not simply one criterion among many that determines whether a candidate is suited for a particular ministry role, though it certainly serves this purpose. Rather, the divine call serves to affirm that the individual is indeed a "legitimate vessel for God's work [for], unlike ordination processes, which are explicitly social in nature, call-experiences are almost always described as a personal journey where the only other participant is God."[101] Pitt continues (in agreement, I believe with Luther, Calvin, and others on this subject) that the perceived experience of a divine call

> is more than [just] a catalyst for the pursuit of a professional credential; it is an essential plank in the argument for legitimacy, especially when other more verifiable evidence is in short supply. Therefore, comprehending the call-experience is a critical component of understanding its impact on both the decision to pursue and the decision to embrace a ministerial identity.[102]

In other words, the experience of a divine call is the *sine qua non* of ministerial legitimacy, and the capacity to provide a compelling retelling of the perception of the experience is the *force majeure* by which the individual makes his or her case as a divinely appointed and equipped candidate.

Though a commonly understood definition of a divine call is lacking, and those in the position of assessing the subjective nature of such lack objective means of doing so, the call of God to ministry remains an essential requisite for ministry roles. And yet, though the focus on the priesthood of all believers dramatically expanded the potential pool of those who could aspire to ministry roles, access to ministry in the church was exclusively limited to men up to and until sometime into the late nineteenth and early twentieth century, and even then, not open to all. Because ministry in the church was largely restricted to men, women were not considered legitimate recipients of a divine call.[103] However, as Western society evolved to grant increasing autonomy to women, together with expanded educational and economic opportunities, traditional gender roles that all but excluded women from public ministry came under increasing scrutiny. Little by little, women were given access to public ministry roles in Protestant denominations and a wide variety of parachurch organizations in response to perceived call-experiences that could not be differentiated from those of men. It was the combination of social change and the lived experience of a divine call that led to increased ministry roles for women, conservative gender roles notwithstanding. This normalizing of women in ministry is worth recounting at length.

Calling and Women

The political, social, and religious factors that led to the settling of the American colonies provided a unique opportunity for the rise of religious pluralism, despite the fact that most who came to settle were Protestant of some sort. Denominationalism in colonial America largely reflected the denominational variations of the European homelands from which the colonists originated. By the mid-1700s, Congregationalists, Presbyterians, Methodists, Anglicans, and Baptists were well, if not equally, represented in settlements from Boston to Jamestown. The real story, however, was not religious pluralism per se, for, after all, that was one of the seminal reasons for embarking on the transatlantic passage to begin with. What marked the early colonial period was the proliferation with which religious variants took root. As Sydney Ahlstrom observes in his volume on the religious history of America,

> A traveler in the 1700s making his way from Boston to the Carolinas would encounter Congregationalists of varying intensity, Baptists of several varieties, Presbyterians, Quakers and several other forms of Puritan radicalism; Dutch, German and French Reformed; Swedish, Finnish and German Lutherans; Mennonites and Radical pietists; Anglicans, Roman Catholics; here and there a Jewish congregation, a few Rosicrucians; and, of course, a vast number of the unchurched—some of them powerfully alienated from any form of institutional religion. With the passing years the variety would increase, and in the year of the nation's officially recognized independence (1783), Ezra Stiles in his famous sermon, "The United States Elevated to Glory and Honor," prophesied that in due course the country would "embosom all the religious sects and denominations in Christendom—and allow freedom to them all."[104]

Though not all who came and settled in the American colonies participated in religion, one cannot deny that religious options were available throughout the settlements. And yet, despite the religious freedom of the colonial era, social norms were decidedly more complementary and conservative. Whereas men assumed the tasks of entrepreneurship, governance, and religion, women—across religious lines—though present in virtually every sphere of commerce and farming, understood that their place was primarily in the home.[105] Much of the grounding for the nurturing of gender-specific societal roles in this early period is no doubt related to the influence of Protestant theology that was dominated by Puritan conservatism and that limited ministerial roles—and hence divine calls to such—to men.

Carol Hymowitz and Michaele Weissman, in their *History of Women in America*, describe the inestimable value that women brought to the establishment of the American colonies, without which the very survival of the initial efforts would have been doubtful. They note, however, that despite the scope of women's involvement in society, which included a wide range of entrepreneurial and commercial ventures, women were nevertheless considered as less than men in many respects. Male-female relationships were ultimately governed by the common understanding of a woman's inferiority to a man, derived from the Puritan comprehension of the story of Adam and Eve. "Scripture told woman that she, like man, was created in God's image and to this degree Scripture recognized a spiritual equality between the sexes. Yet throughout Old and New Testament literature woman was also told that it was her duty and responsibility to be subservient to men."[106] And though some women did contribute to the economic welfare of their families and to the larger society in general, when it came to official ministry roles in the church, women were excluded.[107]

And yet, ministry for women in eighteenth- and nineteenth-century America was not entirely unheard of. The key to ministry outside the home, however, was marriage to a minister or missionary. As Dana Robert notes,

> The most common vocational fantasies of evangelical women in nineteenth-century America involved becoming a minister's or a missionary's wife. Marriage to a minister meant that a woman could function as a minister by leading female prayer meetings, visiting the sick and exhorting; marriage to a missionary meant that a woman could work as a missionary. For some women the choice of a mate was a vocational one.

> The solidification of the doctrine of separate female and male spheres in the early nineteenth century, combined by a religious activism, meant that marriage to a clergyman opened for his wife a realm of public service, albeit one officially limited to work among women and children.[108]

In addition to foreign mission service, the early nineteenth century saw the rise of women engaged in urban social contexts in the US, from soup kitchens to orphanages, from abolitionist movements to prison ministry. This increased activism among women on the "home front" stirred a similar interest on the part of women to organize for foreign service in an effort to mobilize a pent-up female demand and enable ministry that had been frustrated and restricted by the early parachurch organizations of the day. One such organization, the American Board of Commissioners for Foreign Missions, was the first parachurch agency founded for the express purpose of recruiting and sending missionaries from the US to other parts of world. And it did so, provided that the prospective candidate was a male or, if a woman, in most cases, that she be married to another male missionary candidate.

The activism of American Protestant women led to a rush of mission entrepreneurism. According to Marguerite Kraft and Meg Crossman,

> By 1900, over 40 denominational women's [missionary] societies existed, with over three million active women raising funds to build hospitals and schools around the world, paying the salaries of indigenous female evangelists and sending single women as missionary doctors, teachers, and evangelists. By the early decades of the 20th century, the women's missionary movement had become the largest women's movement in the United States, and women outnumbered men on the mission field by a ratio of more than two to one.[109]

Though documentation with regard to how women of this era considered their missionary vocation in light of a particular divine call-experience is limited, it is clear that as opportunities increased, so did the number of women engaged in ministry-related service, service that was commonly related to calling.

Arguably the greatest shifts in ministry in Protestant circles since the nineteenth century have been the birth and proliferation of parachurch ministries and a subsequent surge in the rise of women engaged in ministry. Initially, women served as volunteers under the emerging parachurch organizations and then, more recently, as ministry professionals in local churches—at least, in some denominations. Much of the growth in ministry opportunities for women since the nineteenth century corresponds to societal shifts that also expanded opportunities for women in virtually every domain, from education (first with the rise of women's colleges and then increasing numbers of co-ed academies) to political engagement, with securing the right to vote (1920) and proposals under the Equal Rights Amendment,[110] which increasingly gave women access to employment and equal pay for equal work.

The rapid and widespread inclusion of women in the marketplace (and, in many cases, in jobs that had been the exclusive domain of men) fueled a growing women's liberation movement that pushed against social norms, which had largely relegated women to domestic duties. Though the chicken-and-egg question remains, it is hard to ignore the fact that as opportunities for women in the marketplace increased, ministry opportunities for women also become more common in parachurch organizations and certain church denominations.[111] Kate Bowler in her compelling look at the influence of evangelical women in America cites the Pentecostal evangelist Daisy Osborn, who remarks, "If the Pulpit is the man's Holy of Holies, then the parachurch was like the Temple's Outer Courts, where the women were allowed."[112]

Though local church-related ministry differs from missionary service, in that the biblical roles associated with pastoral duties in the church are often more directly understood as limited to men (see 1 Tim 3:1–13 and Titus 1: 5–9), most Protestant denominations have increasingly opened the door to volunteer ministry roles and, later, professional positions as part of local church staff. Some denominations, such as the Salvation Army, the Church of the Nazarene, and the Quakers have ordained women to pastoral roles from their inception—though these were considered sectarian from the vantage point of the mainline denominations.[113] It is worth noting that apart from the Quakers who date their origin to the mid-seventeenth century, the Salvation Army and the Church of the Nazarene were founded in the late nineteenth and early twentieth centuries respectively, at a time when societal restrictions on women's roles were beginning to loosen.[114]

Despite the fact that evangelical Protestants have been historically less inclined to permit women in pastoral ministry, one creative solution to the cultural push to create ministry opportunities for women in evangelical churches was the creation of women's ministries as a segment of the (especially larger) local churches. This, together with the rise of conferences devoted to women's spirituality and Christian publications focusing on the Christian life and experience of women, created a platform for women's roles in ministry among Evangelicals that operated generally in concert with, but also out from under, the predominantly male authority structures.[115] Today, most Protestant denominations allow some professional role for women, even if they are not considered ordained clergy.[116] In some instances, denominations have developed somewhat parallel tracks to professionalizing these roles by conferring licensing or certification for women in lieu of ordination.[117]

The increased opportunity for women in ministry appears to have resulted in an equilibrium of expectation for women with regard to receiving a divine call of some sort to pursue a role in ministry. This equilibrium of expectation seems to be reflected in survey data of Christian college students described earlier, in which the incidence of a perceived calling is expressed nearly equally by both male and female students (see table 1 above).

And yet, despite this increased participation of women in ministry, the question remains, how does the question of calling relate to women who aspire to ministerial roles in Protestantism? Is a clear description of a call essential for access to a ministry role for women, as has been the case for men? Do women experience calling similarly to or differently from men? Are there other issues (e.g., family responsibilities, social context, etc.) that women need to consider in light of calling experiences?

In their research on women and calling, Barbara Zikmund et al. saw fit to classify Protestant denominations according to how authority is perceived and structured. In so doing, they suggest that there are three types of Protestant denominations:[118]

- *Congregation-centered denominations:* Congregationalists, Unitarian-Universalists, American Baptists, and Southern Baptists
- *Institution-centered denominations:* The Episcopal Church, the Evangelical Lutheran Church, the Presbyterian Church USA, and the United Methodist Church
- *Spirit-centered denominations:* Churches of the holiness and Pentecostal traditions, which include the Church of God (Anderson, IN), the Church of the Nazarene, the Free Methodist Church, and the Wesleyan Church, the Assemblies of God, and other Pentecostal churches

According to Zikmund et al., there is some evidence to suggest that those denominations that can be described as Spirit-centered are more inclined to understand calling as a prerequisite—for both men and women—to any ministerial role in the church (though this may not mean ordained ministry per se) than either congregation-centered or institution-centered denominations. Similarly, those from Spirit-centered denominations who lack a particular experience in which they felt as if God had asked them to devote their lives to ministry are less likely to become clergy than those who are part of the other denominational types.[119] And so, the capacity to articulate a clear call to ministry remains an essential criterion for women who desire to access a public ministry role.

The fact of women in ministry roles in contemporary Western society is no longer in question. Social changes that affected education, employment, and the overall economic marketplace were both served by the influx of women and propelled women into extra-domestic professional roles, including those in church and parachurch organizations of all sizes and types. Though Catholic as well as Protestant denominations often limited public ministry roles to men, women's experience with calling is arguably indistinguishable from that of men. Though some argue that women cannot aspire to a particular ministry role because they are not male, the argument cannot discount the experience of those women who claim that God has called them to pursue ministry. It is this very conflict that raises the question of the nature and value of a genuine call of God. For if God calls, should that calling not serve as the dominant criterion for selection of a candidate, regardless of gender? If not, then on what basis do credentialing bodies discount the presumed call-experiences of some and not others? Has calling in the contemporary context become something other than divine in nature? It is to this question that we now turn.

The Contemporary Evolution

Perhaps the most compelling development with regard to the nature and experience of a divine call that orients a person towards some kind of future role in society is the contemporary evolution of the notion of the call and its increasing use in career counseling in nonreligious colleges and universities as well as in business, especially in the managerial functions of corporations.

On the one hand, the evolution of the concept of calling continues to follow a spiritual path, acknowledging to some degree the idea from Weber[120] that work and calling are interrelated. On the other hand, the notion of calling is taking on an ever-widening meaning in contemporary society by moving away from a dependence on an external spiritual source to other, sometimes intrinsic motivations. Douglas Hall and Dawn Chandler expressly state that the notion of a religious calling is increasingly seen as that which is relegated to the past.[121] For though they acknowledge that some people still perceive a religious call to a particular work or vocation, for many others, if calling factors at all into their consideration of life work, the religious element is not considered essential.[122] This is also the opinion of Michael Novak who contends that many people, especially those whom he describes as "well-educated elites," do not understand life through a religious lens. For these people, "as far as they can see, there is no one or nothing calling them . . . . In addition, religious language may make some of them uncomfortable; it feels false."[123]

Furthermore, they also acknowledge that the exploration of calling is a deeply personal and still largely subjective experience that is inevitably shaped by a host of factors, both personal (i.e., one's social community) and contextual (i.e., historical, political/economic, and sociological).[124] The following table reflects one way of differentiating calling that is primarily religious from that which is primarily secular.

Table 3: Two Views of Calling

Item	Religious View	Secular View
Source of Calling	God or higher power	individual
Who Is Served	community	individual and/or community
Method of Identifying the Call	discernment (prayer, listening)	introspection, reflection, meditation, relational activities, career assessments
Meaning	enacting God's plan for an individual's life	enacting individual purpose for personal fulfillment

Even if the religious view and the secular view of calling differ in their perceived source, they both share some degree of common ground with regard to whom is served, the method of identifying the call, and its particular meaning. Despite the divine source attributed to the call by the religious view, discernment, as a means of identifying a call, is a subjective experience that is fraught with opportunities to misinterpret and misunderstand the call-experience, which makes ascertaining a true call difficult. For those types of calls that emerge within a nonreligious context and for which a religious source is a nonfactor, the arrival at a confident sense of call remains equally difficult. And yet, Novak argues that those who feel pulled by a secular sense of calling have just as strong a conviction as do those who describe calling as originating from a divine source, though, admittedly, the sense of conviction in either case is highly subjective and all but impossible to quantify. For these secular callings, "people speak rather of knowing themselves, seeking their own identity, seeking their own fulfillment or simply doing their own thing" as the core principle of their calling.[125]

Again, descriptions of what is involved vary, but as attempts to provide a working model for this aspect of the human experience increase, definitions tend to coalesce around a collection of cooperative and co-existent realities, which include the recognitions:[126]

1. that each person's calling is unique;
2. that a calling involves preconditions, such as talent (a calling must fit one's abilities), an openness to discovering one's calling, and a love for the work involved;
3. that a calling provides great energy, enjoyment, and vitality to one's efforts;
4. and that one's calling is not easy to discover, requiring much reflection, dialogue with others, trial activities, and persistence.

Work and Calling

One additional aspect of the conversation concerns the relation of calling to work itself. Are all types of employment subject to calls? Or is calling reserved most logically for certain types of employment that seem to satisfy the personal, social, and spiritual aspects often associated with calling? As noted earlier, the evolution of society and individuals' relationship to work is certainly part of this discussion. Contributions to the conversation include works by Max Weber, Richard Niebuhr, and Robert

The Call of God: A Contemporary Understanding 63

Bellah, as well a host of contemporary academic and popular authors, each attempting to articulate a clarifying summary of the current understanding of the concept and offering application to contemporary society. Though differences abound in the ways that calling is explained across the spectrum of contributors, one finds a certain degree of concurrence around the idea that calling can apply to virtually any kind of legitimate work,[127] even though people are perhaps less likely to describe themselves as called to certain work that is menial and low status.

One variation on this effort to associate calling with any and every kind of work is articulated by Pierce Brantley in the argument that calling is really not about the specific job at all but what Brantley calls "the kingdom purpose in it."[128] For Brantley, God gives to all a particular assignment in their work whose purpose is ultimately tied to that of God's redemptive mission—regardless of the nature of the work. This kingdom purpose is best embodied by the Christ whose missional purpose is summarized in Luke 4:18–19:

> The Spirit of the Lord is upon Me because He anointed Me to preach the gospel to the poor. He has sent Me to proclaim release to the captives, and recovery of sight to the blind, to set free those who are oppressed, to proclaim the favorable year of the Lord.

In this summary of Christ's mission, five objectives emerge:

1. to preach the gospel to the poor,
2. to proclaim release to the captives,
3. to proclaim recovery of sight to the blind,
4. to set free those who are oppressed,
5. and to proclaim the favorable year of the Lord.

The Christian then pursues what Brantley refers to as the five fruits of calling, which can be applied to any job or life situation. This, he says, "is your ministry and your calling."[129] In his effort to infuse purpose and passion into the contemporary work experience, Brantley has associated the idea of calling with kingdom purpose and then applied a messianic reference from Isaiah[130] to all believers. In the end, calling is what one finds in one's work and not a divine enlistment to a particular task.

Elizabeth Brewer takes a different approach when seeking to understand calling in light of work. In her article concerning the concept of a *vocational souljourn* paradigm, Brewer first distinguishes vocation from vocations—which she describes as small everyday calls toward wholeness—and defines vocation as that which compels someone to

> transcend the immediate and mortal to serve the highest nature of work: creation, or the sense that all people are called by the Creator to personally contribute to a fecund, productive life on earth. One offers one's originality, not with the focus of earning money, fame, or status but to supplant nothingness with substance, with consequential societal benefits.[131]

Next, Brewer proposes that the concept of work can be divided into four categories that represent points on a spectrum: job, occupation, career, and vocation.[132] She argues that whereas one takes a job or even undertakes an occupation primarily for its financial benefits (and to the extent that one actually has choice over the matter—as will be discussed later), in contrast, one pursues a career and, even more so, a vocation (or calling) out of connection to a higher realm for the realization of ultimate good. In that this pursuit has transcendent objectives, it is not necessarily associated with or equated to one's job or occupation and, in fact, could be pursued simultaneously alongside a remunerative occupation. Duffy concurs and notes that the terms *calling* and *vocation* themselves refer most generally to careers that are not primarily motivated by financial reasons but rather in their capacity to serve a higher good, whether for society in general or a particular aspect of it.[133]

Part of the challenge here, as noted earlier, is the lack of a consistent, commonly agreed-on definition of calling. Lacking such a common reference makes it difficult to discuss the concept and to measure its impact on individuals and organizations to which they are related. In an effort to bridge this gap, Bryan Dik and Ryan Duffy propose the following definition of calling:

> A transcendent summons, experienced as originating beyond the self, to approach a particular life role in a manner oriented toward demonstrating or deriving a sense of purpose or meaningfulness and that holds other-oriented values and goals as primary sources of motivation.[134]

Efforts by Dik and Duffy to define the concept appear as much a quest for clarity as a reluctance to exclude anyone's experience. And so, though they include the possibility that a calling could result from or relate strictly to a sense of duty or collective good, they do not refuse to

The Call of God: A Contemporary Understanding

allow for those for whom calling has a decidedly spiritual source. Interestingly, in an effort to pave the way for clarifying research on the themes and concepts associated with calling, Dik and Duffy propose defining the concept of vocation separately. They suggest that vocation is

> an approach to a particular life role that is oriented toward demonstrating or deriving a sense of purpose or meaningfulness and that holds other-oriented values and goals as primary sources of motivation.[135]

Whereas they acknowledge that the definitional orbit of calling and vocation overlap considerably, they suggest that the difference between the two lies in the nature of the source or impetus. Therefore, "individuals with callings and vocations connect their work to an overall sense of purpose and meaningfulness toward other-oriented ends, but only individuals with callings perceive the impetus to approach work in this manner as originating from a source external to the self."[136]

This notion that calling (and/or vocation) can spring from a non-religious/spiritual source and serve as a motivator and clarifier for finding one's place in the world is increasingly supported by research given to exploring these dynamics. In addition to the sense of calling being seen as a guide to career choice and professional development, research also highlights the correlation between a sense of calling and greater life, health, and job satisfaction.[137]

In an effort to ascertain the role that a sense of calling has on the current generation of college students, Duffy and Sedlacek oversaw research in which over five thousand incoming freshmen to a large, mid-Atlantic public university responded to a series of questions relative to calling.[138] Among their findings are the following:

- Over 40 percent indicated that a career calling was true or mostly true of them.

- An additional 28 percent indicated that they were searching for a life calling.

- Male and female students expressed near equal levels of career calling or search for one.

One finding, seemingly in conflict with that noted in data from the Christian college students referenced earlier, is an apparent lack of connection between calling and religiousness for the students of the nonreligious, public college. One possible explanation for this distinction, which will be explored later, is the idea of social conditioning. In other words, individuals take on the expectations of their social context when describing their place in society.

One aspect of this conditioning is the adoption of the vocabulary and normalized experience of the social group into which the newcomer is welcomed. If, for instance, a college student perceives that the normalized way to proceed towards a ministry role (or any career role, for that matter) is to be able to articulate a perceived divine call, then the experiences of life are filtered through that lens to identify and craft a story that satisfies the expected narrative in terms of vocabulary and themes. The very high percentage of those in the Christian college context (over 80 percent) who indicate that calling is essential for either a ministry-related degree or a non-ministry-related degree suggests that there is a certain degree of conditioning by which students feel an expectation to find in their stories suitable data that add up to a divine call.

In contrast, the college student who perceives that the notion of a call is not expected by the social milieu into which he or she is now circulating is perhaps less inclined to explore the past to craft a narrative that articulates a calling as an explanation for the choice of degree and intended career trajectory. The much lower percentage of students at the public university who express calling as essential to their degree and career choice is indicative of this difference of social conditioning. One note of interest with regard to the study by Duffy and Sedlacek is that the mix of student participants did include 52 percent who self-identified as Christians (27 percent Protestant and 25 percent Catholic). Though their data did not record the correlation between particular religious affiliation and sense of calling, one is left to wonder to what extent those who identified as Christian were more inclined (beyond 40 percent) to indicate that they had a strong sense of calling or were searching for one.

Calling: Is There a Consensus?

Calling, as an aspect of the human experience, has undergone a decided evolution over the centuries, in response, in part, at least, to the changes undergone by society itself. In its medieval conception, calling related exclusively to those engaged in a religious vocation as per the Catholic Church. Under Protestant influence and its commitment to the priesthood of all believers, calling became, on the one hand, more broadly applied to a general purposing of life for virtually any type of work. On the other hand, when it came to church-related ministry, Protestantism struggled to accommodate women who emerged with ambition, gifts, and accounts of divine calling experiences that were similar to their male counterparts. More recently, in response to secular appropriation, calling is understood largely to originate from a nonreligious source and is increasingly becoming a generalized expectation for both employers and those seeking to find their place in the world of work. Those who describe themselves as called and equate their work with their calling attest to greater life and job satisfaction overall.

Those who maintain that calling is best understood as a spiritual encounter that marks them for a particular ministry-related role are differentiated from others for whom calling reflects a personal conviction that orients the individual towards self-fulfillment in contributing to a greater cause.

Despite the challenges that remain with definitions that satisfy those who seek to engage with the concept, the data derived from college students from secular and religious colleges and churches (both Catholic and Protestants) strongly attest to the importance of a perceived calling in screening prospective candidates, as well as in individuals' understanding of their purpose in life. Though there appears to be some debate over the correspondence between calling and religiousness (as suggested by the research of Duffy and Sedlacek referred to earlier), historical engagement with the concept, together with this current research,[139] suggests that calling and religiousness are correlated and that this correlation can affect the choices that students make (e.g., college degree programs, career paths).

And so, what are we left with, after all has been said and done? The definition of calling as proposed by Niebuhr seems to sum up the concept for those who understand calling as originating from a spiritual source. Calling then is "that inner persuasion or experience whereby a person feels himself directly summoned or invited by God to take up the work of the ministry."[140] In keeping with Calvin, then this inner, secret call is validated by an external call granted by a faith-based organization inviting the individual to engage the calling in a professional role.

Similarly, the definition offered by Dik and Duffy seems to sum up the concept as imagined by those for whom calling is not necessarily dependent on a spiritual source. Calling in this context is "a transcendent summons, experienced as originating beyond the self, to approach a particular life role in a manner oriented toward demonstrating or deriving a sense of purpose or meaningfulness and that holds other-oriented values and goals as primary sources of motivation."[141]

Does either of these definitions of the call of God reflect what the Bible prescribes and illustrates in the record of the lives of the men and women of the Old and New Testaments? Do these definitions satisfy the transcultural and transhistorical criteria of a universally applicable aspect of the life of the believer? Is it possible that the term calling has been so influenced by its own historical drama that it has taken on aspects of Western culture at the expense of biblical meaning? It is to these questions that we will now turn.

> While they were ministering to the Lord and fasting, the Holy Spirit said, "Set apart for Me Barnabas and Saul for the work to which I have called them." Then, when they had fasted and prayed and laid their hands on them, they sent them away.
>
> —ACTS 13:2–3

> It is not necessary to undertake a lengthy study to realize that nothing in the Bible allows us to identify work with calling. When the terms that can be translated by the word "vocation" or "call of God" are encountered, they are always concerned with a summons to the specific service of God: a summons to be prophet or apostle, but also King, as was David; and eventually, to serve God by an exceptional act, without even knowing one is serving Him, as the Chaldeans, or Cyrus, or the king of Damascus. It is never a question of work—with the exception of Hiram and the construction of the Temple.... [Work] in any case... does not represent a service to God. It is an imperative for survival, and the Bible remains realistic enough not to superimpose upon this necessity a superfluous spiritual decoration. Moreover, the Bible is not essentially concerned with this situation of work. It is the common and distressing lot of everyone, but it is not particularly important.
>
> —JACQUES ELLUL[142]

Section 2

Biblical, Cultural, and Practical Challenges to the Contemporary Understanding of the Call of God

4

What Does the Bible Say?

Introduction

IN AN EFFORT TO evaluate what has been said to this point concerning the concept of the call of God, it is essential that an exploration of the biblical content be considered. For after all, despite the contemporary interest in a call that is increasingly devoid of a spiritual connection or a divine origin, the Christian understanding of a call is rooted in the Bible. Given the importance that Christian organizations have placed on the experience of a divine call as a prerequisite for Christian service, one would think that the biblical record on this subject would be clear and compelling. But is it?

Conversation around the call of God inevitably draws upon Old Testament examples of Abraham's supposed "call" to leave Ur and to make his way to Palestine where he would become the father of a "great nation . . . [through whom] all the families of the earth will be blessed" (Gen 12:2–4). Or Moses, who, while living in self-imposed exile on the back side of the desert of Egypt, came face to face with God through a burning bush. What transpired between God and Moses in that episode is considered to be Moses's effectual call to deliver the people of Israel out of Egypt from Exodus 3–4. Finally, especially when the call of God is referenced in a missionary context, the conversation moves inevitably to the apostle Paul and either his encounter with God on the road to Damascus in Acts 9 or, later, to what is commonly referred to as the Macedonian call in Acts 16, in which through a vision, Paul "hears" a man from Macedonia urging him to come and help him and his people (v. 9).

In addition to these examples from the lives of particular biblical personages, the concept of the call of God to ministry has been assumed to be part of the transaction when Jesus invites the Twelve to join him in ministry, when Jesus gives his parting assignment to the church in the Great Commission passages, and when Paul puts together a traveling ministry team for each of his missionary journeys. But is this the case?

Is the contemporary understanding and usage of the call of God (the definition that implies a divine source) actually rooted in the biblical record? Does the way that denominations and NGOs make use of the experience of the call of God as a means of establishing whether a candidate is suited for a ministry role find precedent for such in Abraham or Moses, in Paul or the first-century church?

Calling in the Old Testament

The Old Testament is the record of God's creative work as well as the unleashing of his plan to redeem creation and restore uninterrupted worship of himself. To accomplish this plan of redemption, God enlisted Abraham and his descendants to serve as a channel through which God's blessing would ultimately reach all the families of the earth (Gen 12:1–3). This blessing, we learn later, is epitomized in the Messiah, the divine descendant of Abraham, who would become the sacrificial Lamb for all humankind, enabling salvation to be realized, Satan to be crushed, and God to be worshipped as intended.

Throughout the Old Testament account of the unfolding of God's plan to accomplish his eternal purposes, the narrative advances historically as God periodically taps someone to move the divine story forward. And so, readers of the Old Testament are introduced initially to Adam and Eve (Gen 1–5) who give us an introduction to life in the garden, the fall of man, and the early impacts of sin and its effect on the world. A few chapters later (Gen 6–10), Noah and his family arrive on the scene and the reader is given a front-row seat to God's intervention to rescue his creation from complete destruction. Following Noah, Abraham comes onto the stage of history (Gen 11), and with Abraham, several generations of his line are highlighted (Isaac, Jacob and then the twelve sons of Jacob [Gen 16–50]). Once the story of Abraham and his immediate descendants is completed, the narrative introduces the reader to Moses.

The Moses narrative is central to the next segment of Israel's history in Moses's intervention on their behalf before Pharaoh and then as their captain and guide during their forty-year trek across the wilderness. Following the Moses story, which includes the giving of the law and preparations for settling in the promised land, the story runs through several iterations of judges who rule Israel before the introduction of the kings—first Saul, then David and Solomon, and then the rest of them during the time of the divided kingdom.[143] Israel's story under the kings is a tragic one, and in the wake of waves of sinful departure from the law, highlighted by idolatrous escapades, God sends prophets to urge his people to repent and turn back to him. The appeal of the prophets notwithstanding, the people of Israel (both the Northern and Southern Kingdoms) are eventually led off into captivity. The Northern Kingdom was eventually "lost"—assimilated into the kingdom of their captors—as there is no historical indication that these ten tribes were ever granted a return to the land from which they were taken by the Assyrians in the eighth century BC. The Southern Kingdom, which constituted the tribes of Israel and Judah, was carried off to Babylon in the late sixth century and remained in exile for seventy years until the Persian king, Cyrus, granted them permission to return to Jerusalem to rebuild the temple and later the city itself.[144] By the end of the recorded history of Old Testament, Israel has been restored to the land promised to them by God through Abraham (Gen 12:1–3), the temple has been rebuilt, some level of priestly service has been restored (Ezra 6:16–18), and the walls of Jerusalem have been restored (Neh 6:15). And yet, the promise of the coming of the Messiah remains unfulfilled.

Throughout this record of God's dealings with humankind in the Old Testament, focused as it was on his chosen people, the act of enlisting someone to assume a critical role in the unfolding of the divine drama has been often associated with the notion of calling. Those familiar with the Old Testament can identify the sixteen or so individuals who figured prominently in the approximately four-thousand-year account.[145] Of these, the circumstances surrounding the so-called calling of Abraham and Moses are the accounts most commonly cited.

Abraham

The story of Abraham is recorded in Genesis from chapters 11 through 25. In this account, which also includes some of the story of Sarah, his wife; Isaac, their son; Hagar, Sarah's handmaid; and Ishmael, Abraham's son by Hagar, we learn the following:

- Abram (later Abraham) was originally from the land of Ur, which was located in Mesopotamia (modern-day Iraq), to the east of the land of Canaan. The trek which he makes from Haran to Canaan would have been on the order of 7500 miles due to the necessity of traveling in an arc northward around (what is known today as) the Arabian Desert.

- Abraham was likely associated with pagan religious traditions. Joshua 24:2 notes that Terah, Abraham's father, served "other gods"—a reference to tribal deities associated with paganism. In contrast, however, Genesis 31:53 refers to Yahweh as the God of Abraham and of his father Terah. Though there is not much data to analyze, it is possible that Terah and his sons (Abraham and Nahor, his brother) had a knowledge of Yahweh, though they lived in a predominantly pagan context. What is not known is to what extent Abraham or any of his family actually engaged in worship of Yahweh before the encounter in Genesis 12.

- At some point in time known only to God himself, God spoke to Abraham and said, "Go from your country, and from your relatives and from your father's house, to the land which I will show you; and I will make you into a great nation, and I will bless you, and make your name great; and you shall be a blessing; and I will bless those who bless you, and the one who curses you I will curse. And in you all the families of the earth will be blessed" (Gen 12:1–3).

To this command Abraham and his entourage (which included Lot, his nephew, as well as the "persons they had accumulated")[146] respond by leaving and beginning what must have been a many-months journey over unfamiliar territory to a destination that had not yet been revealed to them. As Allen Ross points out, despite our inclination to consider this move by Abraham a simple, though grand, example of obedience on the part of a mature follower of God, it must be seen in light of the context as something else. Abraham's response to the word of God is more than just a relocation for the sake of some divine purpose; it also includes the conversion of a pagan. "This call is the Word of the Lord to the pagan, inviting him to become a Yahwist and enjoy divine blessing."[147]

The rest of Abraham's story is recounted in such a way as to emphasize the realization of the promises in and through his descendants. Whether in the miraculous means by which he is provided an heir in Isaac when Sarah is beyond childbearing years, or the subsequent provision of a substitute for him years later when Abraham is asked to sacrifice him as evidence of his faith, the story is carried forward by the faithfulness of a God who stands committed to his promises. Abraham dies, having passed on the story of God's promise to his son, Isaac, who then takes up the baton to carry it for the next segment of the race.

Moses

Moses, like Abraham, is chosen by God to assume an immensely important role in the outworking of the divine plan of redemption. This plan, by the time it gets to the historical context of Moses, is in a place to respond to the bondage of the Hebrews to the Egyptians that has lasted nearly four hundred years by the time of Moses's birth. The reader of the Old Testament account is given a privileged vantage point from which to see how Moses's mother's attempt to shield the child from the wrath of Pharoah actually puts Moses in a position to be protected and later raised by the ruling family itself. Moses grows up in Pharoah's household, apparently without an understanding of his birth story or heritage until a string of events leads him to discover his connection to the very slaves he was likely commanding. Following an unfortunate attempt at defending his people that ends in the death of an Egyptian, Moses finds himself exiled and alone wandering the fringes of civilization, caring for sheep.

In this place of isolation, God intervenes in Moses's life to enlist him in the task of freeing the Hebrews, leading them out from Egypt and slavery and into a new land and relationship with Yahweh. The specific episode, which is often referred to as Moses's calling, is recorded in Exodus 3. Here, out of a burning bush, God gives Moses a definitive task.

> The Lord said, "I have surely seen the affliction of My people who are in Egypt, and have given heed to their cry because of their taskmasters, for I am aware of their sufferings. So I have come down to deliver them from the power of the Egyptians,

and to bring them up from that land to a good and spacious land, to a land flowing with milk and honey, to the place of the Canaanite and the Hittite and the Amorite and the Perizzite and the Hivite and the Jebusite. Now, behold, the cry of the sons of Israel has come to Me; furthermore, I have seen the oppression with which the Egyptians are oppressing them. Therefore, come now, and I will send you to Pharaoh, so that you may bring My people, the sons of Israel, out of Egypt. (Exod 3:7–10)

With the help of his older brother Aaron, Moses makes his way to Pharaoh and, through a protracted set of encounters, which includes unleashing a set of increasingly onerous plagues, eventually procures the release of the Hebrew slaves. The initial departure of the Hebrews on the morning after the Passover is met with pursuit by Pharoah and his armies, the armies who are then cut off and destroyed by God in the Red Sea. Following their deliverance from Pharoah, Moses leads the people into the wilderness and eventually to Mount Sinai (Exod 19:1–2), where he receives the law of God and invites the people to enter into a covenant with God (Exod 19:7–8).

The final forty years of Moses's life are consumed with his shepherding the people of Israel as they wander in the wilderness as recompense for their lack of faith in God's promise to secure for them the land he had promised them. Despite his years of service as Israel's leader, Moses dies having seen but never having set foot in the promised land after handing over leadership to Joshua (Deut 34:9). Joshua leads the people across the Jordan River to claim that which had been promised (Josh 3).

Though the accounts of Abraham and Moses serve to showcase the enlisting of particular individuals for the sake of the divine plan, nowhere in the accounts do we find explicit reference to calling language. Though it may be assumed due to the context, the explicit idea that God "calls" someone to some kind of ministry role is lacking. Nevertheless, calling language is not absent from the Old Testament text. A survey of the Old Testament usage of calling reveals several interrelated categories which include calling as naming someone or something, calling as a summons or invitation, and calling as causing someone or something to become something else. These categories are described in table 4.

Table 4: Calling in the Old Testament

Use	Passage	Hebrew Word
Naming/ Identifying	"God called the light day and the darkness he called night" (Gen 1:5). "And the man said, 'This is now bone of my bones and flesh of my flesh; she shall be called woman'" (Gen 2:23).	qara (קָרָא)—to call out, to give a name, to pronounce qara
Inviting/ Summoning	"Then the Lord God called to the man and said to him, 'Where are you?'" (Gen 2:23) "When the Lord saw that he (Moses) turned aside to look, God called to him from the midst of the bush" (Exod 3:4).	qara qara
Cause to Become (Something)	"But now, thus says the Lord, your Creator, O Jacob, and He who formed you, O Israel, 'Do not fear, for I have redeemed you; I have called you by name; you are Mine!'" (Isa 43:1) "The nations will see your righteousness, and all kings your glory; and you will be called by a new name which the mouth of the Lord will designate" (Isa 43:1).	qara qara

Some of the most frequent use of calling language to highlight the relationship God has with his people is found in the prophets—especially Isaiah, for whom the idea of calling is referenced over thirty times.

- "I will give you the treasures of darkness, and hidden wealth of secret places, so that you may know that it is I, the Lord, the God of Israel, who *calls* you by your name. For the sake of Jacob My servant, and Israel My chosen one, I have also *called* you by your name; I have given you a title of honor though you have not known Me" (Isa 45:3–4).
- "When Israel was a youth I loved him, and out of Egypt I *called* My son" (Hos 11:1).
- "And it will come about that everyone who *calls* on the name of the Lord will be saved; for on Mount Zion and in Jerusalem there

will be those who escape, just as the Lord has said, even among the survivors whom the Lord *calls*" (Joel 2:32).

From these passages, several observations can be made. Firstly, in the mind of God, calling largely refers to the notion of naming or of summoning, and in the context of God and the people of Israel, the calling is collective (the people) and not directed towards any particular individual. Secondly, the notion of calling includes the past, present, and the future. It is as if God's call directed at his people is timeless in its theological rendering. Thirdly, though there are several instances in which the people of Israel (or a subset thereof) call on God (for help or to self-identify as belonging to him covenantly), it is primarily God who calls, and this calling is rooted in his initial choice to enlist Abraham as a conduit of blessing and the subsequent promises he made to set the program of redemption in motion.

So, if calling in the Old Testament is apparently collective and intended to establish or highlight a relationship between God (who calls) and his people (who respond), how should the experiences of men like Abraham and Moses (among others) be considered? Clearly, they were designated by God for a particular role in the unfolding of God's redemptive drama; but can we say that the circumstances that God used to enlist their participation constitutes a call? And if so, can we deduce from their experience that calling of this nature should be expected for others who (later) aspire to a particular role in ministry?

The Abrahamic account provides little in terms of a common framework that could be applied today for the following reasons. Firstly, if what takes place can be considered a call of God, then it most likely fits the invitation/summoning category from table 4. As noted, this call serves as an invitation to leave a pagan context and join the worship of and obedience to Yahweh. Secondly, if we grant that this does serve as a call of God, the framework of the call is not to some ministry role but simply for Abraham to move to a new location, ostensibly where he can establish a new homestead that reflects faith in the God who calls. Finally, whereas contemporary calling looks for an external call from a local assembly or organization, Abraham's experience has none of that, even though the assurance he receives is directly from God himself.

As in the case of Abraham, the call of Moses is often referred to as a model or example of God's calling today. However, despite the clarity of the divine encounter and directive that Moses receives from God, this experience also fails to provide much that can be applied to a contemporary setting. Firstly, the historical context is unique and pivotal in the history of redemption. God's plan required someone with a unique set of skills, relationship with political authorities, and ethnic heritage to be able to accomplish the task of freeing the Hebrew slaves and then caring for them in their trek to the land of Canaan. That God would raise up someone to fill this role makes divine sense; that an expectation that such a unique role applies broadly to believers at all times and in all places stretches the logic of the historical reality.

Secondly, as in the case of Abraham, contemporary understandings of calling combine an inward call (described as a sense of what God would have me do with my life) and an external call, which is received from a faith-based organization. In Moses's case, the call—if it can be referred to as such—came as a dramatic intervention by God. The text offers no such indication that Moses was feeling as if he should assume some sort of leadership role on behalf of the Hebrews, which, in the meantime prompted him to self-exile to the fringes of civilization and assume a role as a shepherd. In response to the divine assignment, Moses expressed his hesitancy to take on the role for several reasons, not the least of which was his fear that the Hebrews would never believe that he had been sent by God at all. So, in order to reassure Moses, God equipped him with several confirming articles and signs as well as with a companion, his brother Aaron the Levite, who could serve as a spokesman before the Hebrews and Pharoah. Armed with this confirming material, Moses and Aaron made their case to the elders of the sons of Israel and performed the signs intended to accompany and validate their message and assignment. In the end, Moses's role is affirmed by the people (the believing congregation, if you will) but the extraordinary context[148] can hardly be taken as a pattern for today.

If there is a pattern that can be observed in Old Testament literature with regard to the notion of calling, it is perhaps best described in Norman Habel's statement that a pattern related to the public commissioning of Old Testament prophets/judges is initiated in the commissioning of Moses and Gideon. Habel argues that this same pattern then is also found in the story of the sending of Abraham's servant to get a wife for Isaac, as well as the narratives surrounding the enlisting of Isaiah, Jeremiah, and Ezekiel in prophetic service. The pattern, according to Habel, is reflected in a series of six interrelated and chronological steps or phases that begin with the initial encounter with God and conclude with a divine sign, affirming that this word or assignment indeed issues from God. The six elements include: 1) the divine confrontation; 2) the introductory word; 3) the commission; 4) the objection; 5) the reassurance; and 6) the sign.[149]

One helpful way to observe the parallel nature of these elements in the various call narratives of certain Old Testament prophets is to tabulate the passages that apply to each of the elements (see table 5 below).

Table 5: Common Elements in the Call Narratives of Old Testament Prophets

Name	Passage	Divine Confrontation	Introductory Word	The Commission	The Objection	The Reassurance	The Sign
Moses	Exod 3:1–12	vv. 1–4a	vv. 4b–9	v. 10	v. 11	v. 12a	v. 12b
Isaiah[150]	Isa 6:1–13	vv. 1–2	vv. 3–7	vv. 8–10	v. 11a	vv. 11b–13	n/a
Jeremiah	Jer 1:4–10	v. 4	v. 5a	v. 5b	v. 6	vv. 7–8	vv. 9–10
Ezekiel	Ezek 1:1—3:11	1:1–28	2:1–2	2:3–5	2:6–8	2:6–7	2:8—3:11

The pattern revealed in these call narratives confirms a common set of elements that are affirmed over and over again in the stories of those enlisted in service of God's people. However, despite this pattern, many men and women of Old Testament significance cannot point to a similar story that led them into spiritual service, such as Isaac, Jacob, and Saul—and, from the pool of the prophets, Daniel, Hosea, Joel, and Micah—all of whom were notably significant in their service to the people of God and were enlisted into service in some way, but not according to the pattern noted above.

Calling in the Old Testament: A Summary

An investigation of the Old Testament notion of calling yields the following conclusions. Firstly, God is the one who calls. Whether his calling is for the purpose of naming/identifying, inviting/summoning, or causing to become something, God clearly initiates the act, doing so in accordance with mystery of his divine purposes. Secondly, those who are enlisted into service are often surprised by it, and some, namely, Abraham or Samuel, arguably received their summons prior to exercising obvious faith. Calling does not seem to be something that is sought or even anticipated. It comes when God brings it. Thirdly, virtually all who were engaged in service that played out in the history of Israel were men. Apart from a few individuals who stand out as much for their faith as for their scarcity, women were not often designated for special service. Fourth, the reality of being engaged in particular service was highly limited. For every Abraham and Noah and Moses, there were thousands who remain hidden from history and for whom life revolved around sustaining faith in the midst of a difficult subsistence. Though it could be argued that the Levites represent a relatively large number of people who received a call to service, they were selected collectively and not individually via an inherited role once the priestly service was given to the Levites. Otherwise, it is doubtful that the average Hebrew (and certainly not those who endured the four hundred years of slavery under Pharoah) would have considered his or her life and role in any way reflective of some kind of divine calling—apart from, perhaps, the recognition of being part of the chosen people.

Calling in the New Testament

The New Testament record picks up where the Old Testament leaves off. The people of Israel are back in their land, the temple (now that a third temple, known as Herod's temple, is under construction) and the priestly service have been restored. What sets the New Testament account apart from the Old Testament is, of course, the advent of Jesus the Messiah. As Paul notes in Galatians 4:4, "When the fullness of time came, God sent His son, born of a woman, born under the Law." The idea here in the Greek of "fullness of time" can be understood as "just at the right time." That is to say, when God had orchestrated all that needed to be in place historically, then he sent Jesus.

Jesus's arrival and all that follows changes everything from the position of anticipating his coming and what that would mean for the people of Israel (and the world) to one of fufilling the promises God had made across the pages of the Old Testament from Moses to the prophets. In the coming of Jesus, the *missio Dei* takes several steps forward, and in a matter of just a few decades, what Paul refers to as a mystery (Eph 3:3–11; Col 1:25–27)—the salvation of the gentiles and the uniting of Jew and gentile in the church—becomes the new focus of the divine narrative. In this setting, in which the focus of divine activity moves from Israel to the church, the role of individuals enlisted in the service of the divine plan is once again correlated with the notion of calling.

For many, Paul's encounter with Christ on the road to Damascus (Acts 9:1–9) and, perhaps later, the plea from a man from Macedonia (Acts 16:9–10) constitute the definitive example of a call to ministry and, especially, missionary service. Before examining the notion of calling in the life of Paul, some attention should first be given to the notion of calling as generally used by the New Testament writers.

At first glance, the concept of calling as it appears in the Gospels seems to reflect usage noted in the Old Testament. Here, calling is used in naming/identifying, summoning/inviting, and even causing someone to become something. Table 6 summarizes these uses from the Gospel writers.

In the Gospel accounts, the major aspect of calling language refers to the concept of naming/identifying or inviting/summoning. Though several different Greek words are used by the Gospel writers, the dominant term has as its base καλέω, which is used throughout the Gospels for each of the three broad categories. In terms of the use of any of these Greek terms in the sense of designating someone for a particular ministry role, the closest context would be that of Jesus calling his disciples, which is recorded in each of the Synoptic accounts: Matthew 4:18–22, Mark 1:16–34, and Luke 5:1–11.

Table 6: Calling in the Gospels

Use	Passage	Greek word
Naming/ Identifying	"He will be great, and will be called the Son of the Most High" (Luke 1:32).	καλέω—to call
	"But do not be called Rabbi; for One is your Teacher and you are all brothers" (Matt 23:8)	καλέω—to call
Inviting/ Summoning	"And he called ten of his slaves and gave them ten minas" (Luke 19:13).	καλέω—to call
	"And after he called the multitude to him, He said to them, 'Hear and understand'" (Matt 15:10).	προσκαλέομαι—to summon/ invite
	"And He went up to the mountain and summoned those whom He Himself wanted, and they came to Him" (Mark 3:13).	προσκαλέομαι—to call (to oneself), to summon
Cause to Become (Something)	"He brought him to Jesus. Jesus looked at him and said, 'You are Simon the son of John; you shall be called Cephas (which is translated, Peter)'" (John 1:42).	καλέω—to call
	"No longer do I call you slaves, for the slave does not know what the Master is doing; but I have called you friends for all things that I have heard from My Father I have made known to you" (John 15:15).	λέγω—to name, say, or call ἐρεῶ—to call, speak of

In both the Matthew and Mark passage, the author sets the scene by noting that Jesus is walking by the Sea of Galilee, and he spots Simon and Andrew, who are fishing near enough to shore so that, in Matthew's words (which are virtually identical in Mark), "And He [Jesus] said [from the Greek λέγω] to them, 'Follow Me, and I will make you fishers of men'" (Matt 4:19). The Lukan account has Jesus teaching a small crowd from the boat he borrowed from Simon moments earlier. Immediately following the teaching moment, Luke depicts the Jesus-Simon-cast-your-nets-in-deeper-water scene. It is in the wake of the subsequent amazing catch of fish that Jesus informs Simon, Andrew, James, and John that they would be from here on out catching men (Luke 15:10). Mark's Gospel gives the only account of the designation of the remaining disciples[151] when Jesus summons (from the Greek προσκαλέομαι) them to come to his mountain retreat (Mark 3:13–14). Interestingly, immediately following in verse 14, Mark notes that Jesus "appointed [from the Greek ἐποίησεν—to make or accomplish] twelve, that they might be with Him, and that He might send them out to preach." In this passage, we see the combination of the notion of calling together with that of appointment, a combination we will explore again later. In effect, the appointment of the twelve to their apostolic ministry was conditioned upon their response to Christ's summons. Their calling was, if you will, the invitation to follow Christ. The appointment to ministry was a particular designation reserved uniquely for these twelve that was subsequent to their calling to follow him. This idea of selectivity (as opposed to a general appointment or assignment to this role) is reinforced by Mark's phrase "those whom He Himself wanted" (Mark 3:13).

From the Gospel accounts, we learn that the notion of calling reflects much of the Old Testament idea and can be expressed in any of three main categories: naming/identifying, inviting/summoning, and causing to become something. Similar to the Old Testament notion, calling, when it goes beyond common, everyday speech to refer to the particular naming of people, originates in God. What is striking in the New Testament story is that God is now present in Jesus. So when he designates someone or something—as in the case of Simon, when Jesus says to him, "You are Simon the son of John; you shall be called Cephas (which is translated Peter)" (John 1:42)—it carries divine weight. Additionally, all those called in this way are men. Again, women do not seem to figure prominently (yet, anyway) in the unfolding of the *missio Dei*. And finally, Scripture is silent about how the rest of those who exercised faith in Christ perceived their life and role in any way related to a divine calling, apart from Jesus's summons to "come to Me, all who are weary and burdened, and I will give you rest" (Matt 11:28a). Those who listened to Jesus over the course of his three years of public ministry would perhaps have understood that by responding to his summons by putting their trust in him, they would become children of God (John 1:12), his sheep (John 10:9), one of the branches of the true vine (John 15:5), and a friend of Jesus (John 15:13–15), but these realities do not seem to correspond to a particular calling to a ministry role.

As the New Testament story moves beyond the Gospels into the account of the apostles, we are introduced to a turn in the story away from the Jews to the gentiles (i.e., the nations). In fact, Jesus's closing words to his disciples—picked up in somewhat different forms by each of the Gospel writers—make it clear that he has a vision for the world that he wants those who follow him to accomplish, a vision that is inclusive in its reach. Matthew 28:18–20 probably is the most familiar rendering of this assignment: "And Jesus came up and spoke to them, saying, 'All authority in heaven and on earth has been given to Me. Go, therefore, and make disciples of all the nations, baptizing them in the name of the Father and the Son and the Holy Spirit, teaching them to follow all that I commanded you; and behold, I am with you always, to the end of the age.'" Jesus's final words are given here as a command to the church to focus its activity on the task of making disciples of the nations. What is interesting in its absence in this passage, as well as in the other places that the New Testament writers record similar words,[152] is any reference to calling as a condition of participation in the task.

Though debate over the applicability of this passage to anyone but the first-century apostles was largely put to rest with William Carey's famous challenge to the Hyper-Calvinism of the eighteenth century,[153] history indicates, even since the days of Carey, that the church has not always been convinced of its general obligation to the task of making disciples of the nations. In her account of the history of American women in missions, Robert tells the story of the rapid decline in evangelistic witness in the wake of World War I and the realization that the civilizing mission focus, combined with American triumphalism, had badly misrepresented the gospel. One indication of the rapid shift that marked a self-conscious, almost apologetic, turn in American evangelicalism in the 1920s and following is reflected in the shift in programming of the Young Women's Christian Association (YWCA). Robert notes that the

> YWCA reports from 1904–5 showed that twelve mission study classes were held, plus thirteen missionary meetings. In 1919, the Student Volunteer Band had twenty-two members, girls who had signed the volunteer pledge to be foreign missionaries. But in 1925, the "Missionary Department" of the YWCA changed its name to the "World Fellowship Department." In 1929, the YWCA ceased corresponding with missionaries, and the Student Volunteer room was changed to a "World Fellowship Room." Year by year during the 1920s, subtle shifts in emphasis marked a transition from emphasis on missions to international student life.[154]

The decline of women's involvement in missions in America in the 1920s was later negatively impacted by the rise of ecumenism and liberal theology that swept through mainline denominations in post-World War II America and all but choked out active missionary service, which was focused on conversionary efforts. The apex of this turning from Christ's commission is reflected in the 1973 call for a moratorium on North Atlantic missionaries by the World Council of Churches (WCC). Ostensibly, this moratorium (which, in an appeal to the etymology of the term, means "pause" and not "death") was intended as a global appeal to assess the state of the church, particularly in the Third World, in light of what many perceived as theological imperialism issuing primarily from the West. Bert Beach, in his assessment of the ecumenical movement over the last forty years of the twentieth century, made the following observations, which reinforce the conclusion that the church (to be fair, some but not all of the church) has not always been convinced of its obligation to make disciples of all nations:[155]

- The term evangelism (and even more so evangelization) is hardly seen in WCC documents since the New Delhi assembly in 1961.
- Instead of calling people out of the world through conversion, ecumenical evangelism invites people into the world to perform deeds of faith.
- The mission of WCC involves participation in struggle and suffering. This includes the use of power in violent action where nonviolent means have been tried and crushed.

Finally, Beach records that "Eugene Stockwell, the retiring rector (1984–1989) of the Commission on World Mission and Evangelism [of the WCC], spoke on the topic, 'Mission Issues for Today and Tomorrow.' What were the issues? He talked about foreign debt; global annihilation; the pain of war; torture; hunger; poverty; and divisions. He said nothing about the problem of pain of billions lost in sin without salvation. For him, apparently, this was not one of the mission issues for today and tomorrow."[156]

In a more recent exposé of the church in America's feelings about the obligation to make disciples, a 2019 report issued by the Barna Group, entitled *Reviving Evangelism*, indicated that nearly 50 percent of what they identify as "practicing Christian Millennials" consider it wrong to share their faith, a first step towards making disciples.[157] With the commitment to disciple-making fading from prominence in the church in general and, more strikingly, among Evangelicals (!), the notion of calling to any kind of ministry role that is associated with evangelism seems that much less likely. How would someone process a call to something that one feels is illegitimate?

The concept of calling in the Gospels seems largely to carry over meaning from Old Testament usage. Examples can be found in which calling is used to name/identify, invite/summon, or cause to become. For those who became Christ's apostles, calling to salvation is paired with appointment, such that those who responded to the summons to follow Jesus were subsequently given a ministry assignment. Calling in the Gospels seems to be limited to the stories of the apostles. Though calling and appointment (to ministry) seem to be distinct aspects of grace, a discussion of calling that relies on the experience of the apostles as the model could reflect a conflation of the logical sequence of calling relative to appointment. Lastly, the fact that calling seems to be absent from all of the Great Commission passages suggests that the idea that calling refers to and is necessary for a ministry assignment may be a misunderstanding of the concept.

Calling and the Early Church

Not long after Jesus's final words to the apostles in Acts 1:8, the story tells of the annual celebration of Pentecost, the Jewish festival commemorating the fiftieth day following Passover. This time, as described by Luke, the Spirit moves, men speak in unlearned tongues, people are amazed, some mock, Peter preaches, others sincerely inquire as to what it all means, and, in the end, "those who had received his [Peter's] word were baptized; and there were added [to the Church] that day about three thousand souls" (Acts 2:41).

Immediately following these events, Luke in Acts 2:42–47 records what is likely a condensed summary of what many believe to be the beginnings of the early church. The description can be boiled down to several main items: the people who believed 1) devoted themselves to the apostles' teaching, 2) were amazed at the miraculous signs, 3) met together regularly, and 4) shared their possessions. In closing, Luke notes that "day by day the Lord added to their number those who were being saved" (v. 47b).

Leadership of this early gathering of those who would later be called Christians falls naturally to the apostles who carried over their authority from their time with Jesus to this new phase of the unfolding story. It was likely that no one really knew what exactly was happening nor what the next steps were. The church had been mentioned by Jesus only twice before (see Matt 16:18 and 18:15–17), and if Jesus gave the disciples any other information about this new community of faith before his ascension, it is not recorded anywhere. Regardless, leadership for the early church was an inherited role for the apostles. If one admits that they were called to be apostles, then calling to this church leadership role would, ostensibly, follow.

As we learn just a couple of chapters later in the account by Luke in the book of Acts, the apostles are soon overwhelmed by the people's demands on them, in part because of the responsiveness of the people to their message. At some point, a conflict erupts between Hellenistic Jews and native Hebrews over the question of the distribution of daily food. Apparently, the native Hebrews, who might have considered themselves "better" than their Hellenistic brethren, were not treating them well (Acts 6:1). In response, the apostles gathered the assembly and urged them to select from among themselves those who could faithfully and equitably serve the entire body so that they, the apostles, could devote themselves to the spiritual aspects of the ministry.

In the request issued by the apostles for the selection of those who would serve the rest—the office that later became known as the office of a deacon—the qualifications for selection include 1) gender—male, 2) reputation—good, 3) spiritual life—full of the Spirit and wisdom. The account continues by noting that the congregation chose Stephen, Philip, Prochorus, Nicanor, Timon, Parmenas, and Nicolas. And when these were selected, the congregation presented them to the apostles, after which the apostles prayed and laid their hands on them (Acts 6:5–6).

This solution seemed to please everyone, including the apostles. In verse 7, we read that in the wake of this reorganization of the early church, "the word of God kept on spreading; and the number of the disciples continued to increase greatly in Jerusalem, and a great many of the priests were becoming obedient to the faith." Despite the care that the apostles took to consult with God and lay out a process by which suitable servants would be found, what is lacking in this description of the identification and appointment of the first church leaders after the first apostles is any reference to some internal sense that the individual selected was called to this task. Nor do the apostles in their affirmation of those selected by the congregation suggest that they have affirmed or validated such a call. Was calling so obvious that it didn't need to be acknowledged? Is the lack of an acknowledged call as an indicator that calling was not pertinent to the early church merely an argument from silence?

Paul and the Call of God

The conversion of Paul and his subsequent appointment as "a preacher and an apostle as a teacher of the Gentiles" (1 Tim 2:7) is commonly cited as the example of what a call to ministry looks like. Sills attests to this when he states, "Paul is actually more of a prototype for missionaries of the twenty-first century than any previous time in modern mission's history."[158] Paul's repeated reference to this aspect of his life story[159] is a reminder to himself and others that his life was dramatically changed due to his encounter with Christ. Not only does he acknowledge that the events on the Damascus Road resulted in salvation, but they also served to redirect his life's work. Whereas Paul had been in the service of the Jewish people as a Pharisee (Acts 22:3–5, Phil 3:5–6), his conversion made him into an apostle to the gentiles (Rom 11:13, Eph 3:1–11).

On two occasions in his letters to the churches, Paul describes his new assignment of apostolic service to the gentiles in terms of calling. In his introduction to the church in Rome, he writes, "Paul, a bond-servant of Christ Jesus, called as an apostle, set apart for the Gospel of God" (Rom 1:1). Similarly, in his introductory remarks to the church in Corinth, he writes, "Paul, called as an apostle of Jesus Christ by the will of God" (1 Cor 1:1). Paul reiterates this relationship between his salvation and his apostolic ministry to the gentiles in his letters to Timothy. In 1 Timothy 1:12, Paul says that God "put him into service." Though the object of his service is left open here, in 2:7, he acknowledges that he was "appointed a preacher and an apostle . . . of the Gentiles." He repeats this same description in 2 Timothy 2:11, when he says, "for which I was appointed a preacher and an apostle and a teacher." From these statements, it is clear that Paul understands that his new ministry role as an apostle to the gentiles is a God-given assignment that follows from his new identity in Christ. However, when examining Paul's conversion, several questions arise, including, "How does Paul understand the concept of call? Is Paul's calling to apostleship part of his conversion or is it subsequent to it? How does the idea of being appointed fit with calling?"

The Greek term most commonly used in the New Testament to convey the idea of calling is καλέω. The term, in its various forms, occurs nearly 150 times. As noted in table 4, καλέω is used in the New Testament to convey a range of actions. Paul, in his writings, employs καλέω some 33 times, primarily in the context of a divine action. In other words, for Paul, καλέω refers particularly to something that God does to or for someone. For example, in Romans 9:23–24, Paul states, "And He [God] did so to make known the riches of His glory upon objects of mercy, which He prepared beforehand for glory, namely us, whom He also called, not only from among Jews, but also from among Gentiles." And again, in Galatians 1:15–16, he says, "But when He [God] who had set me apart even from my mother's womb and called me through His grace was pleased to reveal His Son in me so that I might preach Him among the Gentiles"—God is the agent of calling.

In addition to divine agency, for Paul, καλέω is almost exclusively used in the context of salvation.[160] For example, in Romans 8:30, Paul says, "And these whom He [God] predestined, He also called; and these whom He called, He also justified; and these whom He justified, He also glorified." Another example is found in 1 Thessalonians 2:12, Paul says, "So that you would walk in a manner worthy of the God who calls you into His own kingdom and glory." For Paul, calling is mostly understood as the means by which God exercises salvation or a summary of the salvation experience itself. And here, though the range of possible uses of the term includes the idea of invitation/summons, the suggestion that an invitation or summons could be refused raises theological questions related to the efficacy of the call. Klein, in his work on Paul's use of καλέω, argues:

> The whole idea of an "effectual summons" may be problematic. A summons seems implicitly to contain some tentativeness. It is a request, an invitation, albeit a commanding one. To add a causative component to the sense of "summons" must result in either "God caused Paul to be summoned" or "God caused Paul to respond positively to the summons." It seems that the first does not really say anything different from the simple "God summoned Paul." But the second also seems problematic. Here the summons becomes such as to be unrefusable. But if this is the case, must we speak of summons? If God is unquestionably causing some one or some ones to become his own children—to attain salvation—that is an act of fiat designation or

appointment. He is causing them to be his own. "Calling" here is the application of, not invitation to, salvation.[161]

And so, for Paul, it seems, the calling of God is associated more fully with the act of God that, by grace through faith, results in salvation. The call is effectual and, in this respect, irrefutable.

From the moment that marks Paul's conversion (Acts 9), Paul is made aware that his conversion also involves a new ministry role that will be marked by two elements that Jewish thought would have considered to be well beyond the norm for spiritual service: redemptive efforts among the gentiles and suffering.[162] On more than one occasion Paul takes great pains to try to convince his hearers that his ministry to the gentiles is not only appropriate, because God promised to Abraham that the nations would also be blessed, but legitimate, because his ministry assignment was given to him by God himself. To this end Paul argues in Galatians 1:11–12, "For I would have you know, brothers and sisters, that the gospel which was preached by me is not of human invention. For I neither received it from man, nor was I taught it, but I received it through a revelation of Jesus Christ." Later in this chapter, he goes on to recount his journey to Damascus to highlight the supernatural nature of conversion experience and how his ministry assignment to the gentiles was tied up in it. Furthermore, in many of the introductions to his letters, he underlines the fact that his apostolic ministry has divine origins. A comparison of how Paul makes this case is summarized in table 7.

The point of all of this is simply that, for Paul, both his calling to salvation as well as his ministry assignment as an apostle to the gentiles were of divine origin. They both came from God, and they did so when he was not looking for them. In fact, he makes the point that he considers himself the "least of all the apostles and not worthy to be called an apostle because he persecuted the Church of God" (1 Cor 15:9). Paul was actively seeking to destroy the church and the witness of the gospel when God visited him with this twofold grace that changed his life, both temporally and eternally.

Table 7: Paul's Statement on the Divine Origin of His Apostleship

Reference	Statement on the Divine Origin of His Apostleship
Rom 1:1	"Paul, a bond-servant of Christ Jesus, called as an apostle, set apart for the gospel of God"
1 Cor 1:1a	"Paul, called as an apostle of Jesus Christ by the will of God"
2 Cor 1:1a	"Paul, an apostle of Christ Jesus by the will of God"
Gal 1:1	"Paul, an apostle (not sent from men nor through human agency, but through Jesus Christ and God the Father, who raised Him from the dead)"
Eph 1:1	"Paul, an apostle of Christ Jesus by the will of God"
1 Tim 1:1	"Paul, an apostle of Christ Jesus according to the commandment of God our Savior, and of Christ Jesus, who is our hope"
2 Tim 1:1	"Paul, an apostle of Christ Jesus by the will of God, according to the promise of life in Christ Jesus"

In addition to, or perhaps because of, the divine origin of his ministry, Paul understood that his apostleship was permanent and something to which he was obligated. This is evidenced in his comments in Romans 1:14, when he says that he is "under obligation both to Greeks and to the uncultured, both to the wise and to the foolish." The sense of the Greek term rendered here "obligation" is that of owing a debt. On the one hand, Paul understands that his life in Christ was such an underserved gift that he is indebted to God for it. At the same time, he has grasped that as a Jew and therefore one who has had access to the covenants, the law, and the promises (Rom 9:4–5), he also has a debt to the gentiles to bring them the good news that opens the door for them to the blessing of God promised to Abraham (Gen 12:1–3). Furthermore, in his letter to the Galatians, Paul reminds his readers of the nature of his commitment to his task when he says that he had been "entrusted with the gospel" to the uncircumcised (i.e., gentiles) (Gal 2:7). And finally, in perhaps his most colorful language on this subject of all, in 1 Corinthians 9:16, Paul makes his obligation to his apostolic ministry unequivocal: "For if I preach the gospel, I have nothing to boast about, for I am under compulsion; for woe to me if I do not preach the gospel."

Throughout his letters, Paul regularly urges his readers to do all that they can to nurture faith individually and corporately. As he does so, it seems in some of his exhortations to maintain the faith, that there is more than a hint of a reference to his own apostolic obligation to the gentiles. And so, in 1 Corinthians 9:24–27 where Paul describes the Christian life as a race and a boxing match that are to be undertaken with the intent to win, he goes on in verses 26 and 27 to point to himself and his efforts as an example of how to do so. In his Second Letter to Timothy, probably his last letter before his eventual death, Paul gives a brief summary-evaluation of his life since he met Christ. In 4:6–7, he picks up the metaphors from 1 Corinthians 9 and again applies them to himself: "For I am already being poured out as a drink offering, and the time of my departure has come. I have fought the good fight, I have finished the course, I have kept the faith." Though he does not explicitly connect his fighting the good fight, finishing the course, and keeping the faith with his apostolic ministry, it is hard to imagine that Paul would have given himself such a favorable assessment had he not done so. And so for Paul, both his call to salvation as well as his appointment to apostolic ministry share divine origin as well as divine obligation.

One final thought pertaining to the relationship of calling to salvation and apostleship concerns the chronology of the elements of Paul's call. It goes without saying that, logically speaking, Paul could not have undertaken his apostolic assignment until he was in Christ. This is especially true, because Paul, in fact, was an active persecutor of the church and hence an anti-apostle prior to his conversion. So, conversion has to come first. This first step Paul describes in his three conversion accounts in Acts 22, Acts 26, and Galatians 1–2. Once Paul undergoes conversion, he can then be given his apostolic assignment. The introductory comments to some of Paul's letters (see table 7) seem to suggest that his conversion and apostolic assignment were concurrent. In two of the cases, the text seems to suggest that the calling applies directly to the secondary feature. In Romans 1:1, we read, "Paul, a bond-servant of Christ Jesus, called as an apostle, set apart for the gospel of God." Similarly, in 1 Corinthians 1:1, Paul says, "Paul, called as an apostle of Jesus Christ by the will of God."

However, whereas Paul's conversion results from calling, Paul's apostleship results from appointment. In both Romans 1:1 and 1 Corinthians

1:1, the Greek term rendered "called" is κλητός which, though it shares the meaning of invitation/summons with καλέω, here it carries the idea of being appointed to the discharge of a particular office (ministry). That it takes on this meaning here is based on two arguments. Firstly, in the account of his conversion in Acts 26:16–17, which is part of his defense before King Agrippa, Paul argues that his apostolic ministry to the gentiles came from Jesus himself who said to him,

> But get up and stand on your feet; for this purpose I have appeared to you, to appoint you as a servant and a witness not only to the things in which you have seen Me, but also to the things in which I will appear to you, rescuing you from the Jewish people and from the Gentiles, to whom I am sending you.

In this retelling of the events of that fateful day, Paul argues that Jesus appointed (προχειρίζομαι—to put into one's hand, to appoint) him to this task and consequently sent (from ἀποστέλλω—to send) him to the gentiles. This same term for "sent" or "sending" is used in Matthew 10:5, when Jesus sends out the twelve. "These twelve Jesus sent forth (ἀποστέλλω) and commanded them saying, go not into the way of the Gentiles, and into any city of the Samaritans."

Secondly, in at least two of his introductory comments, Paul makes it clear that his apostleship was something other than an invitation or summons. In 1 Timothy 1:1, he notes that he is an apostle because of "the commandment of God our Savior, and of Christ Jesus, who is our hope." In 1 Corinthians 1:1, 2 Corinthians 1:1, Ephesians 1:1, and 2 Timothy 1:1, Paul claims that his apostleship was the result of the will of God. For these reasons, it seems reasonable to conclude that Paul's apostolic assignment was granted separately from his calling to salvation.

The concept of calling as seen in the life and letters of Paul provides us with significant insight as to the function and relationship of the concept of calling. For Paul, calling is almost always associated with conversion. Calling in this sense marks the

> concrete and historical realization in a person's life of God's foreordained plan. It is the point at which God's purposes become actualized in the life of the person. In God's mind, His purposes on behalf of the person may be foreknown and predestined. But it is not until the action of "calling" that the person actually becomes a recipient of and participant in God's purposes for him.[163]

Calling is therefore of divine origin and, as such, is irrefutable. Calling "makes us" into children of God.

Calling, as noted in and by Paul, precedes ministry appointment. Whereas Paul was called to salvation, he was appointed to ministry. The two elements are nearly concurrent in Paul theologically but are logically separate divine actions. So, where we read that Paul was "called as an apostle" in Romans 1:1 and 1 Corinthians 1:1, it should be read as, "Paul, called to salvation so that I could be appointed as an apostle," to reflect the chronological and logical outworking of God's grace in his life.

Other New Testament Considerations

The New Testament account is taken up with the life of Jesus and his disciples in the Gospels. The book of Acts, which chronicles the emergence of the church, largely traces the life and ministry of Peter and Paul and introduces us to a handful of other significant individuals such as Luke, Timothy, Aquilla and Priscilla, Titus, Lydia and a few others. The Epistles and Revelation, given that they serve a more didactic role, are less given to historical data and thus introduce few key people to the story of Christianity in the first century. So, apart from Paul, what do we glean about the concept of calling from the rest of the New Testament?

Calling and Church Ministry

Ever since Luther and Calvin made their theological break from the Catholic Church and elevated the priesthood of all believers, the question of who could serve in the church was ignited. As discussed earlier, though these men and many of their contemporaries made significant theological strides in helping to restore a more biblical understanding of the church and the believer's relationship to it, they both were still products of their time and culture, and their understanding of calling reflected such.

Whereas Luther was primarily fixated on countering Catholic dogma (and trying to stay alive!), Calvin undertook to remake the church in a renewed biblical framework. In an effort to do so, he articulated an understanding of calling that he applied to church-related ministry. It is worth noting that for a number of reasons that were as much about theology as sociology, the Protestant Church under Calvin did not mobilize a significant missionary community nor make a recognizable missionary impact in the world. In fact, apart from a few exceptions such as the Moravians,[164] Protestant missions cannot be said to have been a visible part of the church until the mid-1800s.[165]

For Calvin, calling had both soteriological realities as well as vocational ones. He, with Luther, argued for the evidence of the presence of God in the lives of all humankind through the sovereign appointment of men and women to the stations and tasks in life he ordains that they should fill. For Calvin, calling was intimately tied to the sovereignty of God that left nothing to chance or beyond the purveyance of the divine. And this applied specifically to vocational or occupational calling. "Underlying [the] point of Calvin's biblical view of occupational calling is the biblical truth that God places individuals where He wants them to be and that every person's occupation is a post and a station assigned to him by God. [In this argument,] Calvin and other Reformers freed vocation from the confines of the Church's walls."[166]

It follows then, that if Calvin understood calling to apply to all vocations, then it certainly applied to those associated with the church. Calvin argues in his commentary on Acts 13:2 that "no man is to be counted a lawful pastor of the Church save he that is called of God."[167] And again, in his commentary on Ephesians 4:11, Calvin remarks that "true pastors do not rashly thrust themselves forward by their own judgment, but are raised up by the Lord."[168] As noted previously in the discussion of how Calvin applied this notion of calling to the emerging Protestant Church, he insisted on both the internal call by which the individual is convinced of a divine appointment to church ministry as well as an external call extended to the qualified candidate by the local church. This external call then affirms and confirms the secret call and sets the person apart for church ministry. What is curious about Calvin's position on this issue and the legacy he left the Protestant Church thereafter is the lack of anything similar in the New Testament texts that addresses qualifications for church leaders.

The longest passage in the New Testament that addresses qualifications for church elders and deacons is found in 1 Timothy 3:1–13. Here Paul says,

> It is a trustworthy statement: if any man aspires to the office of overseer, it is a fine work he desires to do. An overseer, then, must be above reproach, the husband of one wife, temperate, self-controlled, respectable, hospitable, skillful in teaching, not

> overindulging in wine, not a bully, but gentle, not contentious, free from the love of money. He must be one who manages his own household well, keeping his children under control with all dignity (but if a man does not know how to manage his own household, how will he take care of the church of God?), and not a new convert, so that he will not become conceited and fall into condemnation incurred by the devil. And he must have a good reputation with those outside the church, so that he will not fall into disgrace and the snare of the devil.
>
> Deacons likewise must be men of dignity, not insincere, not prone to drink much wine, not greedy for money, but holding to the mystery of the faith with a clear conscience. These men must also first be tested; then have them serve as deacons if they are beyond reproach. Women must likewise be dignified, not malicious gossips, but temperate, faithful in all things. Deacons must be husbands of one wife, and good managers of their children and their own households. For those who have served well as deacons obtain for themselves a high standing and great confidence in the faith that is in Christ Jesus.

Whatever else Paul sets forth as requirements for those who he says "aspire to the office," one looks in vain for any reference to the necessity of either the inward, secret call or the external call extended by the local church. Elsewhere in the ministry of Paul, when it came time for him to move on from a place of successful ministry, he would appoint leaders to take his place. One example of this is found in Acts 14:20–23.

> The next day he left with Barnabas for Derbe, and after they had preached the gospel to that city and had made a good number of disciples, they returned to Lystra, to Iconium, and to Antioch, strengthening the souls of the disciples, encouraging them to continue in the faith, and saying, "It is through many tribulations that we must enter the kingdom of God." When they had appointed elders for them in every church, having prayed with fasting, they entrusted them to the Lord in whom they had believed.

The point in contrasting the actions taken by Paul and Barnabas in appointing elders with the procedural pattern of Calvin is not to suggest that somehow Paul and Barnabas made poor choices or undermined the future stability of the church in so doing. Nothing leads one to believe that Paul's practice of appointing elders as part of his departure plan was somehow detrimental or of secondary value to some other means of procuring qualified leaders. The point is rather that one looks in vain to find the pattern recommended by Calvin in the New Testament church.

The same can be said of Paul's missionary journeys. From the records provided by Luke, primarily, Paul is accompanied by a number of different individuals, including Barnabas, Silas, and a handful of others.[169] Though admittedly not much detail is given as to how Paul selected those who would accompany him, what is missing in every case is any reference to calling for any of those who do so. Take the case of Paul's search for a replacement for John Mark. While Paul and Silas were in Lystra, they heard of a young disciple named Timothy (Acts 16:1–2). According to Luke's narrative, Timothy was "well-spoken of by the brethren" (Acts 16:3). Though there may have been more to Timothy and his qualifications, the text never reveals that Paul inquired of Timothy's calling. Was this because calling was so essential that Luke could ignore commenting on it? Or was it because calling as a means of being set aside for some kind of ministry was not part of how the average Christian understood life in the New Testament era? Garry Friesen concludes that this idea of calling, despite the importance attached to it in the contemporary era, just does not show itself to have been of the same importance in the New Testament church. He concludes his review of the New Testament data by saying, "In the actual practice of the New Testament church, the decisions concerning timing, destinations, and personnel were all made by the appropriate people with a view to obeying God's moral will in the most effective manner possible. There is a remarkable absence of any reference to the call of God beyond Acts 16."[170]

What about Acts 13:2?

In Acts 13, Luke sets the stage for what would become known as Paul's first missionary journey. Paul and Barnabas, fresh from a trip to Jerusalem, return to Antioch and resume life and ministry among the believers there. At some point, Luke records the following scene (Acts 13:1–2):

> Now there were prophets and teachers at Antioch, in the church that was there: Barnabas, Simeon who was called Niger, Lucius of Cyrene, Manaen who had been brought up with Herod the tetrarch, and Saul. While they were serving the Lord and fasting, the Holy Spirit said, "Set Barnabas and Saul apart for Me for the work to which I have called them.

The importance of this scene cannot be overstated. Immediately following this pronouncement, Luke records the response by both the church and Paul and Barnabas as follows (Acts 13:3–5):

> Then, when they had fasted, prayed, and laid their hands on them, they sent them away. So, being sent out by the Holy Spirit, they went down to Seleucia and from there they sailed to Cyprus. When they reached Salamis, they began to proclaim the word of God in the synagogues of the Jews; and they also had John as their helper.

Though Luke does not explicitly connect what happened on the island of Cyprus with the prophetic word from verse 2, the chronology of the narrative suggests that what took place is what God intended by the "work to which I have called them." So what is happening here?

Grammatically speaking, the Greek word that is rendered "I have called them" is προσκέκλημαι, whose root is καλέω, the term most commonly used in New Testament literature to refer to calling. Various forms of this verb appear throughout the New Testament as well as in Acts to signal a summoning or an invitation to someone to make an appearance or respond to an appeal. This is the term also used in Acts 16:10. In this instance, Paul recognizes that the unusual appeal from the man from Macedonia signaled that "God had called us to preach the gospel to them." It is within the norms of Greek grammar to conclude from these two instances that the term can be defined as "to call to a specific task or office," as noted by Russell Penney.[171] In that this calling of Paul and Barnabas takes place in the context of a local church who could affirm their apostolic gifts for the task to which they were apparently called, this fits neatly with Calvin's suggested pattern for procuring qualified ministers.

Theologically speaking, two issues must be addressed, the first of which is simply the question of essentiality. If this pattern of divine calling to a particular office or task plus some kind of local church confirmation is necessary, why does this pattern not receive any attention in the epistles to the churches? If this is a prerequisite for spiritual ministry, why is Jesus all but silent on the issue? It is difficult to suggest that a particular behavior be normalized for the church when the New Testament instructions to the churches make no mention of it.

Secondly, one cannot ignore the fact the prophetic appeal to Barnabas and Paul to set out for Cyprus was unique, not only in that it came to them through a prophet in Acts 13 and then in a vision in Acts 16 but also in that it launched them on the first missionary journey. This missionary journey was arguably the initial act on the part of the church to preach the gospel to the gentiles. It served as a historical marker not only in its impact on the church that now becomes both a Jewish and a gentile spiritual haven but also for Paul who is given the opportunity to be part of the initial harvest of gentiles into the kingdom. Following this journey, Paul and Barnabas made their way back to Jerusalem. On their way, they passed through both Phoenicia and Samaria, where they "described in detail the conversion of the Gentiles" (Acts 15:3). Next, they made a visit to the church in Jerusalem where they "reported all that God had done with them" (Acts 15:4).

Luke notes that the reports that Paul and Barnabas made concerning the response of the gentiles to the gospel bothered some of the Pharisees, which prompted the apostles and elders of the Jerusalem church to "look into this matter" (Acts 15:5–6). At some point in the proceedings, following comments by Peter (Acts 15:7–11) who defended ministry to the gentiles on a number of points, Paul and Barnabas made their case. In so doing, they related "what signs and wonders God had done through them among the Gentiles" (Acts 15:12).

The response of the gentiles to the gospel and the church decision to make believing gentiles full members thereof were crucial steps in the fulfillment of the *missio Dei* and provided a visible realization of the promise God had made to Abraham back in Genesis 12. As such, it is not out of the question that God would have extended a unique appeal to Paul and Barnabas—calling them to a specific task, if you will—much as he had done across the historical record whenever he saw fit to advance the kingdom storyline. This is the conclusion that Friesen draws in reflecting upon the nature of this divine appointment given to Paul and Barnabas. He writes,

> each "vocational call" was issued only to certain individuals at certain times. The book of Acts makes it clear that the Holy Spirit was carefully superintending the opening stages of the Church's growth. Only at decisive moments and in decisive ways did God intervene supernaturally to commission a worker, chart a particular course, or point in a specific direction. The rest of the time, He accomplished His purposes through saints obeying the moral will of God.[172]

In short, the Bible makes it clear that God did and likely still does intervene to enlist individuals for particular roles in salvation history. His intervention to set aside Paul and Barnabas for the "work to which I [God] had called them" is one such example. Nevertheless, the testimony of the rest of Scripture makes it clear that such divine interventions were rare.

What about Mary?

Unlike any other woman in the New Testament, Mary, the mother of Jesus, is given ample attention, especially in the early chapters of Luke's Gospel. In the account of her coming to realize that she is destined for a unique role as the one who would be the mother of Jesus, it is clear that she is set apart uniquely for the role. When the angel Gabriel meets her to break the news, he says that she has been given this task because she "has found favor with God" (Luke 1: 30). From the historical context, we also know that Mary was a descendent of Abraham through Judah and also of David, which enabled her to be in a position to serve as the one to whom Jesus would be born, thus making it possible that Jesus was truly a son of David (Matt 9:27, 12:23, 15:22, 20:30, 21:5, 21:9). Additionally, from Matthew's genealogy, we learn that Joseph, the one to whom she was espoused, was also a descendant of Abraham as well as David, which made it possible for Jesus to be an heir to the throne as King of Israel. For these reasons and more, Mary was truly a unique individual in a matrix of unique circumstances, which arguably made her out to be one in a million in terms of possessing the character and social characteristics necessary to bear Jesus as her son.

As Luke tells the story, Mary is initially visited by Gabriel who gives her the news. She then makes a visit to her cousin Elizabeth who, she finds out, is also pregnant with the one who will become John the Baptist. Amazed by all of this, she no doubt must at some point become a bit bewildered by how she is going to live out this pregnancy in the midst of a very conservative family and relationship with Joseph. For his part, Joseph gets his own angelic visitation (Matt 1:18–25) in which he is informed of Mary's condition and instructed to take her as his wife, despite the apparent look of impropriety.

In all of this, neither Matthew nor Luke describes the role of Mary or Joseph as a calling, nor is their place in the divine narrative ever described as such by anyone else. It is certain that they played a unique and essential part in the unfolding of God's plan and the fulfillment of the *missio Dei*, but no one who speaks of them during or after the fact equates their contribution as calling.

Calling in the New Testament: A Summary

The New Testament, in its treatment of the concept of calling, accommodates the range of meaning found also in the Old Testament. As such, calling can refer to naming/identifying, an invitation/summons, or, more rarely, a cause to become something. Though latent in Old Testament theology in the promise to Abraham, for example, calling as an agency of salvation takes center stage in the New Testament, where it is shown to be important to the soteriology of Paul, Peter, Luke, James, Jude, and the author of the book of Hebrews.[173]

Though calling in a soteriological sense is common to New Testament writers, the notion of calling to a particular task or ministry role is rare. Neither Jesus in the several renditions of his Great Commission exhortation nor Paul in his description of qualifications for ministerial candidates make mention of calling as a prerequisite. Furthermore, nowhere in the run-up to his missionary journeys does Paul make a point to suggest or identify calling as part of the criteria that separates his companions from others in the church. Finally, though Paul and Barnabas are said to have been called by God for a particular missionary role, it is likely that this is a unique case for the advancement of the gospel and fulfillment of the *missio Dei* as it relates to the inclusion of the gentiles in the church.

Calling in the Bible: A Summary

Calling in the Bible is a broad concept that carries social and/or theological weight. In its purely social usage, calling is understood in terms of naming or identifying, inviting, or summoning someone. Calling is how someone gets the attention of someone else. In its theological usage, calling is associated with the activity of God who reaches out towards his creation and either collectively or individually names/identifies, invites, or summons. Additionally, God can call in the sense of causing or making something or someone to become someone or something else.

What Does the Bible Say?

Tradition contends that the idea of a divine call is displayed in God's enlistment of men such as Abraham and Moses to play essential roles in the unfolding of redemption. Some have observed a particular pattern by which some of these individuals receive their assignment, though not all. Interestingly, the notion of calling, despite not being explicitly associated with a particular role, is evidenced almost exclusively by men.

The New Testament carried forward much of the range of meaning of calling from the Old Testament. Here, however, the association of calling with salvation became much more prominent. The early church was initially led by the apostles whose authority to lead was carried over from their apostolic role under Jesus. However, the first leaders in the emergent church to be chosen were done so without mention of calling. The account of Paul's conversion, which is often held up as the epitome of the call to service, clearly set him apart for an apostolic role by which the church among the gentiles was able to take root. Despite the tradition of assigning a calling to ministry in the pattern of Paul, it is not obvious that even he understood his calling in this way. For Paul, God's calling was first to salvation, which paved the way for an assignment to ministry as an apostle. Finally, as gospel preaching by Paul and his companions gave birth to new churches across Asia Minor over the course of Paul's missionary journeys, local church leaders were identified, trained, and coached by Paul. And yet, in none of these instances, does he make an appeal to calling as a criterion for church leadership or as grounds for refusing a candidate who nevertheless "aspired to the office."

Cross-cultural critiques repeatedly emphasize that existing career theories are predominantly U.S.-biased and do not effectively account for the experiences of women, racial/ethnic minorities, and individuals coming from more collectively oriented cultures with an interdependent self-concept.

—ANDRE PEKERTI

How one finds entry into ministry as a vocation and what one understands that vocation to be is as much a sociological question as a theological one. In the stories that people tell about how they came to be "chosen" for this particular vocation—a story that few people outside of a religious context ever feel compelled to share—can be found a description of and an accounting for the social action and social identity that is born from the experience. A phenomenological perspective suggests that religious communities are embedded in the common everyday society, but that have their own meanings, which are not shared by other people and other circumstances. This idea of calling to a kind of labor (e.g., ministry) may be both defined and limited to this social microcosm.

—RICHARD PITT

5

Cultural Challenges

Introduction

FROM THE HISTORICAL ASSESSMENT of the evolution of the concept of calling, it is evident that calling has taken on aspects of the cultural climate in which it is interpreted. And so, for Luther, calling was all about responding to the Catholic understanding that limited calling to the ordained clergy. Calvin moved the needle on this some in his era and sought to associate calling with all that God gives men and women to do on this earth. Nevertheless, for both of these men, calling related to church ministry was limited to men, in keeping with the social norms of the day.

As political, social, and economic structures changed in the West, moving from monarchies and feudal arrangements to nation-states and increasingly free market economies, the nature of work and man's (and woman's!) relationship to it also changed. Though the waning of traditionalism with regard to gender roles varies from culture to culture, the last fifty years have seen a massive shift in the push towards egalitarianism in the Western world between men and women in virtually all walks of life. In many respects, this is also true in the church and church-related ministry. Though the Catholic Church, together with some Protestant denominations, still restricts priestly roles to men, many avenues to church-related ministry have been opened to women, allowing women to pursue and satisfy their calling.

The contemporary understanding of the concept, however, even if we grant the definition that assumes a divine origin, is visibly marked by two interrelated elements that limit the application of calling to a minority of humanity. The first of these is the opportunity to choose a career path that includes a ministry option. Such economic and related social mobility are largely effects of the Industrial Revolution and the evolution of Western economic and societal structures that gave rise to the possibility of career choice. The second of these is the expectation that the pursuit of a particular career will provide a degree of self-actualization and personal fulfillment. The emergence of this increased focus on the self, fueled as it was by a merit-based social standing, is derived from the Enlightenment's contribution to the rise of the individual as the central component of society. Both of these elements work together to answer the question "What do you want to be when you grow up?"

That these factors have influenced the notion of calling as argued in previous chapters is highlighted by the fact that in most early societies, one's place in society was inherited. Upward mobility was limited by a host of social factors and norms. Education, a historical wild card that offered knowledge, power, and a context of relationships upon which to build an upgraded economic and related social context for oneself, was restricted to an extremely small segment of the population and only very recently made available universally to include both genders and, more or less, any economic class. Furthermore, depending on the era and locality, large numbers of men and women were relegated to slave status or, a half-step better, that of indentured servant or tenant farmer. For this group of people, the idea of career choice was an unknown possibility. And so, given the restrictions associated with social and economic mobility in these cases, can we say that calling, as we understand it today, also applied to them? Apart from Moses and Aaron, did any of the other Hebrew slaves consider what God wanted them to do with their life? Did the tenant farmer in the British countryside, under the watch of the local baron, ask his son or daughter, "What do you want to be when you grow up?" Did Christian women in colonial America feel free to pursue a career path in the church, convinced that it was God's call on their life to do so?

In his letter to the Ephesians, Paul argues that in the coming of Christ, what had been hidden had now been revealed (Eph 3:1–13). This radical mystery that God had hidden from ages past and now revealed was the granting to both Jew and gentile unity (as one body) in the church through the riches of the gospel (Eph 3:6). Paul in effect makes this argument in Galatians 3:28 when he says, "There is neither Jew nor Greek, there is neither slave nor free, there is neither male nor female; for you are all one in Christ Jesus." Paul's point is that the reach, effect, and access to the gospel as a portal to salvation had never intended to be limited by social class, gender, or ethnicity. In fact, God had always intended that his divine provision in both this world and the world to come should be available to all.[174] This is what the promise to Abraham in Genesis 12:3 was all about, when God said "in you all the families of the earth will be blessed." Some 1800 years later, in Revelation 7:9, John records his vision of the end of the age to give us a picture of the future realization of this truth:

> After these things I looked, and behold, a great multitude which no one could count, from every nation and all the tribes, peoples, and languages, standing before the throne and before the Lamb, clothed in white robes, and palm branches were in their hands; and they cried out with a loud voice, saying, "Salvation belongs to our God who sits on the throne, and to the Lamb."

Salvation, from its seminal reference in God's promise to Abraham in Genesis 12 to John's account of his vision of the end of the age in Revelation 7 is inclusive: whosoever believes in him will have eternal life (John 3:16). As a divine grace, salvation yields what Calvin refers to as the "twofold righteousness" or the "double grace" of justification and sanctification.[175] As the fruit of salvation, it follows that justification and sanctification then are both equally inclusive in the sense that no one is preemptively excluded from their virtues as a result of personal status. So how does this relate to calling?

Justification is understood as the act of declaring a person righteous or just. As such, justification is applied at a point in time, and its effects endure indefinitely. In contrast, though sanctification carries a similar punctual or positional aspect (cf. Acts 20:32, 1 Cor 1:2, Heb 10:10), it also is understood in a developmental or progressive sense by which the believer grows in grace (2 Pet 3:18) and increases in holiness (2 Cor 7:1, 2 Tim 2:21) with the goal of becoming more like Christ (Rom 8:29, 2 Cor 3:18). This progressive aspect of sanctification is the spiritual lens or grid through which the individual processes daily life. Sanctification then, in its progressive sense, is the lived spiritual experience of the believer.

Calling, in the contemporary understanding of the term, represents the divine assignment or realm of the believer's contribution to society, especially with regard to a ministry-related occupation. If one adheres to an understanding of calling whose origin is not divine, calling represents a summons to a life role that is oriented towards demonstrating or deriving a particular sense of meaningfulness. In either case, calling can be conceived of as the professional domain through which the called individual makes his or her life contribution. In this way, calling becomes the domain through which the believer expresses his or her spiritual life. Calling, in effect, provides the role in society in and through which the believer progresses in sanctification. If this relationship between calling and sanctification is justified, then it follows that just as sanctification is inclusive in its reach, so then calling must equally reflect a similar inclusiveness. For if sanctification is inclusive and calling is not, then some who are sanctified would be deprived of the very domain of their lived spiritual experience. If sanctification comprises the domain of spiritual transformation of the individual into the person of Christ (2 Cor 3:18), one's calling comprises the social and economic domain in which one's spiritual life is lived out. In this way, then, if sanctification is an inclusive reality for all believers regardless of personal status, so calling, as an aspect of such, must be so as well.

The pattern with regard to God's dealing with humankind seems to be that access to the provision and blessings of God is made available to all, social class, ethnicity, and gender notwithstanding. This is evidenced in the application of salvation through justification and sanctification, which are granted without restriction to any and all. If this is indeed the case, then the application of calling should serve the people of God in the same way. For if calling is indeed of divine origin, and part of the essential make-up of the divine-human relationship in sanctification, then it must also be available to all and not exclude some on the basis of social class, ethnicity, or gender.

But this is where the contemporary application of calling is confronted by the limitations of its cultural context. For as has been argued in previous chapters, the biblical notion of calling has largely been shaped by the evolution of Western society at the expense of other cultural frameworks. As a result, calling, as we understand it today, really functions only in the context of a twenty-first-century, First World Western culture that assumes career choice and an individualized, self-fulfillment objective. How believers in the West understand calling just does not fit with most of the world.

In opposition to the two key assumptions underpinning the contemporary notion of calling, notably, that career choice is possible and that individuals are free to make such choices, societies made up of cultures that do not embrace career choice as a value or for whom it is not possible cannot comprehend and apply calling in a similar way. The following section examines a number of societal contexts that militate against the practice of career choice as an individual right.

The Case of Filial Piety

Filial piety refers to the obligation of children to reverence parents and older relatives. It emerged from and remains intimately tied to the teachings of Confucius. According to David Yau-Fai Ho,

> for centuries, filial piety has served as a guiding principle governing Chinese patterns of socialization. As a cornerstone of the Confucian ethic, it goes far beyond the demand of simply obeying and honoring one's parents. It makes other demands that are no less stringent; providing for the material and mental well-being of one's aged parents, performing ceremonial duties of ancestral worship, taking care to avoid harm to one's own body, ensuring the continuity of the family line, and in general to conduct oneself so as to bring honor and not disgrace to the family name.[176]

Filial piety prescribes the expectations and exchange between children and parents and influences everything from education and occupational choice to marriage and child-rearing. In the modern era, as a result of the evolution of Chinese society and the influence of Western values through immigration and globalization, filial piety as a societal norm has lessened its central influence on socialization of young people. Nevertheless, filial piety remains a factor that influences behavior from early childhood to the end of life.[177] It is worth noting that scholars have identified filial piety as influential aspects of other Far Eastern societies (e.g., Korean, Japanese, Filipino), as well as Latino and Arab-Israeli cultures. Additionally, filial piety has been shown to be an integral social value in Islam.[178] Likewise for Judaism, the command to "honor your father and mother" is embedded in the law of Moses as the fifth of the foundational Ten Commandments (Exod 20:12). For Christians, Paul appeals to the fifth commandment as part of a series of exhortations concerning the

Christian home (Eph 6:1–4). Given the breadth of influence of filial piety on social norms, it is essential to consider how this could influence the aspect of occupational choice as it affects calling.

Examples of filial piety are grounded in the fourteenth-century compilation written by Guo Jujing during the Yang Dynasty (AD 1271–1368). This collection is known as the *The Twenty-Four Paragons of Filial Piety* and recounts specific examples of how filial piety should be applied in varying contexts. Since its inception, the text was used to teach Confucian moral values in Asian societies. Major themes treated in the examples range from economic to personal (physical or emotional) care. In that the economic sphere overlaps to some degree with occupation, examples associated with that aspect of filial piety fall within the scope of calling as well. One example from the ancient collection that refers to the economic sphere of filial piety is referred to as "Taking on Menial Labor to Support His Mother" and is recounted in full below.

> During the Later Han Dynasty, a filial son named Jiang Ge supported his widowed mother. As his father had passed on years ago, the son and mother got along as best they could. Bandit gangs roamed the countryside nearby, and Jiang Ge resolved to take his mother to safety, far from the chaos and trouble of his home. Having no cart or horse, the young man simply carried his mother on his back along the highway, escaping the onslaught of the brigands. As luck would have it they promptly ran into first one, then another group of rebels. When the leaders demanded that Jiang Ge join their number, the young filial son knelt down and pleaded for mercy, crying, "If I run off with you, my old mother will starve. She needs me to take care of her; please let us travel on in peace."
>
> Touched by his sincere plea, the bandits would always let them go. Traveling in this way, the two eventually reached the county of Xiabi in Jiangsu province. They had spent all their money, and their clothing had grown tattered and torn beyond repair. Lacking relatives in Jiangsu to support them, mother and son could only fashion a lean-to of grass and camp out with the other refugees from the civil war to the North.
>
> Jiang Ge would go out each morning in search of odd jobs. Whatever bits of cash he earned would go to supporting his mother in the style she was accustomed to before her husband had passed on. Jiang Ge wore ragged clothes and went barefoot, he ate wild greens and broken rice himself, but the clothing and food he provided for his mother was the finest he could afford.

He was not the least bit remiss in the care of his mother. Their neighbors praised his selflessness in service to his mother, and urged him to relax the ascetic hardship he imposed upon himself. Jiang Ge would only smile, and say, "A son's duty is to care for his parents."

At long last he found a secure, salary-paying job that promised a comfortable living for his mother. Peace had returned to their home-land by this time, and his mother wished to return. The ride in a horse-drawn cart would have proved too strenuous for her, so Jiang Ge passed over the good job that could have brought him a luxurious life. Instead he found a sturdy cart, settled his mother comfortably within, and pulled it himself all the way back home. Good people all along the way praised his devotion as a genuine model of filial compliance. A verse in his praise says,

Bearing mother on his back, he fled the troubled land.
Evil bandits caught them on the road.
A plea for mercy saved their lives, as always,
He labored hard to treat his mother well.[179]

As the story goes, Jiang Ge sacrificed a good job that, according to the text, "brought him a luxurious life," in order to be able to care for his mother. The idea here is that the obligation to the parent—the mother, in this case—was more important than the security of a good job. One of the takeaways from this example is the stark commitment to self-sacrifice that is expected for the sake of the senior family member. Though in much of the modern era, societies have progressed beyond horse-drawn carts, the notion of parental preference in the choice of occupations is still in vogue in some instances. One extreme example is taken from the research by Olwen Bedford and Kuang-Hui Yeh in this report:

> Until the 1990s, some young girls in Taiwan from impoverished families were indentured by their parents to brothels, usually to cover family medical or gambling debt. Parents appealed to their daughter's sense of filial piety to obtain her consent to indenture. Although they had little choice, the girls reported that they had not been forced; they had willingly agreed. These girls were admired by their family, and also for the income they provided . . . . These girls had internalized their parents' values and felt they were demonstrating love for their parents by supporting them.[180]

The example is clearly extreme, but it highlights the powerful sense of self-sacrifice that is understood as a cultural norm in societies influenced by filial piety.

When it comes to occupational choice, a condition that appears to have become intertwined with the contemporary concept of the call, personal characteristics and the family context combine with cultural and work values to direct the individual towards what is possible.[181] Some personal and family factors include such things as gender, sibling position, emotional and physical health, degree of traditionalism/conservatism, parental occupation, family coherence, and social status. In addition to the individual context, societal values as well as structural factors influence the range of possible occupational choices. Structural factors include such things as the degree of modernization, the availability of necessary education and training, economic and social stability and traditional values governing male and female roles.[182] Clearly, not every possible occupational outcome is possible for every member of society, even if one supposes an egalitarian, First World, Western context.

Now, some might argue that calling would be just what is needed to overcome the limitations of filial piety. Having heard the voice of God, what reason would there be not to follow it? After all, isn't this what Jesus meant when he said, "If you *love* your *father or mother* more than you *love* me, you are not worthy of being mine" (Matt 10:37, emphasis added)? One solution to the apparent conflict is to embrace the option that submission to Christ and his cause supersedes all other commitments for the Christian. In this case, then, calling would seem to presuppose generational conflict, an outcome seemingly anticipated by Christ when he said,

> Do not think that I came to bring peace on the earth; I did not come to bring peace, but a sword. For I came to turn a man against his father and a daughter against her mother and a daughter-in-law against her mother-in-law; and a person's enemies will be the members of his household. The one who loves father or mother more than Me is not worthy of Me; and the one who loves son or daughter more than Me is not worthy of Me (Matt 10:34–37).

Another solution would be to postpone response to the call until after the elder's passing, much like the man's response to Jesus's invitation to follow him recorded in both Matthew 8 and Luke 9. The Matthew passages reads as follows: "And another of the disciples said to Him, 'Lord, allow me first to go and bury my father.' But Jesus said to him, 'Follow

Me, and let the dead bury their own dead'" (Matt 8:21–22). In this case, the postponement would seemingly allow the man to avoid generational conflict and shame and, theoretically, still fulfill his calling. And yet, this solution seems unacceptable to Jesus.

If, as noted by Bedford and Yeh, filial piety remains a strong cultural value but is evolving to adapt to certain aspects of the modern era,[183] then perhaps the rendering of appropriate responses can accommodate creative solutions. Vanessa Hung, in her article on "Filial Piety and Missionary Calling,"[184] gives three examples of creative solutions to fulfilling filial obligations while pursuing a missionary calling. In one case, a group of women from a local church committed to visit the missionary's mother on a weekly basis, bringing her food and friendship. The mother was glad to have exchanged one daughter for a host of surrogate daughters. In another instance, a friend moved into the family home to provide care in place of the departing missionary. In the third example, the mission agency arranged for satellite phone service to enable the missionary to be in regular voice contact with his parents while out of the country.

The ReMAP study of missionary attrition that was published in 2007 is one of the first of its kind to acknowledge that filial piety is a cultural factor that must be acknowledged and addressed by NGOs seeking to enlist candidates from strong filial piety cultural contexts. In their compilation of survey data from agencies across Old Sending Countries (OSC), which are dominated by Western nations of North America, Europe, and Australia, versus New Sending Countries (NSC) from Africa, Asia, and Latin America, they acknowledge that the data shows that missionaries from NSC experience a much stronger impact of family obligation than those from OSC. In some instances, sending agencies in NSC require that the financial support of new missionaries include sufficient funds to provide for both the missionary family and satisfaction of filial obligations to parents.[185] In contrast,

> OSC did not rate family blessing highly and there was no correlation with retention. This is because the Western world sadly places less emphasis on family ties and in this global village whilst communication is much easier and brings people together across the distance, many individuals increasingly make decisions with little regard to the wishes of the wider family.[186]

Discussions in Western literature concerning the application of the call to ministry all but ignore the challenges afforded to those whose cultural context is influenced by the notion of filial piety. Undoubtedly, the affect of filial piety on any given individual is influenced by a host of factors related to the degree of traditionalism/conservatism of the family of origin, the religiosity of the individual and of the family (and whether religious affiliation is shared or opposed), and the personality of the individual. Because of the mix of these factors, the sense of filial obligation will be felt and play out differently in different personal and ethnic contexts. Nevertheless, a conception of calling that leans heavily on Western values of career choice and individual self-fulfillment fails to take into consideration other cultural values, such as filial piety, sacralizing a particular understanding of the concept. In so doing, it inadvertently establishes a norm that leaves those who are influenced by a strong sense of filial piety faced with a choice not to honor Christ above family but to adopt Western values at the expense of their own.

The Case of Caste

The caste system is a socially rendered organizational construct that classifies members of society into a particular, semi-permanent hierarchy, which, though officially no longer a legal concept in Indian society, still dominates the cultural landscape. Though some believe that the caste system was initially created by Brahma, others contend that the concept emerged following the invasion of the Vedic Aryans to the Punjab region around 1500 BCE and has since evolved over the centuries to what it is today.[187] Originally established on the basis of separating the slave population from the conquerors, it later adopted an economic basis by which to classify members of society.[188] In its historical formulation, the caste system was comprised of the following classifications: Brahmins—priests and teachers; Kshatriyas—warriors and rulers; Vaishyas—farmers, traders and merchants; Shudras—laborers; Dalits (outcasts)—street sweepers, latrine cleaners (who are not technically considered part of the caste system). Over the centuries, political and religious influences served to further subdivide the primary caste distinctions into subcastes known as *jatis*, each of which is associated or defined by a particular social function or job.[189] Caste, which serves as a system of social stratification, is marked by three fundamental aspects: repulsion, hierarchy, and hereditary specialization.[190] The implications of these characteristics affect the social status and intercaste social interactions. For example, in that caste was considered a closed system, the practice of endogamy dominated the cultural practices surrounding marriage. Additionally, in that *jatis* were associated with particular social functions (jobs), the rigid nature of caste effectively resulted in inherited job status with little or no possibility for occupational choice or migration.[191] Furthermore, cultural notions of purity and pollution influenced social mixing such that lower caste members were required to separate from upper caste members in virtually every social context.[192]

One example of how caste influences the nature of occupation and social status mobility is depicted in an article published as part of the "Caste in America" series by *WGBH News*.[193] The article tells the story of Suraj Yengde, a thirty-year-old, single, male Dalit. What makes Yengde's story remarkable is that he is also a Fellow at the Shorenstein Center at Harvard's Kennedy Law School, where he has completed graduate and post-graduate studies in law since arriving in the US in 2016. Yengde admits that he is a "proud beneficiary of reservations," by which he means government-endowed and constitutionally mandated educational and employment quotas for members of the lowest segments of India's social hierarchy, which were initially enacted as part of India's Constitution as adopted in 1950.

Aided by these affirmative action policies, Yengde was able to attend primary and secondary school and later the University of Mumbai. Early in his college career, he received a scholarship to attend and eventually earn a law degree from Birmingham City University (England) in 2012. Following completion of his law degree, he made his way to South Africa and earned his doctorate from the University of Witwatersrand, finishing the dissertation while in the US at Harvard. Despite this success, when speaking of the kids he knew from grade school, Yengde acknowledges, "If you don't go abroad, what happens once the student graduates from his 12th grade? Look around. When the guys I grew up with ... knew I was here, they came up to me to talk to me, and I could see they are doing exactly like what my father was doing and they have very limited future options." Though Yengde's future would seem to be securely tied to other, non-caste dynamics, he admits that "even today, I'm still an untouchable. You have to understand. [Despite] being at Harvard or being at the Kennedy School or being anywhere in the world, my primary identity for some reason is not going away."

Though caste is gradually slipping from its dominant place as the defining means of classifying and discriminating in Indian society, the lessening of the practical aspects related to occupation, marriage, and social status is not felt equally across the country. Urban areas, which are much more cosmopolitan and influenced by globalization and modernization, tend to see a greater lessening of attachment to caste system values and applications. Additionally, upper castes with greater access to educational and business opportunities, often in multicultural and international contexts, experience a more significant lessening of caste system norms. In contrast, rural areas and lower castes with more traditional/conservative family and cultural values and limited access to cultural influences beyond their local community still retain ancient commitments to caste system-related social norms.[194]

So, how does calling work in a caste system context? When occupation and social status are dominated by caste system norms, what does it look like for a Dalit to consider pursuing a cross-cultural missionary career as a result of a call of God? Without denying the capacity of God to reach down and touch someone from any one of these untouchable communities—like Yengde—and make it possible for him or her to pursue and fulfill a missionary calling, despite the cultural and social norms, is it understood by Dalit Christians that this is possible, even normal? When we consider that upwards of 40 percent of all college students at a public university in the US and over 80 percent of students at Christian colleges in the US consider calling as part of that which influences their career trajectory, can it be said that what they understand as calling is at all grasped by the street sweeping members of the Balmiki caste—even those who align with Christianity?[195] Perhaps it could be understood that this is what Jesus was getting at when he said,

> The Spirit of the Lord is upon me, because He has anointed Me to bring the good news to the poor. He has sent me to proclaim release to the captives, and recovery of sight to the blind, to set free those who are oppressed, to proclaim the year of the Lord. (Luke 4:18–19)

Does Jesus's intent to proclaim release to the captives refer to those who are captive in oppressive social structures? Does his reference to setting free those who are oppressed refer to those who remain under societal and cultural oppression? Surely the primary theological import of Christ's words here is to be understood in a salvific sense, but are there also social and cultural implications related to deliverance from corrupted social systems? And if the latter is true, what does this look like for those intending to pursue a calling to ministry beyond the limits of their *jatis*? Do the words and work of Jesus actually set them free from social conventions?

Conceptions of calling in a Western context do not consider the impact of communal systems in which job assignment and social status are assigned with very little room for upward or outward mobility. To be fair, the dominance of caste is lessening for many as modernization and globalization continue to influence conservative/traditional social norms towards individualism and egalitarianism; and yet, even for those who profit from government programs of affirmative action and acquire advanced education and international experience, their identity with caste is not entirely erased. If calling is going to fit in a world in which social interaction is prescribed, economic roles are assigned, and upward social mobility is highly restrictive, it must find a way to accommodate these realities. Failing to do so makes calling out to be a perk available only to those of upper castes for whom a degree of educational and occupational freedom is accorded.

The Case of Gender

The relationship between gender and calling, especially with regard to the limitations for women as calling is applied to public ministry roles, has been discussed earlier. The reason to revisit this subject here is not so much to rehash what was previously described but rather to identify the challenge that gender limits on calling is to the notion of calling itself.

As previously argued, calling, when associated with ministry, has from its earliest conception been mostly, if not exclusively, reserved for and applied to men and their roles. In addition to Abraham and Moses, Old Testament patterns of call narratives described earlier almost exclusively relate calling to male participants in the unfolding of Israel's story. In the New Testament, despite the inclusion of gentiles into the story, those who are recognized as making major contributions to the emergence of the church are, with few exceptions, men.[196]

With the rise of the church following the age of the apostles and into that of the church fathers (late first century to fifth century), women in official ministry roles are all but unaccounted for. Social custom, combined with a male-leaning biblical framework that excluded women from heads of Israel's tribes, schools of prophets, and disciples, left women on the sidelines of official church ministries. This is not to say, however, that women were not involved in ministry. Old Testament history through to the modern era is replete with examples of women who served God in every conceivable manner, though, for the most part, in unofficial roles. With the rise of the importance of Mary, mother of Jesus, to the Christian experience, women found an advocate and example of piety and humility that inspired them to turn their lives into avenues of ministry. The rise of monasticism provided some of these women with an outlet for their spiritual energies.

In the wake of the confrontation with the Catholic Church led by Martin Luther (among many), which eventually gave rise to the Protestant Church, calling was liberated from its clergy-only status. And yet, the Protestant Church, for all that it recovered in terms of biblical priorities, actually offered less for women in terms of official roles, because they simply had nothing equivalent to the monastic orders of the Catholic Church. Calvin's contribution to the development of the concept of calling helped to raise the legitimacy of all occupations and all men and women to an equal status of calling before God, and yet, for Calvin as for Luther, church ministry roles were still limited to men.

As described at length previously, the most significant shift in terms of women's conception and application of calling with regard to ministry roles corresponds most directly with social changes in the West from the 1800s forward that, little by little, opened doors for women beyond homemaking to occupations such as nursing and teaching. In the US, additional gains for women were acquired in the wake of the Civil War and the two World Wars that took able-bodied men out of the employment stream. In many cases, women took the place of men so that farms and factories wouldn't fail. Following the wars, though men reclaimed their place in society and at work, the pendulum never completely swung all the way back to where it had been before, and some of the advances in employment outside the home were retained by women. According to Hymowitz and Weissman,

> Six million women took paying jobs during the War [WWII]. The proportion of women in the labor force increased from 25 to 36 percent. Two million of these women went to work in offices—half of these for the federal government, handling the flow of paper created by the war. An even greater number of women went into the factories. Heavy industry alone created nearly two million jobs for women during the war . . . . Three-quarters

of the new women workers were over thirty-five years old, 60 percent were married, and the majority had children of school or pre-school age. For the first time married women were a majority of working women, and most Americans supported their right to work.[197]

War-inspired employment opportunities for women were not in and of themselves sufficient to engineer a wholesale shift in cultural values regarding the place of women in society; nevertheless, women's real contributions to the war effort and their proven capacity in a host of occupations for which they had previously been deemed unfit "let the genie out of the bottle." Over the last half-decade of the twentieth century, waves of social reform regarding the social identity of women were pushed by organizations such as the National American Woman Suffrage Association (NAWSA) and the National Organization for Women (NOW). These organizations rallied women, lobbied congress, drafted resolutions, held community gatherings, and advocated in every imaginable way for the rights and opportunities of women without limits.

As society embraced these changes in the social status of women, church denominations began to open their doors to women as well. In some cases, denominations ordained women and gave them priestly duties. Others who retained a more conservative distinction between male and female roles and withheld primary priestly duties from women nevertheless often created new pathways in women's and children's ministries in an attempt to respond to the growing interest among women in serving in official ministry roles, ostensibly following their calling to do so.

Interestingly, the rise of the modern Protestant missionary movement (1800s forward) offered a new set of career options for women. At first, women who felt called to such were obliged to find a mission-oriented husband in order to play a role in ministry. Eventually, however, mission agencies began to enlist single women workers who were able to serve the communities beyond the reach of men.

Arguably, women's expanding role in ministry paralleled changes in the wider social context in Western society in general and the US in particular. In that access to such roles was predicated on calling, those who allowed access to public ministry roles were, in essence, validating that a woman was as equally receptive to a ministry call as was a man. However, in the debate that ensued between so-called liberals (or progressives) and conservatives over this issue, what was lacking was an articulate argument from Scripture to address the issue. Attempts by liberals/progressives to argue for an egalitarian position for women vis-à-vis men were met by complementarian arguments from conservatives, arguments that failed to address calling as a potentially divine experience and instead relied on appeals to Old Testament and New Testament role distinctions and their application to transcultural and transhistorical contexts.

In the early 1990s, John Piper and Wayne Grudem edited a volume of collected articles intended to provide a response to what had become known as evangelical feminism. The overall purpose of the work was to provide a discussion of the range of biblical roles that are genuinely afforded to women. In an early section of the book, Piper and Grudem respond to a number of common questions concerning the role of women in the church and society. One question was, "If God has genuinely called a woman to be a pastor, then how can you say she should not be one?" Their argument in response is as follows: firstly, the Bible teaches that God has determined that only men can fill the role of pastor in the church. Secondly, because the Bible limits the pastoral role to men, by implication then God does not select or call women to serve in this role. Thirdly, church history shows that an individual sense of calling is not enough; it must be somehow validated by the church. Therefore, if a woman believes she has received a divine call to be a pastor, the call is a priori untenable for the reasons noted. She cannot be a pastor, because the role is reserved for men, so, by consequence, her calling is not and cannot be what she thought it was. Finally, Piper and Grudem argue that a personal sense of calling needs to be carefully considered in light of other revealed truth. It is for this purpose that Scripture warns pretenders and churches to beware of those who think they are sent by God but are not.[198] As noted in Jeremiah 23:32, "I [God] did not send or appoint them." Though this response summarizes the overall position with regard to calling and women in ministry, nowhere in the rest of the collected articles in the book (of which there are more than twenty-five) is the question of calling discussed.

Though the conclusions offered by Piper and Grudem served to clarify the position of some of the evangelical church, by no means did they bring an end to the debate over the role of women in the church, and the conceptualization of the issue—complementarianism vs. egalitarianism—has not remained static either.[199] Since the first publication of *Recovering Biblical Manhod and Womanhood* in 1991, a number of conferences,[200] publications,[201] and various forms of digital communication (e.g., blogs, vlogs, etc.) have taken up the question of women's roles in the church and society, as they continue to voice various positions on this complex matter. If anything can be observed from this historic debate, it is that the ever-shifting nature of society will continue to shape how women and their role in society are understood.

Joan of Arc: A Fifteenth-Century Example

About midway through the terrible Hundred Years War that pitted England against France in a fight over territorial and political/religious prominence in fifteenth-century Europe, a peasant girl was born who would become both a flash point and a heroine in political and religious history for centuries to come.

According to history, around the age of thirteen, the girl began to receive visions that she ascribed to St. Michael, St. Catherine of Alexandria, and St. Margaret of Antioch, during which she heard voices exhorting her to lead a virtuous life and to assist the dauphin, Charles VII, to be named the rightful king of France. Eventually, making her way to Charles, she convinced him to let her fight. Dressed as a man, she led the French army in the liberation of Orléans from the English. Other battles and victories followed, and in 1422, Charles VII was crowned king of France.

Some time later, after failing to secure the liberation of Paris in 1430, Joan of Arc, as she had become known, was taken captive by the duke of Burgundy—a rival to Charles VII and claimant to the throne. Under the duke, Joan was put on trial and charged with seventy counts of heresy in addition to other charges, including witchcraft and dressing like a man. In her defense, Joan claimed, as she had argued to the dauphin at the beginning, that she had been chosen and sent by God. In short, she had received a divine call to a very particular, monumental task.

The trial, in addition to its potentially highly charged political outcomes, centered around the credibility of Joan and whether God could and would use such an instrument for such an important task. In one of the counterarguments put forth by an unnamed Parisian cleric, the basis for the rejection of Joan as a legitimate instrument of God is given in seven points:

> First, the lack of sufficient evidence of her divine mission; second, the wearing of men's clothes and her usurpation of a masculine role; third, doubt as to whether God intervenes on behalf of nations, in particular, that he would aid one Christian

nation against another; fourth, Joan's nonobservance of holy days; fifth, her lying predictions (failure to realize her miracles); sixth, idolatry; and seventh, the use of spells.[202]

As Deborah Fraioli points out, the case against the credibility of Joan was compromised because of politics from the beginning. For if her claims of divine calling were determined to be legitimate and Charles VII was indeed the rightful king of France, then that would invalidate the English claim to France—and provoke the duke of Burgundy, who aimed to prosper from this arrangement. If her claims of divine calling were determined to be false, this would undermine Charles's claim of legitimacy and give room for the English to claim France as their own. But what made the case against her more complex was the fact that she was a woman. Again, as the Parisian cleric argued, "all masculine office is prohibited to women, for instance, preaching, teaching, bearing arms, absolving from sin, excommunicating, etc." Despite the reaction that this kind of sexism elicits today, Fraioli is right to note that the priest was following canon law, which drew from Aquinas's application of Aristotle to maintain that women were deficient mentally and therefore inferior. Further, as we saw in Luther who lived at this same time, the accepted worldview of the day promoted the notion that God assigned people to a certain role or vocation in the world that they were to occupy,[203] and refusing to remain and fulfill one's vocation would be considered rebellion against God himself.

In the end, Joan of Arc was condemned of heresy and burned at the stake in 1431. Though the official charge against her was heresy, a crime for which the death penalty was prescribed, her sentence was commuted to life imprisonment in response to her promise to submit to the wishes of the church with regard to her comportment in keeping with female identity and modesty. However, within days of the commutation of her sentence she was found again dressed in men's clothing in response to words of censure she said to have heard from St Catherine and St. Margaret. She was immediately turned over to the secular authorities who carried out her execution. In effect, her call-experience was invalidated by her refusal to maintain her vocation as a woman.

The Church of God in Christ (COGIC): A Twenty-First Century Example

One denominational example of the conflict raised by the contemporary understanding of calling with regard to the role of women comes from Richard Pitt's description and analysis of calling in the Church of God in Christ (COGIC), a primarily Black Evangelical Protestant denomination whose origins can be traced to the Azusa Street Revival of 1907 and the resultant holiness movement that emerged. Pitt notes that built into the function of the denomination are instructions regarding how to identify and validate those who wish to be considered for a public ministry role. In his analysis, several characteristics of these instructions are highlighted. Firstly, those who aspire to ordained ministry must be men. The COGIC understands the ordained ministry as that which is reserved exclusively for men, in the pattern of Jesus's disciples. And, secondly, selection and validation of a candidate must assess the validity of his calling to the ministry.[204]

As Pitt points out, the COGIC, in its insistence on calling as part of the prerequisite for a public ministry role, is in line with other Protestant denominations who also affirm the essential nature of a call of God that compels people to pursue ministry as a profession. Furthermore, the call of God serves to legitimize the notion that professional ministers have somehow been selected by God for this work. Pitt comments:

> Unlike ordination processes, which are explicitly social in nature, call-experiences are almost always described as a personal journey where the only other participant is God.... Yet this moment [of the call] is the foundation for everything that follows it. The call-experience is more than a catalyst for the pursuit of a professional credential; it is an essential plank in the argument for legitimacy, especially when other more verifiable evidence is in short supply. Therefore, comprehending the call-experience is a critical component of understanding its impact on both the decision to pursue and the decision to embrace a ministerial identity.[205]

Finally, in the interplay between the candidate who presents himself for consideration and the church who seeks to ascertain the qualifications of the candidate, the nature of the supernatural experience is at the same time compelling and problematic. For though the call-experience must be noted, the capacity for assessing its legitimacy is all but unknown.[206] How exactly does one measure the veracity of a divine encounter, especially when the very nature of the experience and the way it is described to have happened is itself conditioned by the very community for which it was intended? In other words, the call-experience itself is described in terms that fit what the church community considers to be legitimate carriers of a religious message, such as a call. Pitt explains that

> the calling experience and the narratives that follows must be recognizably canonical [in agreement with biblical themes, motifs, and theological orthodoxy], but they are interesting because they aren't a normal experience for the callee. Canonical experiences are those that are "culturally comprehensible" inasmuch as the religious culture that the callee is imbedded in gives her the imagery, icons, or other symbols that she recognizes as components of a religious message. Doves are canonical; pigeons are not. A dream about fishing is canonical; dreams about playing baseball are not.[207]

Here Pitt, together with others who have studied the effect of the believing community on newcomers,[208] argues that to some degree the community of faith not only provides a new social network but also a means of understanding the cosmos by offering a vocabulary of words, themes, symbols, heroes, and experiences deemed to be legitimate and normative. As the worldview of the newcomer takes shape, it may result in a reimagining of the newcomer's past experience in light of this new framework and, in some cases, "they might then experience a dream, or remember a past dream, as part of a call to ministry that may not, in reality, be there."[209] In the end, what matters is not really that which took place, per se, but whether it fits with what the church deems as canonical. Fundamentally,

> these clerical aspirants have learned what a call to Protestant— and particularly, Pentecostal—ministry looks like. It is clear that they recognize that the calling has a particular set of cultural markers. They mobilize cultural tools in a way that gets them over the important hurdle of convincing church leaders and other parishioners that they are the "real deal." The church has expectations of both a calling narrative and a called individual. Whether God or man, the originator of the impulse to pursue a call to ministry uses those expectations to create the interesting and canonical components of a recognizable narrative description.[210]

But this is where the definition of calling, canonical cultural markers, and gender collide in the COGIC. For in that they have limited calling and ministry by gender and task, and have codified as canonical certain symbols, heroes, and images that qualify as calling, they have inadvertently established a system that automatically disqualifies certain candidates for public ministry solely on the basis of gender, despite their canonical call-experience that they (the church) deem to be illegitimate.[211]

In light of this reality, women in the COGIC who are convinced of a divine call to ministry construct other avenues for service, which allows them to fulfill their divinely appointed task in an unofficial, nonclerical capacity. Here, in these nonclerical roles, the women contend that the call is in and of itself a legitimizing factor above and beyond the validation of the church. They claim that the God who called them endows them with supernatural knowledge and abilities that they may need. Secondly, they argue that if God called them and they are unable to exercise this calling within the church, then God must be content to have them exercise this calling external to it.[212] These extra-clerical avenues for ministry for women in the COGIC make for an interesting picture of parallel realities that bely the very experience that is claimed to be at the core of the qualifications of ministers in the first place.

For if public ministry roles are limited to those who are called to them, and if calling is defined as "that inner persuasion or experience whereby a person feels himself directly summoned or invited by God to take up the work of the ministry,"[213] which we take from Niebuhr, then those organizations that were denying ministry roles to women were, in effect, denying that these ministerial candidates had heard from God at all. The conflict that then ensued was not just over whether or not a particular woman was qualified for a particular role (for with the advent of access to higher religious education to women, this became a non sequitur) but whether what she considered to be the call of God was actually legitimate. To say that this conclusion is problematic is an understatement. In effect, those who denied a ministry role to a woman were denying the legitimacy of her call-experience, not because it was necessarily any less objective than any other male candidate but because the very impossibility of giving the role to a woman predisposed the conclusion that her calling was illegitimate.

Conclusion

The point of this argument concerning the case of gender with regard to calling is not to suggest that women should or should not be given public roles of ministry, but that withholding such roles from them on the basis of calling cannot be substantiated biblically. Firstly, as argued previously, because the biblical notion of calling to ministry lacks clear connection to selection of candidates for church offices, it is hard to see how lack of calling limits access to ministry roles. Secondly, if calling is indeed of divine origin, then to disallow someone to fulfill one's calling would be to stand in judgment of a divine approbation. Thirdly, if calling is used to prequalify male candidates for a public ministry role, by rejecting a woman candidate who brings an equivalent calling experience, the decision itself belies its innate gender bias and demonstrates in so doing that it considers calling to be merely supplementary to the actual hiring process.

This is really what was at the core of the Joan of Arc condemnation. Joan of Arc was not tried and executed because she had an illegitimate supernatural experience that rendered her insane, as some argued. Though the church was struggling to contend with self-proclaimed apostles and various heresies at that time,[214] others from that era—both male and female[215]—made references to not dissimilar experiences and were subsequently revered for their contribution to the church's agenda. Joan of Arc was tried and executed because she was a woman who pursued her calling in the midst of a politically charged set of circumstances in violation of certain cultural norms of femininity. It was by virtue of her gender that her calling was determined to be categorically illegitimate.

Other Factors

Besides the challenges presented to the contemporary notion of calling described above, other social factors impact the capacity for a given individual to pursue a perceived calling. Two additional factors to consider are poverty and physical/mental disabilities. What makes these two factors significant is the fact that they cut across virtually all modern societies and affect people regardless of gender, religious affiliation or age demographic. Furthermore, these two factors have been part of the human condition from time immemorial and thus offer up a potentially long-standing challenge to the notion of calling as it is understood today.

The Case of Poverty

According to Webster's dictionary, poverty is defined as the "state of one who lacks a usual or socially acceptable amount of money or material possessions." On the one hand, those who are poor are those who do not have the minimum needed to function normally in society. On the other hand, poverty is much more than just the lack of resources; it is also the incapacity to make things better. Lack of money is inextricably tied to deficient educational programs and facilities, insufficient access to safe and affordable housing, unavailability of competent and proximate health care, and limited opportunities for suitable employment. With this lack of resources and the incapacity to make things different comes the sense of helplessness, shame, fear, and failure.[216] Fundamentally, poverty, especially intergenerational poverty, is a major hindrance to social mobility. Those who are poor feel as if they are trapped within their personal and social story.

The debate over what causes poverty and its solution(s) rages between those who maintain that poverty is largely a result of systemic conditions that favor some over others and those who argue that poverty is a failure on the part of the individual to make the most of himself or herself.[217] The debate is essential, because if the cause can largely be determined, then, in theory, solutions can be derived and applied to respond appropriately.

Historically, poverty has been a part of human society almost since the beginning.[218] As noted in Webster's definition, poverty is what results when individuals, families, or larger groups lack the resources necessary to lead a functionally normal life in a given society. The definition of the term is not cause-specific, and so, whether poverty results from human intervention such as war or from natural causes such as drought, the results can be similar. And yet, not all poverty is the same. Researchers denote at least six different kinds of poverty.[219] These include:

1. Situational poverty—poverty caused by a sudden crisis or loss that is often temporary and reversible.

2. Generational poverty—the status when two or more generations of a given family are born into poverty. In these cases, families lack the tools to escape.

3. Absolute poverty—being unable to afford the country-specific minimal standards of food, clothing, health care, and shelter.

4. Relative poverty—the economic status of a family whose income is insufficient to meet its society's standard of living.

5. Urban poverty—describes inhabitants of metropolitan areas of at least 50,000 who are unable to secure adequate employment, housing, and education and who are also at risk of unhealthy and violent conditions with few or no social protections.

6. Rural poverty—economic and social conditions particular to rural areas, which are subject to factors of particular impact on rural economies (e.g., agriculture), such as harsh weather (storms or drought), infestations, fire, etc., with limited access to social services.

Causes of poverty are varied and often intertwined or compounding and can be categorized as accidental (birth defect), historical (colonialism), economic (energy prices), political (corruption), international (war), social (racism), individual (irresponsibility), demographic (overpopulation), geographic (infertile land), and environmental (pollution).[220] Despite the range in types and causes of poverty, what is common is the effect that poverty—especially sustained, systemic poverty—has on social mobility.

One example of the interplay between poverty and social mobility is described in detail by Stephan Thernstrom in his book *Poverty and Progress*. Thernstrom's research centered on the economic evolution of the American urban setting in the 1900s in the wake of the Industrial Revolution. In this work, Thernstrom chronicles the rise and fall of economic fortunes (and misfortunes) as industries came and went, profiting at times and struggling at other times to compete in a largely unregulated market that was largely driven by emergent, unbridled consumerism and technological advancement. What is striking in his description of the era is the conditions of the common laborer, those that made the machinations of industry and profitability possible. Firstly, employment was unstable. On any given day, a laborer might be hired for an extended season or for the week, day, or time it took to perform a task.[221] Secondly, wages were minimal, and with minimum wage guarantees a figment of some future era, employers could offer whatever they wished and trust the ebb and flow of the employment pool sufficient to guarantee minimum costs associated with wages. At times, an influx of immigrants to a community would drive wages down even further as the suddenly expanded pool of potential workers meant that there was always someone willing to work for less than the going rate.[222] Thirdly, the effect of irregular, unstable employment and the suppression of wages meant that women and children were pressed into economic service as soon as possible. In this way, the pooling of resources could potentially stave off dire circumstances and fatal outcomes.[223] But this meant in many cases that children's education (if even available) was surrendered for the sake of wage earning.[224] A lack of education meant lack of social skills related to economic progress such as the basics of literacy and mathematics. And whereas parents may have lacked education-related skills, they could not in many circumstances conceive of the benefit of education for their children.[225] One additional factor that seemed to cement the acceptance of the poor as an economic, social necessity that needed no relief was a particular reading of the Bible that understood the division of class as a matter of divine providence. A community of the 1780s

> contained four churches—two Congregational, one Episcopal and one Presbyterian. The ministers of these churches were men of unquestioned elite status, and spokesmen for the entire community. Members of their congregations were seated according to social status. Merchant, craftsman, laborer, and servant, each in his appropriate pew heard sermons which identified the Newburyport social system with the will of God. The Lord had created the existing class structure and His providence presided over the affairs of men to preserve the various orders, ranks and conditions of society.[226]

In this example, not only is poverty a result of economic instability, but social and religious conventions worked together to perpetuate it from generation to generation. And for those of the labor and servant classes, whose access to basic life necessities consumed the vast majority of their existence, other social norms associated with education and occupational choice were all but unattainable luxuries.

American economic norms have certainly evolved since the colonial era. Virtually every generation of worker since has seen improvements to working conditions and expanded social opportunities as a result. However, though economic and social progress were enjoyed by many in early America, the benefits of the industrial progress were not evenly shared. Those who were born into families that did not enjoy social privilege, those who were generally of non-European heritage, bore the costs of such progress without reaping the benefits. Two groups in particular who suffered hardship, groups marked from the start by what became generational poverty, are the Native Americans and African slaves.

Section 2: Biblical, Cultural, and Practical Challenges

Native Americans

With the arrival of increasing numbers of colonists in the early 1800s, progressive expansion into the so-called Indian Territory became an inevitable necessity for the realization of the American experiment. Fueling this expansion were two somewhat parallel philosophical tenets that influenced everything from politics to religion. The first was the notion of European superiority and, with it, the conviction that Europeans embodied the epitome of civilization. It was this assumed inherent superiority or cultural maturity that justified the displacement of or, if religiously motivated, the civilizing of the Indian.[227] The second was encapsulated by the conquering impulse known as Manifest Destiny, which ascribed to the European white man a providential right, so to speak, to acquire all that could be acquired.[228] The acquisition of territory on the North American continent by displacing its historic inhabitants was understood to be both justified and inevitable. Its eventual realization stood then as its own justification for the means and methods employed to see it through.

One example of how this philosophy took shape in actual governmental policy is epitomized in the 1830 Indian Removal Act that was signed into law by President Andrew Jackson. This act authorized an exchange of lands inhabited by Native Americans east of the Mississippi for land west of the Mississippi as designated by the US government. As part of the legal decree, the law stipulated that those Native Americans who surrendered their lands east of the Mississippi would be granted title to their new lands in perpetuity, aid and assistance in moving and resettling in the new territory, and protection from others (including other Native Americans) who may have objected to this exchange.

In the end, some of the northern tribes gave up their homelands and made the trek westward to be resettled in tracts of land that were deemed useless for the white man. The challenge to the relocation policy came largely from tribes in the southeast known as the Five Civilized Tribes (Chickasaw, Choctaw, Seminole, Cherokee, and Creek). These tribes, who arguably had become accommodated to European ways,[229] refused to trade their cultivated farms for the promise of strange land in the Indian Territory with a so-called permanent title to that land. Many of these Native Americans had homes, representative government, children in missionary schools, and trades other than farming. In the end, some 100,000 tribesmen were forced to march westward under US military coercion in the 1830s. Historians of this era suggest that up to 25 percent of the Native Americans, many in manacles, perished en route. The trek of the Cherokee in 1838–1839 became known as the infamous Trail of Tears. Even more reluctant to leave their native lands were the Florida Native Americans, who fought resettlement for seven years (1835–1842) in what became known as the Seminole Wars.[230] Displaced tribes struggled to reestablish a semblance of life in the new context but often faced discriminatory reactions from their new neighbors without recourse to US governmental assistance.[231] In 1887, Congress passed the Dawes Act, which established a federal policy for allocating lands for tribal resettlement. The Act gave Native Americans a bounded territory to inhabit but under the jurisdiction of state governments whose laws sometimes discriminated against them.[232] The forced removal of the Native Americans and eventual allocation of tribal lands didn't put an end to Native American-US government conflicts. As the nineteenth and twentieth centuries unfolded, a series of diplomatic efforts along with US legal decrees contributed to additional marginalization and dehumanization of the Native Americans.[233]

One stark example of the efforts made to remove Native Americans from the social context was the introduction of boarding schools for Native American children for the purpose of assimilating them into the new American culture.[234] The first of these schools was founded in 1879 in Carlisle, Pennsylvania, on the premises of the Carlisle military barracks. The Carlisle Indian Industrial School became the model for a rapidly expanding system of educational facilities known as the Native American Boarding Schools or Indian Residential Schools. The purpose of these schools was to aid in the assimilation of the Native American into the dominant white culture of the US by eradicating and denigrating the culture of the Native American and inculcating a Western, so-called "Christian" culture through a strict military-style regimen that left nothing unaffected.[235] It is recorded that Captain Richard Henry Pratt, who was appointed to the task of developing and supervising the system of schools, expressed that his aim for the schools was to "kill the Indian, save the man" in every pupil.[236] At the height of the program, the Bureau of Indian Affairs oversaw some 350 of these schools in the US. From their inception in 1879 until the present day, hundreds of thousands of Native American children passed through these schools.

The legacy of the schools is nothing less than horrific. Accounts of insufficient facilities, nonexistent health care, and lack of basic food and adequate clothing were systematically ignored by the US federal government.

Worse, reports of excessive corporal punishment and verbal, physical and sexual abuse were suppressed, while perpetrators were rarely, if ever, reprimanded, let alone prosecuted. The systemic abuse amidst degraded living conditions gave rise to a "cluster of psychological dysfunctions" known as "Residential School Syndrome" (RSS) among survivors of these schools.[237] What is striking is that the symptoms of RSS are "virtually interchangeable with those attending the so-called Concentration Camp Syndrome (CCS) manifested on a collective basis by survivors of both the Nazi facilities and their counterparts in the Soviet Union."[238]

Admittedly, cause and effect are notoriously difficult to prove, but current socioeconomic data of Native American communities reflect the devastation that was in part effected by these Indian Residential Schools. According to the 2018 US Census, Native Americans have the highest poverty rate among all minority groups, at 25.4 percent. The African American poverty rate stood at 20.8 percent, while the white poverty rate from the same report was given as 8.1 percent.[239] The Bureau of Labor Statistics data from 2018 list the unemployment rate for Native Americans at 6.6 percent, just slightly higher than that of African Americans (6.5 percent) but nearly double the unemployment rate for whites, which was noted at that time at 3.5 percent.[240]

One closing comment on the social context of the Native American concerns the sense of hopelessness that has been identified by others as a by-product of intergenerational poverty. This hopelessness is demonstrated by studies that have shown that nearly one in every two adult Native Americans suffered from acute alcoholism during the twentieth century. Recent studies indicate that this self-destructive behavior has morphed, so it seems, into other, more nefarious behaviors, which involve inhalation of gasoline fumes and solvents by children of these alcoholic parents.[241] One Canadian study showed that "by the early 1990s, [those who were inhaling fumes] included seven in every ten indigenous youngsters in Northern Manitoba, and, by the end of the decade, all the children between nine and twelve years of age in several villages in Labrador where, instructively, virtually every adult was both a residential school survivor and an acute alcoholic."[242] From this data it is clear that Native Americans continue to struggle with economic and social challenges to a degree that sets them apart from other minority groups. Equally concerning is the reality that despite the progress made in some of these social conditions, generational poverty continues to stand as an obstacle to full participation in the wider benefits of society related to social mobility.

African Americans

America's introduction to slavery was perhaps unintended as such. When a Dutch trading vessel with twenty or so slaves landed off the coast of Virginia in 1619, it was not because the ship was delivering an order for cheap labor but rather that the Dutch were looking for a market for the slaves they had acquired from a Portuguese slave ship. Regardless of the unintentionality of this exchange, this was not the first instance of slavery in the Western Hemisphere. French, Portuguese, Dutch, English, and Spanish merchants had been transporting slaves from Africa to support growing plantations of rice, sugar, and coffee in such places as Haiti, Jamaica, and Brazil for over a hundred years. Harsh conditions in many of these operations resulted in high mortality rates, and owners opted for male slaves over female because of their capacity to endure harsher working conditions for longer periods of time.[243]

In North America, slavery developed differently. At first, many Africans were engaged as indentured servants, meaning they were contracted to an employer for a period of time related to a certain debt load. In principle, once the debt was satisfied, the indentured servant would be set free to pursue his or her own interests. Indentured servants, in contrast to later slaves, could also marry and save money and generally appreciate some measure of controlling their own destiny—as long as they first satisfied their contract.[244]

The shift from indentured servitude to slavery was largely the product of economics. With the success of the tobacco industry, the demand for cheap labor increased. The Native American population, the most likely choice to satisfy the labor pool, had been nearly wiped out as a result of disease and conflict resulting from encroachment of European settlers on Native American lands. Furthermore, Native American labor proved to be more difficult to manage due to the natives' familiarity with the local terrain, which facilitated escape and support from nearby allies. Compared to North American indigenous peoples, African slaves were less of a flight risk and were without local allies that might threaten European exploitation.[245]

As African slavery took root in the emerging colonial economies, slave codes were drafted for the purpose of regulating the rights and obligations of slaves and their owners. These slave codes determined the social status of a child based solely on the mother's social status (slave or free), vacated legal rights of slaves, denied matrimonial freedom to slaves, and prohibited slaves from carrying arms, among other things. The result was that African slaves were effectively defined as chattel—the private property of a slave owner with no more rights than livestock.[246] Despite the impassioned support for slavery by many in both Southern and Northern states, impassioned opposition to the institution was able to eventually pressure Congress to end the Atlantic slave trade in 1808 (though it did not put an end to slavery itself). In 1820, in an effort to appease both pro- and anti-slavery factions, Congress passed the Missouri Compromise, which admitted Missouri as a slave state and Maine as a free state in order to preserve the balance of power between slave and free states. This decision served to guarantee the presence of slavery in the US for the immediate future.[247]

In the wake of Lincoln's Emancipation Proclamation (1863) and the passing of the Thirteenth Amendment, African Americans sought to finally realize their part of the American dream ensconced in the "life, liberty and pursuit of happiness" formula of the Declaration of Independence. In an effort to reunify the country and restore economic and social cohesion between the North and the South following the Civil War, Congress instituted Reconstruction, which was codified by the Civil Rights Act of 1866 as well as the Thirteenth, Fourteenth, and Fifteenth Amendments to the Constitution. As a result of these legislative acts, blacks were for the first time, in many cases, able to purchase land, travel freely, establish businesses, hold public office, vote in elections, and participate in society without limits and under the protections of federal laws.

The emancipation of the slaves was almost immediately followed by the adoption of freedom-restricting local and state laws in Southern states designed to limit black access to the freedoms ostensibly guaranteed by Reconstruction. These ordinances spread across the US and eventually became known as Jim Crow laws. One of the maxims of Jim Crow statutes were the separate but equal provisions, which were designed to establish and maintain racial separation in public spaces and contributed to the creation of black urban ghettos as blacks moved to the cities in search of better jobs. These provisions, in some form or another, remained in place and governed black and white interaction until the Supreme Court decision in Brown v. Board of Education (1954) ended public school segregation.

The end to public school segregation was one visible step in a long journey towards granting to black men and women in the US the keys to unencumbered opportunity, as was intended in the Reconstruction Era.

The struggle for removing legal obstacles culminated in the passing of a second Civil Rights Act in 1964 prohibiting discrimination based on race, color, religion, gender, or national origin. This legislation was subsequently followed by the Voting Rights Act of 1965 and the Fair Housing Act of 1968, each of which reinforced provisions granting particular rights to blacks in America.

The story of the African Americans is long and complex. The events, circumstances, and people who shaped this story in the US are myriad and remain mostly unknown to most of us. What is however evident and confirmed by study after study is that, despite the legal efforts to level the playing field and grant an obstacle-free existence to black Americans, the reality is that the effects of slavery, Jim Crow, and racial segregation remain. Today, despite the fact that Barack Obama became the first black president, and others like Oprah Winfrey, Michael Jordan, and Madame C. J. Walker made their fortunes in an otherwise white-dominated society, the average black family is far behind the average white family in virtually every social indicator.

According to a 2018 report by the Economic Policy Institute, the black poverty rate in the US recently was 21.4 percent, as compared to the white poverty rate of 8.8 percent. Another way to look at this economic data is to note that African Americans are nearly two-and-one-half times as likely to be in poverty as whites.[248] The unemployment rate (pre-COVID-19 pandemic) for black Americans was approximately 6.6 percent, in contrast to the white unemployment rate of 3.5 percent.[249] Black students have made substantial gains in terms of high school graduation rates, from 54.4 percent in 1968 to 92.3 percent in 2018, and just over 54 percent of blacks have earned a college degree, a figure effectively unchanged since 1968.[250] In terms of home ownership, the percentage of black homeowners is roughly 40 percent—almost unchanged from 1968, the year the Fair Housing Act was passed, which put an end to racially biased rental and home purchase policies. Black homeownership lags white homeownership by a full 30 percentage points and stands as the most significant factor in racially biased wealth disparity. Because of historically low home ownership in black families as compared to white families, the median white family has nearly ten times the wealth ($171,000) of the median black family ($17,409).[251] With regard to the long-term financial outlook, it is estimated that "one-fifth of African American families have a net worth of $0 or below, 75 percent have less than $10,000 for retirement."[252] A summary analysis of the persistent wealth gap between blacks and whites in the US concludes by saying, "Unless current economics change, black families will be poorer on the 175th anniversary of Emancipation than they were in 1980."[253]

One final statistic sheds a different light on the long-term outlook for black families. Since 1968, the number of African Americans incarcerated nearly tripled. Today, African Americans are nearly six times more likely to be incarcerated as whites,[254] and incarceration rates are positively associated with greater need for social assistance and poor social, psychological, and academic outcomes of children.[255]

As noted earlier, assigning cause and effect is notoriously hard to do. It is no secret that the relationship between education, employment, wealth/income, and race/ethnicity is a complex one. Furthermore, any given person or family is also affected by physical or mental health, geographical location, and a host of other factors related to social networks, natural or acquired skills, and opportunities. And yet, the sum of these elements shows that black Americans continue to struggle to fully participate in and benefit from the opportunities in American society. According to a 2016 report by the Sentencing Project, on racial and ethnic disparity in state prisons, "Sixty-two percent of African Americans reside in highly segregated, inner-city neighborhoods that experience a high degree of violent crime, while the majority of whites live in highly advantaged neighborhoods that experience little violent crime."[256] Furthermore, as a result of what is referred to as "structural differences," "youth of color are more likely to experience unstable family systems, exposure to family and or community violence, elevated rates of unemployment, and more school dropout."[257]

Calling and Poverty

What does this all have to do with calling? Given the contemporary understanding of the term, together with its use by ministry-related organizations (e.g., local churches, mission agencies, etc.), societal challenges that leave people with limited education, wealth, and family role models make it difficult for calling to be perceived and pursued. One example comes from recent reports from the Southern Baptist Convention (SBC), the largest evangelical denomination in the US. A 2020 ministry report from the SBC indicates that less than one-half of 1 percent of their career missionaries were African American.[258] To what can this disproportionate representation of African Americans be attributed? The complete answer is surely complex and a function of a number of interrelated factors, but one cannot ignore the fact that the history of social relations in which whites kept black Americans from accessing education and employment opportunities must have played a role.[259] David Roach, elsewhere in his report on the efforts of the Southern Baptist Convention to actively recruit African Americans for cross-cultural mission activity, notes that "black Christians historically have been segregated from seminaries, white mission agencies, and some denominations with a focus on world missions"[260]—including the Southern Baptist Church itself, which was established in 1845 in a reaction to the apparent pro-freedom position of Baptists from Northern states.

Calling, as has been argued, operates in twenty-first century America as a means of orienting an individual towards a choice of career options that are legitimately within reach of the individual. In most cases, in addition to the experience of a divine call, these career options require education and skills commensurate with the career of choice and operate within a scheme of social mobility that both allows and enables someone to aspire to and assume a particular role (job, occupation, career, or "calling"). And though a number of church denominations and socially focused nonprofits draw from predominantly African American communities (e.g., the Church of God in Christ), candidates for roles within these organizations need to possess and display the necessary attributes in order to be considered as legitimate candidates, a divine call notwithstanding.

The question of access to career options that are the fulfillment of a person's calling presumes an antecedent that asks, "Is such a career (calling) option even available to me?" The question posed is not intended to negate a moment of divine intervention in which God speaks to someone, such as we see in the case of Saul in Acts 9. Rather, the question underlines the observed reality that the contemporary notion of calling is shaped by the social context in which it operates, both generally and specifically. This is why 80 percent of Christian college students who are pursuing a ministry-related degree speak of calling as part of their story, whereas only 50 percent or fewer (depending on the specific demographic) of college students at secular universities do the same.[261] To some degree, the social context influences the perceived reality by setting out expectations for normative experiences.

Conclusion

Studies confirm that, for the poor, ideas related to success and advancement are highly conditioned by perceptions of the possibilities of upward mobility that are often encoded in childhood and reinforced over time through personal experience.[262] The perceptions of upward social mobility are often clouded by a prevailing mindset that attributes poverty to a function of personal effort (or lack thereof) or to structural societal matters. In the first case, poverty is the fault of the poor who, if they made an effort, could rise above it and, ostensibly, aspire to and assume any legitimate societal role. In the latter case, poverty is the fault of society, and the poor have little, if any, hope of breaking free. To this point, in his analysis of intergenerational social mobility that compared data from twenty Western European countries, Alexi Gugushvili shows that downwardly mobile individuals are more likely than upwardly mobile individuals to explain poverty by external factors such as societal injustice and, as a result, are less optimistic about rising above it.[263] Because the possibilities to go beyond poverty are perceived to be hindered by societal issues that are beyond the scope of the individual to overcome, the perception of inevitability can feed a pernicious cycle of low expectations, minimal personal effort, and social stagnation. If calling is in turn functionally defined as the process by which an individual follows a spiritual leaning towards a particular career, the poor who are unable to perceive the notion of career possibilities and unlikely to obtain the commensurate education, skills, and experience to be considered a viable candidate are effectively left out of the process. For them, calling is essentially meaningless.

The Case of Disability

According to the 2016 "Morbidity and Mortality Weekly Report,"[264] nearly one in four noninstitutionalized adults in the United States, or nearly 61 million persons, are considered disabled. Disability is described as manifesting limitations in one or more of the following characteristics: hearing, vision, cognition, mobility, self-care, or independent living. The degree of disability in any of the categories varies in severity from person to person but is also more prevalent among older adults, those living at or below the poverty line, those living in the Southern US, and women.[265]

Despite the prevalence of disability in the general population, the social stigma associated with disability shows a long history of exclusion. In 1990, the US Congress passed the Americans with Disabilities Act (ADA) which, among other things, "prohibits private employers, state and local governments, employment agencies and labor unions from discriminating against qualified individuals with disabilities in job application procedures, hiring, firing, advancement, compensation, job training, and other terms, conditions, and privileges of employment."[266] In addition, employers are obligated to provide accommodations to employees with disabilities in order to enable them to perform their work assignments without undue barriers based on their disability needs. Adoption and implementation of the ADA, though still ongoing and imperfect, made possible a degree of economic integration for many disabled and opened doors of possibility even wider to the next generation of disabled Americans who would benefit from the changes made to everything from education to transportation, employment to entertainment.

With regard to the church, not unlike secular corporations, people with disabilities have not often found themselves granted access to ministry roles. According to David Deuel and Nathan John, the church's attitude towards persons with disabilities has been one of compassion over competence. In other words, the church has considered persons with disabilities to be the focus of ministry to, rather than ministry by. Deuel and John argue that the idea that the church leader needs to display wholeness and strength and represent the "ideal" comes from a misunderstanding of the Old Testament purity laws. In effect, God's directive to make certain that a priest was ceremonially clean in order to carry out the sacramental duties was assumed to suggest that he also be physically able in every respect. This misunderstanding, they argue, eventually made it such that persons with disabilities were not even allowed to enter the synagogue to hear the reading of the Torah in the Qumran community just a couple of centuries before Jesus's birth.[267]

As a result of this able-body mentality, disability in mission has been all but impossible, at least in the modern era. Much of the unspoken bias against people with disability in missions is rooted in the assumption that able-bodied candidates who express a call of God to missions have the necessary gifts, skills, and overall capacities (cognitive, emotional, physical and spiritual) to make a contribution to the advance of the gospel. This may be the case. But conversely, those who present themselves for a similar assignment but who bring a disability with them are assumed to be unable to make a similar contribution, regardless of whether they express a similar calling. Deuel and John ask if this unspoken bias against persons with disabilities is not only a failure of the church to adopt the commitment to accommodating such persons as per US society but a much greater failure to actually believe what the Bible affirms about the value and usefulness of every individual in God's sight.

As an example, Deuel and John make an interesting case for the disability of Moses. They note that in the exchange between Yahweh and Moses at the burning bush recorded in Exodus 3–4, Moses states, "Please, Lord, I have never been eloquent, neither recently nor in time past, nor since You have spoken to Your servant; for I am slow of speech and slow of tongue" (Exod 4:10). It is easy to read right past this admission of Moses and chalk it up to "he's just admitting he's a bit nervous when it comes to speaking in front of a crowd." But Deuel and John note that commentators disagree over the exact meaning of the Hebrew terms translated as "slow of speech" and "slow of tongue," and they could indicate a real speech impediment that would have compromised Moses's appeal to Pharoah, at least in Moses's eyes.[268] In response to Moses's admission of weakness, God says,

> "Who has made the human mouth? Or who makes anyone unable to speak or deaf, or able to see or blind? Is it not I, the Lord? Now then go, and I Myself will be with your mouth, and instruct you in what you are to say." But he said, "Please, Lord, now send the message by whomever You will.
>
> Then the anger of the Lord burned against Moses, and He said, "Is there not your brother Aaron the Levite? I know that he speaks fluently. And moreover, behold, he is coming out to meet you; when he sees you, he will be overjoyed. So you are to speak to him and put the words in his mouth; and I Myself will be with your mouth and his mouth, and I will instruct you in what you are to do. He shall speak for you to the people; and he will be as a mouth for you and you will be as God to him. And you shall take in your hand this staff, with which you shall perform the signs. (Exod 4:11–17)

The point of this example, according to Deuel and John, is to show that God was able to make use of a disabled person, even at a moment so pivotal to the story of the people of Israel. If he was able to do so then, there is no reason to suggest that he cannot do so now.

But, as noted in the discussion of the historical challenge of including women in ministry roles from chapter 2, the church tends to adopt and apply societal norms more so than biblical truth. In the end, many of the accommodations the church has made to women in ministry took place because of societal shifts in the push for equality for women. In so doing, churches followed one of three paths: 1) continued to limit public ministry/sacerdotal roles to men only, 2) allowed women equal access to all ministry roles, or 3) established both official and unofficial roles for women that allowed them to lead but in a particular and restricted sense.

This also seems to be the pattern in the church with regard to persons with disabilities, but to a point. Despite societal progress in terms of granting access to persons with disabilities to the church's activities, the stigma of disability inhibits such persons' inclusion in the full community. According to a 2018 report on religion and disability, children with disabilities are less likely than other children to attend religious services, even, depending on the disability, far less likely.[269] Furthermore, one in three families with disabled children have changed churches because they felt excluded, and nearly 46 percent of families with disabled children have never been asked how their child could be made to feel more included.[270] This able-bodied bias is not just felt at the congregational level but also still influences the credentialing process and leadership in the church. Lamar Hardwick recounts how this anti-disability bias influences perceptions of potential leaders. He writes,

> A few years ago, I was invited by a member of my church to join an educational task force in our community. The task force was made up of local businessmen and businesswomen, former and current educators and administrators, clergy and community activists, and concerned citizens . . . . When my seat at the educational task force was questioned, it was a question that assumed incompetence. It assumed that autism prevented me from being an active, contributing member of an important gathering of professionals who had the power and influence to shape the educational system in our country. [Similarly,] when Tom's ordination was repeatedly denied because of his epilepsy, it was an assumption of value. How can he possibly be any value to the Church?[271]

Hardwick laments that the church continues to struggle with the notion of disabled leaders because of the assumption that only those without disabilities are competent to lead. For Hardwick this is because, "we [the church] have surrendered to the seduction of society's seating-arrangement strategy, and it shows. Our [the church's] structures support symbols of honor that can only be housed in bodies displaying a lack of disability."²⁷² This sentiment is seconded by Deuel and John in their assessment of candidacy requirements for cross-cultural ministry assignments. They note that the measures of success and the assumed characteristics necessary to guarantee such are derived from secular ideals of the able-bodied.

> This success-oriented approach can cause us to squeeze our potential missionaries into rigid molds in which they have to be intelligent, strong, agile, and have high energy: the type A personality. This can mean that the missions movement selects only missionaries who have certain personality types, or alternatively it can tend to squeeze people who are different shapes into the same mold.²⁷³

In the 1980s and early 1990s, the West experienced a relative increase in the number of long-term, cross-cultural missionaries who were sent by traditional mission agencies and by large churches who took on the roles of both the sending and administering agency. In response to increased information about unreached peoples and the interest in Muslim ministries, many of these workers set out for difficult, often hostile places.²⁷⁴ In the years following, many workers returned earlier than anticipated, often because of debilitating physical, emotional, mental, or spiritual health. Deuel and John note that in the wake of this wave of brokenness, mission agencies and sending churches developed member care strategies that ranged from pre-field preparations to on-field processes to assist workers in managing stresses and enable them to remain on the field and productive in their work for as long as possible. These member care strategies led to better awareness of what was involved in caring for workers in cross-cultural contexts that contributed to well-being and retention. However, they argue that this emphasis on member care preemptively fostered a risk-averse attitude towards enlisting candidates with potentially challenging characteristics, including those with disabilities.²⁷⁵ As a result, it was not uncommon that

> those with a perceived defect or disability that might impede ministry were turned away, seemingly for their own good or for the good of the field team, without agencies stopping

to realize the discriminatory nature of this. It was, after all, well-meaning.²⁷⁶

This effort to seek to assure long-term success and the well-being of the missionary individual or family is, as Deuel and John note, well meaning and probably served to keep many workers successfully engaged for longer. However, the discriminatory nature of the selection process all but ignores the issue of calling, as if one's sense of call were not enough to overcome the perceived challenges to service that the disability raised. To be fair, stories can be found of cross-cultural workers impacted by disability who nevertheless found a way to be appointed to a ministry role and who served faithfully and successfully despite their disability. Deuel and John recount the story of George Scott (1835–1889) who approached the eminent British missionary Hudson Taylor about missionary service in China, where Taylor had made a name for himself. What was unique about Scott was the fact that he only had one leg. The exchange between Taylor and Scott is recorded to have proceeded accordingly:

> Hudson Taylor asked, "With only one leg, why do you think of going as a missionary? Stott replied, "I do not see those with two legs going, so I must."²⁷⁷
>
> Scott was accepted for missionary service and went on to become the first missionary in the Wenzhou Province of China where he spent twenty-four years as a highly effective mission leader.²⁷⁸

Though statistics are lacking, it is evident from the observation of missionary workers that people like George Scott and others with disability who make it to a cross-cultural ministry assignment are a decided minority. This is not so much because they lack the necessary skills and education—which, thanks to the accommodations of society that emerged since the passing of the ADA (1990), are now widely available and accessible—but because of the anti-disability bias that influences how people perceive the meaning and importance of calling. If calling is truly divine in origin, then nothing should be able to stand between the person called and the task or role to which that person has been called. If nothing else, this is what we learn from the stories of men like Noah, who built the ark to survive the flood; or Moses, who led an estimated two million men, women and children for forty years in the wilderness; or Paul, who, although a former antagonist, became the preeminent first-century missionary. But if, as has been argued throughout, calling in the contemporary sense functions largely as a spiritualized tool of career choice, then careers that are culturally beyond reach, for whatever reason, become effectively unavailable. In short, the minimal representation of people with disabilities in church and cross-cultural ministry reflects not a lack of calling per se but that organizations are making credentialing decisions based on corporate-minded, human perceptions and not taking into consideration the full impact of a divine call. This sentiment is summarized by Deuel and John in their own assessment of the current state of mission efforts to engage with the disabled. They note,

> The [mission] agency is called to support those who are called. The agency should not be seen as a panel to weed out people who are not perfect. Instead, the agency needs to walk beside the person/family with disability in exploring their calling.... If God is calling an individual or family to serve in mission, we need to consider all possible means to enable them to do so, for his glory.[279]

Cultural Challenges—A Summary

The examples of Native Americans, African Americans, and the disabled call into question the contemporary notion of calling that functions primarily as a spiritualized career choice tool. Because calling is often perceived to be the key to ministry, some who have an interest in a particular ministry role may resort to reconstructing their stories to try to fit with the expectations of an appropriate calling experience. For others, the fact that their social status all but prevents them from acquiring the education, skills, and experience needed for a ministry role, a legitimate call-experience is considered insufficient to secure the ministry assignment.

For the credentialing agency, calling is an essential criterion for potential candidates. However, calling as understood in the contemporary sense seems to take a back seat to other criteria perceived to be more telling with regard to an individual's fit for the role and long-term success. So, whereas calling is deemed essential, it is often effectively relegated to a secondary role in candidate selection. This is not to say that candidate screening and benchmarks of essential skills, education, and character are unimportant in the selection process. The world is complex and ministry is often hard, but those who purport to represent Christian enterprises must reflect upon the actual value they assign to such things in comparison to the perceived calling of the candidate.

This state of affairs seems to present at least three possible scenarios. First is that of a candidate who articulates a compelling call-experience but lacks the requisite education, skills, and able-bodied characteristics essential to the role. Second is that of a candidate who lacks a legitimate call-experience but possesses the education and skills essential to the role. Third is that of a candidate who both articulates a compelling call-experience and possesses the requisite education and skills. In the first case, the candidate could be required to acquire the necessary education and skills before being reconsidered. But this assumes, of course, that the candidate is in a position to actually do so—a condition that assumes a certain degree of social mobility and access to education and skill development. In the second case, an otherwise qualified candidate may be rejected because of the lack of a compelling call-experience; but if calling as understood in the contemporary sense is more of a cultural construct than a biblical reality, has an otherwise qualified candidate been rejected? The third case seems to be the ideal; and yet, what actually qualifies as a legitimate call-experience? Does the credentialing body possess the objective tools to validate the often subjective experiences of others? If so, on what basis? If not, then on what grounds can they legitimately reject the candidate who possesses the education and skills but no calling? These questions highlight a number of the practical issues related to calling as it operates in the contemporary context. And it is to these questions that we will now turn.

It would seem that there is no means by which we can know. Our intellect perceives things through the senses, but their unreliability is signaled by 2 Corinthians 11:24: "For Satan himself transformeth himself as an angel of light." . . . [Additionally, there is] the difficulty of judging from external signs . . . [for] false prophets can simulate true prophets, and that any act a prophet can perform, a false prophet can counterfeit.

—JACQUES ELLUL

Whether clergy are truly called in an interaction with God or not, a relationship with a religious community is an important element of that interaction's transcendence from experience to action and, ultimately, to identity. Like the family of origin for a child, the congregation-of-origin plays an important socializing role for these aspiring clergy. It is these congregations, not the ones that eventually hire them, that inform, confirm, and affirm the future cleric's belief that he or she has had a meaningful encounter with the divine that, from their perspective, affects who they are and what they are to do.

—RICHARD PITT

6

Practical Challenges

Introduction

THE PRECEDING CHAPTER MADE an attempt to describe the challenges to pursuing a perceived call of God based on one's particular cultural or social context. As described, the way calling is understood and used in twenty-first-century America inadvertently excludes large numbers of those who are unable to meet the conditions essential to fulfilling their call. For different reasons, those who find themselves in social contexts that limit social mobility are effectively unable to pursue a perceived call. One particular example worth recalling here comes from the work of Dana Robert in describing the history of American women in mission. Robert points out that in nineteenth-century America, in the wake of the modern missionary movement launched by the likes of William Carey (among others), "regardless of their personal qualifications, most women in [nineteenth-century] New England could live out a missionary vocation only if they married male missionaries."[280] In other words, even if a woman experienced what she considered to be a call of God, acquired the necessary education, and honed the essential skills associated with mission activity, the social context of the day prohibited her from pursuing that call unless she was married to a missionary.

In addition to cultural challenges to the pursuit of one's perceived calling, there are a number of practical challenges. These challenges are no less paralyzing than certain cultural changes to the individuals who desire to fulfill what they believe God has asked of them, but these sets of obstacles differ in that they apply more broadly to men and women alike regardless of social standing, geographical location, or historical context.

The Call of God—What Is It?

The initial practical challenge and one that stands as the elephant in the room in this discussion of calling is simply this: "What exactly is calling?" As argued previously, the contemporary conversation around calling lacks a common definition. Not only do religious organizations differ on how they define it, but the concept is growing in its secular usage, which further complicates the issue. Many describe calling as a type of two-step formula that includes an internal call together with an external call. The internal or secret call is the result of some kind of personal divine encounter that orients the individual generally towards a particular ministry-related public role, though not exclusively, however, for calling is also commonly attributed to the teaching, medical, and other nonreligious service domains. The external call is an organizational approbation that a candidate possesses and exhibits the characteristics essential to the job as a validation of the candidate's calling-experience. As noted previously, for some, calling is highly mystical and subjective; for others, it is an obvious directive towards a particular objective. For some, calling is a long, sinuous journey; for others, calling is instantaneous. Regardless, the literature suggests that however one perceives calling, the experience and the means of describing it are to a greater or lesser extent influenced by the social context to which the individual belongs and its relationship with calling. And so, the experience of calling looks different for Pentecostals and others who belong to "Spirit-centered" denominations and retain a strong connection to divine intervention in everyday life, than for those who are part of more "congregation-centered" or "institution-centered" denominations for whom direct, spiritual intervention is less expected.[281]

From the review of the literature on the subject, however, two essential definitions seem to have emerged: one that appeals to divine, supernatural origin and the other a sort of obligation to the common good. For those who perceive that calling is rooted in a divine dimension, calling as defined by Niebuhr seems to approximate a common sense of the term. In his discussion of the purpose and work of the church, Niebuhr says that calling is "that inner persuasion or experience whereby a person feels himself directly summoned or invited by God to take up the work of the ministry."[282] Despite this succinct definition, even Niebuhr sandwiches this aspect of calling between a general call directed to all Christians to discipleship, a providential call whereby the individual exhibits the capacity to actually perform the duties of the ministry role, and an ecclesiastical call that serves as the summons to the individual to engage in the work of the ministry.

For those who understand calling apart from any sense of a divine imperative, calling is equally directive, compelling, and profound. Furthermore, its increasing presence in vocational counseling and management theory makes calling not just an anomaly but a significant contributor to overall corporate culture. As the research notes, those who consider their work as the outgrowth of a personal calling experience more contentment, longer tenure, and overall increase in general well-being.[283] Those who traffic in the meaning and application of the concept struggle to settle on a definition that satisfies everyone. Nevertheless, the definition provided by Dik and Duffy seem to reflect the essential aspects of the concept. Dik and Duffy conclude that calling is "a transcendent summons, experienced as originating beyond the self, to approach a particular life role in a manner oriented toward demonstrating or deriving a sense of purpose or meaningfulness and that holds other-oriented values and goals as primary sources of motivation."[284] Here, for the secularist, calling provides the means to connect a particular interest in a particular role with a sense of purpose that extends beyond the individual's personal benefit. However, in contrast to those for whom calling has a decided religious origin, the secular notion of calling can apply to virtually any legitimate type of work and not just that which is religious or ministry-related.[285]

In the end, what is the meaning of calling? Is that which Niebuhr articulates sufficient? If so, is it necessary to experience all four of the aspects that he outlines in order to say that one has had a legitimate call-experience? What if, having experienced what one believes to be a divine call, one is unable to acquire or demonstrate the commensurate skills of what Niebuhr refers to as the providential call? Does the call become stalled and remain a potential reality until or if the skills are acquired? What if, having acquired the skills, one never receives the external call from the organization that serves as the final validation of sorts and opens the door to the actual pursuit of the call-experience? What happens to a call that remains unfulfilled?

Or, is the secular definition, which roots the call not in the divine but in something "beyond the self" and which opens the door to any and all kinds of work as calling, a better description? In that the secular call definition excludes the necessity of an external call and leaves the validation of the call-experience to the individual, does this simplify the notion and make it so broadly available that it effectively loses its meaning? If a calling is available to all and can apply to any and all sorts of work, does calling become the norm and those without a call become those who are left out and out of touch with their deeper self? Is calling in this sense simply a repackaging of the notion of the responsible citizen who works for the betterment of humankind? This seems to be what Robert Bellah argues in his description of how individualism and commitment play out in American society. With regard to the intersection of calling with the social impact of one's work, he says,

> In the strongest sense of a "calling," work constitutes a practical ideal of activity and character that makes a person's work morally inseparable from his or her life. It subsumes the self into a community of disciplined practice and sound judgment whose activity has meaning and value in itself, not just in the output or profit that results from it. But the calling not only links a person to his or her fellow workers. A calling links a person to the larger community, a whole in which the calling of each is a contribution to the good of all . . . . The calling is a crucial link between the individual and the public world. Work in the sense of the calling can never be merely private.[286]

In Bellah's assessment, calling seems to equate to the obligation carried by a citizen to care for and contribute to the welfare of those around him. Calling in this sense, like social responsibility, is meaningless if it is separated from and provides no benefit to others. Here the general call emerges from the needs of society, and a particular call is defined by the application of an individual's interests, skills, education, and opportunities in response to the general call. From this understanding, it follows that calling would be the societal norm, common to all, and not the exception.

Regardless of the meaning that is adopted, do either of these definitions function broadly beyond the First World, Western context? Is the pursuit of one's calling experience even possible when not also supported by robust individualism and occupational choice, regardless (at least in theory) of gender, race, or creed?

The Call of God—How Do You Know?

In addition to the difficulty in understanding and agreeing on a common understanding of calling, the next question that arises is how exactly does one know if a calling has been received? Calling, by either definition, is largely a subjective notion. Whether one operates from within a worldview that includes God and the possibility of divine communication or not, determining whether one has experienced a call requires some degree of interpretation of the events, feelings, and perceptions that accompanied the call-experience. Furthermore, the pursuit of one's calling, to some degree or another, is related to the real social context to which one belongs. In other words, a call-experience that presupposes unreal circumstances or "impossible" outcomes self-adjudicates. That which cannot be, cannot be pursued. It is also noted that the call-experience itself, as well as how it is described, is influenced by the social context of the recipient. Pitt notes that

> there is an on-going debate among social scientists that takes the form of a kind of chicken-or-egg argument: which is really operating here—social structure or individual agency? It would be easy to suggest that the entirety of the call—from incident to interpretation, from affirmation to accomplishment—is a function of environmental influences. I certainly would not argue that the complex matrix of cultural, organizational, and theological forces acting upon these men and women plays no role in setting boundary markers for the calling. Even the symbolism that makes the calling experience noticeable is born out of a relationship with a religious community. These clerical aspirants have learned what a call to Protestant—and particularly, Pentecostal—ministry looks like. It is clear that they recognize that the calling has a particular set of cultural markers. They mobilize cultural tools in a way that gets them over the important hurdle of convincing church leaders and other parishioners that they are the "real deal." The church has expectations of both a calling narrative and a called individual. Whether God or man, the originator of the impulse to pursue a call to ministry uses those expectations to create the interesting and canonical components of a recognizable narrative description.[287]

In short, people experience or seek to experience what they feel is essential to fit the perceived social roles to which they aspire. In so doing, they also adopt the language (words, symbols, and rites/rituals) of the community that they use to confirm the experience. This is not so say that "real" encounters with God do not happen in these contexts, but it does suggest that care must be taken to ascertain a genuine call from an imagined or mistaken one. One final comment with regard to the notion of the individual's perception of a call concerns the reimagining of past experiences. Lewis Rambo cautions against the subtle adaptation of one's story to conform to the perceived norm of the community. Rambo notes that the process of language transformation and biographical reconstruction is particularly present in conversion narratives or testimonies of converts. In this process, the convert adapts his story to align with the universe of vocabulary and acceptable range of experiences of the new religious community. He notes that "although all of ordinary human life can be seen as a subtle process of reorganizing one's biography, in religious conversion there is often an implicit or explicit requirement to reinterpret one's life, to gain a new vision of its meaning, with new metaphors, new images, new stories."[288] The expectation of calling can result in the same effect. If it is perceived that a call of God is essential to access a particular ministry-related role, a concerted effort to reinterpret past events to fit the call narrative is possible, especially if calling is normative in the community.

But the validation of a call-experience does not lie only with the individual. For ministry-related roles, calling is a standard criterion for candidature. And those responsible for interviewing and selecting candidates for organizational roles are faced with the challenge of determining if someone's description of the call-experience sufficiently satisfies the assumed criteria. But how is this done? How does an organization validate a uniquely personal experience that is often highly mystical?

In order to begin to address the validity of a divine call-experience, several worldview level elements must be acknowledged. Firstly, the idea that God exists. If one relies upon a divine call for life direction, then God, the Divine One, must exist. Secondly, in order for calling to be realized, it must be acknowledged that God must speak. He must be able to communicate his will to humankind. Thirdly, it must be acknowledged that divine communication must be comprehensible and relevant. To the extent that the divine call directs, compels, or leads the recipient to do something, that something must be "possible" and valid. The validity issue demands that what God "calls" someone to do must be compatible with the divine moral framework. It is nonsensical therefore to submit that God has called me to perform something that he has elsewhere and otherwise condemned.

In addition to these parameters for determining the validity of someone's call-experience, some have argued that secondary elements such as signs or testimonials be considered as means of validation. As noted in chapter 2, both the Catholic Church and Protestant denominations look for evidence that the individual is suited for the role by virtue of the acquisition of commensurate skills, education, and character. In some cases, the process of evaluating these secondary elements can be long and involve multiple interviews, medical and emotional screenings, and internships, which place the individual into real or simulated circumstances that approximate the role aspired to by the candidate for the purpose of gauging the candidate's suitability. Despite the degree of sophistication of these screening processes that have become standard practice in modern-day Western society, they cannot offer any real certainty that a calling has been received. But this is not new. The historical events that epitomize this challenge are found in the story of Joan of Arc.

Joan of Arc: Reprised and Expanded

In chapter 4, the tragic tale of Joan of Arc was recounted through the lens of how the social context of fifteenth-entury Europe played a role in her eventual condemnation. In effect, much of what she was accused of was related to the fact that she was a female who had assumed a role of prophet-warrior that was considered to be out-of-bounds for a woman—even one who claimed to have divine authority to do so. This reprise of her story will focus on the nature of the effort to validate her call as an envoy of God sent to deliver the French monarchy from destruction by England.[289]

As noted earlier, Joan's revelations, which she ascribed to Michael the Archangel, Saint Margaret of Antioch, and St. Catherine of Alexandria,[290] directed her to make her way to the dauphin and to inform him that he alone was the "true king" of France and that she should be allowed to lead the French troops against England in order to rid France of them and restore Charles VII to his rightful throne.[291] Though her family doubted her mission and tried to stand in her way, she eventually made her way to the town of Chinon (a journey of some three hundred miles, which, according to tradition, she made on horseback at night) where the dauphin resided. Upon discovering her identity and mission, the dauphin and consort hesitated but eventually, after confirming her virtue and modesty, gave her leave to prove that she was who she said she was—a servant sent by God to rid France of the English and restore the rightful king to the throne. Though opinions were divided and the debate heated, Joan was insistent that the proof that she had indeed been sent of God lay in her capacity to accomplish what she had been sent to do. As Helen Castor notes, the French, following their defeat at Agincourt, were recoiling before the relentless pressure of the English. Furthermore, the dauphin was all but powerless to mount a definitive defense on his own, and Orléans, a sizeable city, was under siege. Those who saw the possibility of Joan as a divine envoy seemed compelled to trust her divine commission, fearing that if they did not and opposed what God had sent, things would only be worse.[292] As Castor explains,

> an attempt to relieve Orléans would be a finite task, requiring only a minimum of resources to be committed by the king, that could stand as a practical test of the girl's mission. Success, if it came, would be a miraculous vindication of her claims; failure would provide an incontrovertible judgement against her. Either way, God would have spoken—and, even if the verdict were negative, there was relatively little to lose by trying.[293]

Remarkably, Joan initially accomplished what she set out to do. In her first test, the battle of Orléans, Joan led French troops against the English and, in a matter of weeks, was able to break the siege and deliver the town. Over the next several weeks, Joan led other successful expeditions against the English and, in July, captured the city of Reims,[294] where Charles VII was later that month crowned king of France.[295] In May 1430, following her failed attempt to liberate Paris, Joan was captured by the English and jailed for more than a year pending trial. The initial charges against Joan (which eventually swelled to over seventy) included heresy, witchcraft, and violating divine law of dressing like a man.[296]

The trial of Joan of Arc cannot be divorced from its political and religious context. For at least the two years prior to her trial, Joan had been a remarkable force, not just because of her military prowess (though Joan didn't actually engage in battle) but because of her inspirational power. Her presence on the battlefield inspired the French and led to extraordinary victories against the English. But what was at the core of the trial debate was this: had God actually sent Joan? Though the context is unique and dramatically different from today, this question is essentially the same question that is at stake when seeking to validate an individual's call-experience and to know: "Has God really directed you to do that?"

In order to determine whether or not Joan had really been sent by God, the English organized a tribunal led by the bishop Pierre Cauchon and some forty-two other clerics, some of whom were the leading theologians of the day. These interrogators undertook the evaluation of Joan via a process referred to as *discretio spirituum*—the discerning of spirits—which drew its biblical inspiration from 1 John 4:1: "Try the spirits if they be of God." The objective of the tribunal was to determine if Joan had indeed heard from God and hence was serving as a prophet of the Lord. According to ecclesiastical tradition, the validation of a prophet rested on two issues: 1) an exemplary life marked by extraordinary virtue and moral purity and 2) miraculous signs.[297] The tribunal, however, could not answer those questions until they were first able to satisfy several other issues: 1) was Joan truly human; 2) if so, were her actions human and, therefore, accomplished solely by her own person or supernatural; and 3) if her actions were supernatural, then was she sent from God and under the direction of a good spirit, or sent from Satan and under an evil one.[298]

The church of the medieval era readily accepted the notion that the gift of prophecy was consistent with the Christian faith and had been so throughout biblical history.[299] Additionally, the highly unlikely possibility of a teenage girl serving as a military deliverer was itself not completely without precedent. Those in Joan's defense argued that God had used Deborah as a deliverer of Israel (Judg 4–5), and David had been called upon while still a youth to take down Goliath (1 Sam 17). That Joan potentially stood in the line of prophet-deliverers of the people of God was therefore not an impossibility.

The accusations against Joan that were levied by the tribunal ranged from questions of her moral character to her failure to measure up to the standards associated with legitimate prophets. Joan was obliged to repeatedly mount a self-defense to these accusations that both flustered and provoked her interrogators. In the end, however, the central question that haunted the proceedings remained: was Joan of Arc actually sent by God? In one set of arguments, the archbishop of Embrun, Jacques Gelu, who was also a supporter of Joan, concluded that the proof of the matter is all but unknowable. He argued,

> It would seem that there is no means by which we can know. Our intellect perceives things through the senses, but their unreliability is signaled by 2 Corinthians 11:24: "For Satan himself

> transformeth himself as an angel of light." . . . [Additionally, there is] the difficulty of judging from external signs . . . [for we know that] false prophets can simulate true prophets, and that any act a prophet can perform, a false prophet can counterfeit.[300]

The trial lasted from January until the end of May 1431. On May 24, as she was facing imminent execution, Joan signed a retraction and submitted to the will of the tribunal. In response, her execution was commuted, and she was returned to prison. Five days later, on May 29, Joan was found to have retaken to wearing men's clothing. She was returned to the tribunal, and all twenty-seven of the trial masters agreed to reapply her death sentence. She was burned at the stake the following day.[301]

The story of Joan of Arc is of particular significance to the question of discerning calling today for the very reason that this incident rallied the top theologians to determine the validity of a young person's perceived divine call. In the end, the tribunal was unable to render a clear verdict on this issue. As Gelu argued, men just cannot always know what God is doing, because our intellect is limited (even corrupted) so that we cannot clearly discern. Additionally, when it comes to signs, even false prophets are at times able to counterfeit true signs.

Gelu's conclusion is seconded by Pitt. In his discussion of the nature of calling in the Church of God in Christ (COGIC) denomination, Pitt notes that few credentialing bodies admit to having the discernment necessary to ascertain true calling.[302] For all intents and purposes, as least as far as the human condition is concerned, calling remains ultimately unverifiable.[303] Due to a lack of certainty, Pitt notes that the COGIC has adopted a process by which they give the otherwise acceptable candidate the benefit of the doubt and allow them to move through the credentialing process with a "wait and see" approach. Instead of denying the individual's claim to a divine call, the church grants a certain trial period to ascertain if the performance of the candidate (to show evidence, "signs," if you will) supports the supposition that the individual has indeed been called of God.[304] In this way, they echo Calvin's conclusion when Calvin argued that "those whom Christ calls to the pastoral office he likewise adorns with the necessary gifts, that they may be qualified for discharging the office, or, at least, may not come to it empty and unprovided."[305] This also aligns with what Niebuhr refers to as the providential call, "which is the invitation and command to assume the work of the ministry which comes through the equipment of a person with the talents necessary for the exercise of the office and through the divine guidance of his life by all its circumstances."[306]

All of this is in part an admission that validation of someone else's divine call-experience appears to be beyond the scope of what is possible. For want of discernment that is able to certify these highly personal and often mystical encounters, credentialing bodies have adopted processes that explore the candidate's experience, character, and skills—not too unlike what took place in fifteenth-century France. But in the end, these processes don't actually verify the calling so much as satisfy the credentialing body that the individual is capable of satisfying the demands of the job. Despite the good intentions of fifteenth-century inquisitors or modern-day interview panels, validating supernatural encounters remains a difficult, if not impossible, task.

The Call of God—How Specific Does It Need to Be?

From the accounts of those who seek to articulate a divine call-experience, one thing that stands out (among other things) is the range of specificity. Some describe their call in terms of a specific task such as preaching or working with children or, as in the case of Joan of Arc, of delivering nations from invaders and restoring rightful kings to the throne! Others describe their call in terms of a particular location for future service, like China or the inner city. Still others describe their call in terms of a particular ministry role such as pastor or teacher. But for others, the sense of calling is vague, leaving them to wonder what the next steps should be. And so the question that emerges is this: "Is specificity an essential component of a divine call?"

If we look back at the biblical record and consider those who were given particular divine assignments, we are drawn to people like Abraham, Moses, and Jonah. In Abraham's case, though the first part of the directive was clear—"Go from your country and your kindred and your father's house" (Gen 12:1a)—the second part of the directive "to the land that I will show you" (Gen 12:1b) was not. Still, Abraham set out in faith and God showed him along the way what he had in mind for that second, less clear, part of the directive.

As for Moses, the divine directive was somewhat more clear:

> And the Lord said, "I have certainly seen the oppression of My people who are in Egypt, and have heard their outcry because of

their taskmasters, for I am aware of their sufferings. So, I have come down to rescue them from the power of the Egyptians, and to bring them up from that land to a good and spacious land, to a land flowing with milk and honey, to the place of the Canaanite, the Hittite, the Amorite, the Perizzite, the Hivite, and the Jebusite. And now, behold, the cry of the sons of Israel has come to Me; furthermore, I have seen the oppression with which the Egyptians are oppressing them. (Exod 3:7–10)

In Moses's case, though what God had asked of him was clear, what was lacking was an explicit description of how he (Moses) was going to be able to accomplish the task. Yes, God had promised to be with him and had given him particular signs and symbols (i.e., his staff), but the how of what would happen next was not yet revealed. Despite the lack of certain details, the biblical account makes clear that as Moses went forward in an effort to see this through, God intervened as necessary to guarantee the outcome.

Finally, Jonah also received a clear, straightforward directive. Jonah 1:1 recounts that "the word of the Lord came to Jonah the son of Amittai, saying, 'Arise, go to Nineveh, the great city, and cry out against it, because their wickedness has come up before Me.'" Jonah, as we know, fled from the directive and intended to escape his responsibility. God turned him around, and Jonah finally made his appearance in Nineveh, only to have the inhabitants—from the king to the lowest servant—repent and become recipients of God's grace, the very thing that Jonah did not want to happen.

New Testament examples of those who received recorded divine assignments are best illustrated by the life of Jesus and Paul. Jesus acknowledges that he came to do his Father's will (John 6:38) and to seek and to save those who were lost (Luke 19:5, 9–10).[307] For his part, Paul came to realize that he was "a bond-servant of Christ Jesus, called as an apostle, set apart for the gospel of God" (Rom 1:1) and, more specifically, as "an apostle to the Gentiles" (Gal 2:8b).

From these few examples, it would seem that some degree of clarity is essential to the call that God gives. Though some details and aspects of the assignment may be lacking, the recipients from the biblical record knew enough to take the initial steps to follow through. Abraham, Moses, Jonah, Jesus, and Paul all had enough of the specifics to get them started and enable them to clearly articulate what they were sent to do, even if all the details of the where and how were not initially obvious.

But here is where the substance and validation issues associated with a perceived call of God resurface. For if the perceived call of God is general and lacks sufficient detail concerning where or how or with whom, how can the recipient be certain that a particular vague notion is actually a divine directive? Additionally, what hope does a credentialing body have of ascertaining the validity of a divine call if the candidatse can describe only a vague sense of what they perceive? With this in mind, it is telling that when students attending Christian colleges in the US admit to receiving a divine call, they describe that call in the following terms:[308]

- to "be a disciple of Jesus anywhere in the world"
- "my life's work is to be set aside as service to God"
- "to lay down my life to bring the gospel to people that can't get it for themselves"
- "to participate in God's big picture to draw every nation to himself"
- "a desire to live for God"
- "redirected passion to kingdom issues"
- to "impact others and lead them to know God"
- to "do what God wants you to do to glorify him"
- "to serve others"

All these descriptions fit clearly into the core of what it means to be a Christian, in that they all describe aspects of the general call to obedience that is fundamental to the average, normal Christian life. Not one of these is inherently unique to the person, nor do they seem to rise to the same kind of call-experience that is attributed to Abraham, Moses, Jonah, Jesus, or Paul. But this is not because they lack transcendence or impact. Many of the recipients can recall the exact circumstances surrounding when they became conscious of this conviction. These common descriptions of calling do not rise to those of the biblical record because they lack particularity. They reflect an understanding of the general obligation of the Christian to obedience to all that Christ commands, but they are not unique, compelling directives. They reflect an experience that has displaced an otherwise cognitive issue of faith commitment to a category of personal application that may or may not apply to them.[309] In other words, certain cognitive issues of faith do not apply to them solely because they are Christians and are therefore obliged to keep the commands of Christ (see John 14:21, 23; 15:10; 1 John 2:3; 5:3). They apply only if they have an experience that they define as a particular call of God that compels them to do so.

Here then is the crux of the challenge with regard to a divine call. A culture (in this case, a religious culture) that demands a certain experience to validate an individual's spiritual condition may substitute emotive experience for cognitive assertion. In other words, when experience becomes more important than propositional truth, having an experience replaces knowledge and becomes the interpretive key to the applicability of a particular aspect of faith. This dependence upon experience as a gauge of what is true and real for in individual is actually a reflection of postmodern thinking for which experience is the arbitrator of truth. On the flip side, if I do not have an experience that compels me to consider a particular cognitive aspect of the Christian faith, then I am not responsible to follow through on it, because God has not "called" me to do so. To make this even more specific, as noted in chapter 4, nowhere does Jesus attach divine calling as a condition to engaging with the Great Commission. And yet, having a perceived call of God related to missions has become a substitute for—and a convenient excuse to avoid—an understanding of a general obligation on the part of all believers to take the gospel to the nations. This is exactly what J. Herbert Kane was concerned about when he said,

> The term missionary call should never have been coined. It is not Scriptural and therefore can be harmful. Thousands of youth desiring to serve the Lord have waited and waited for some mysterious "missionary call" that never came. After a time they became weary in waiting and gave up the idea of going to the mission field.[310]

When the "missionary call" becomes an expected prerequisite to engaging with the Great Commission, the lack of a mystical experience provides a convenient excuse for not being involved. Or, as intimated earlier by Rambo and Pitt, because of the expectation of such a call, a candidate could look to interpret life experiences to fit the perceived universe of expectation of what the organization expects to hear. Much of what is described as a call of God in contemporary accounts seems rather to be a mystical impression, so that what was otherwise foundational to the faith has now become personally applicable only to those who have received a call.

The Call of God—Is Calling a Predictor of Long-Term Success?

As noted earlier, both the Catholic Church and Protestant denominations agree that a call of God to ministry is an essential criterion for potential candidates for roles both official and public (vocational), as well as, in many cases, for lay workers and volunteers. Similarly, mission agencies and some NGOs also include the necessity of a call-experience for candidates for which they have devised more or less complex procedures to validate. But why? What exactly does a perceived call contribute to the capacity of the candidate? Does calling serve to prepare candidates for the desired role/task and then give grounds for credentialing bodies to identify those who are capable? Does calling make someone more effective? Does calling actually help keep someone on the field of service longer? Does it correlate at all to long-term success?

The REMAP II report entitled *Worth Keeping: Global Perspectives on Best Practices in Missionary Retention* summarizes an investigation of retention of overseas workers in addition to factors related to attrition. The study differentiates between what it refers to as Old Sending Countries (OSC) and New Sending Countries (NSC) and seeks to identify differences between the two. Interestingly, the report notes that whereas calling was considered important, even essential for both the long-term missionary as well as the mission agency, the relationship between calling and retention is hard to assess. The report affirms that

> we have yet to meet a long-term missionary who has not felt that call and a personal sense of call was utterly vital to their own missionary journey. Everyone thinks that call as a concept is no longer widespread, and yet everyone believes it is vital for them personally.[311]

Furthermore, analysis of the data suggests that having a clear sense of calling is co-related to retention.[312] However, this apparent correlation belies the reality that, as they note in the introductory comments to the report, OSC "lose" about one in fourteen missionaries every year. That is to say, approximately 7 percent of missionaries leave their field of service every year. For NSC, the percentage of those who leave the field of service each year is only slightly better.[313] The report goes on to ask mission agencies from both OSC and NSC to identify and rank which factors they considered to be of most importance to (improving) retention of overseas workers. For both OSC and leaders, a clear sense of calling is considered to be the most important single factor to improving retention of workers. However, this perspective is paradoxical. For if a clear sense of call is considered to be important for both the missionary and the agency, then how does one account for the fact that nearly 7 percent of missionary workers leave their field of service every year and the vast majority do so for preventable reasons, of which calling is a part?[314] Can it be said that those who leave their field of service each year were really not recipients of a clear call of God? Can this be concluded, despite the fact that the agency made sure to validate the call-experience as part of the candidating process? Is it better to say, perhaps, that those who leave their field of service each year may have been mistaken or that those who sought to validate their call were not able to categorically state that the candidate(s) were indeed not called? This raises the conundrum pointed out by Pitt[315] and Catholics,[316] in that for lack of a clear means of denying someone's call, the credentialing organization puts the candidate on hold either until such time as God can further reveal next steps or until the rest of the credentialing process plays out as a type of litmus test of suitability.

Because of the multiple and complex issues that influence the retention of a missionary, the contribution of calling is difficult, if not impossible, to actually determine. Despite anecdotal testimonial evidence to the importance of calling for keeping an individual engaged in the work, especially during difficult times, calling is but one piece of a multipiece puzzle. Furthermore, even if it was possible to determine the degree of objective correlation between calling and retention, it is quite another thing to associate calling with long-term success. For like retention, ministry success—whether in a local church, an overseas missionary context, or a domestic NGO—is a function of a host of factors, only some of which are under the influence of the individual engaged in the ministry role. Additionally, the notion of success in ministry-related roles is debated. Is success a function of the specific task, a measurable output of results that correlates to the ministry task? Is the fact of having served one hundred malaria-infected patients in two weeks to be considered a success? Or is it the eradication of malarial infection in the region altogether? Is handing out water to families with whom you are unable to communicate in a refugee camp for three days a success? Or is it the fact of passing the language proficiency exam, which allows you to begin teaching in the local church? Fundamentally, ministry success is notoriously difficult to determine and even more difficult in many cases to quantify. Whereas one can count the number of patients served and the number of water bottles distributed, it is all but impossible to measure the spiritual progress of new disciples in their emerging faith in Christ. And again, even if one could find a way to measure success, does calling have anything to do with it?

The Call of God—What If My Spouse Doesn't Feel Called?

Calling as we have discussed thus far is an intensely individual notion, especially for those who are culturally American. And in that the events that are considered to contribute to an individual's perception of calling are seemingly randomly occurring and may draw from a number of otherwise unrelated incidents, the timing and impact and sense of direction of an individual's call reflects a complex, dynamic aspect of the individual's personal and spiritual life. Because of this relatively elastic and often highly mystical nature of calling, it is very possible and, in fact, not uncommon for spouses to end up on different sides of the calling fence. Even if they both were to live some of the same spiritually formative experiences, they are just as likely to understand the importance of these events differently than to find agreement in them.

One of the most well-known stories of this mismatch of calling comes from the life of A. B. Simpson, the founder of the Christian and Missionary Alliance denomination. Somewhere around 1878, Simpson had what he perceived to be a call to missionary service in China. He and his wife Maggie had just had their fourth child, The church he had been ministering in was thriving and advancing, he believed that now was the time to go to China if he was to have enough time to learn the complexities of ministering cross-culturally while caring for a wife and raising four children. To his surprise, his wife refused and mentioned that he could go ahead if he wished, but she and the children would be staying behind in Canada.[317] Despite Simpson's perceived call to China, he did not go.

Later, as Simpson reflected on the reach of the gospel in light of the composition of the major metropolitan capitals of North America, he felt an increasing call to move to New York City to perhaps engage the nations that had come to the shores of North America. Again, his wife, Maggie, objected. It is reported that when she came across his journal entries in which he described his interest in moving to New York City that she tore them out and threw them away,[318] wondering why her husband would ever consider moving to a place that he himself had described as "a corrupt sin-committing, Sabbath-breaking, mammon-loving, God-defying Gotham."[319] Diary entries from Simpson in the weeks that follow their move to New York City indicate that Maggie had taken the move badly, resulting in a severe strain on their marriage.[320]

The conflict that emerges in a story like that of A.B. Simpson is real and can be fatal to a marriage (though it was not ultimately so in their case), largely because this mismatched scenario raises an interesting dilemma. How should a couple consider the importance of calling as it relates to their commitment to unity as a couple? How exactly does one reconcile the notion that one spouse feels called and one does not? Does the called spouse oblige the not-called spouse to submit and follow, or does the not-called spouse's lack of call determine the outcome? Unfortunately, it appears as if the Bible is all but mute on this issue. For though the man is instructed to love his wife as Christ loved the church and the wife is instructed to submit to the husband (Eph 5:22–33), there is no answer to the question of an apparent mismatched sense of calling.

If calling is an all-or-nothing divine obligation, then it would appear that a sense of calling trumps other conditions, including a lack of call for the spouse. And so, we would expect that Sarah would in fact follow Abraham to go to "the land that I [God] will show you" (Gen 12:1). And so she did—though the Bible does not say if Sarah also received any kind of message from God as well. Assuming she did not, then her submission to Abraham's call would be one example of this kind of response. This seems to be the case for all those who are typically considered to have received a divine calling, whether one speaks of Abraham or Moses, Noah or Jonah, Peter or Paul. Their call superseded any and all other social conditions. A divine call effectively operates as a divine obligation.

If calling is, however, a spiritualized tool for determining a particular career path among a range of options, then a negotiated alternative that satisfies both spouses would seem to be appropriate. And yet, in the contemporary era, where everyone's voice counts and everyone is inclined to hear for themselves what the will of God is for their lives, this may be more easily said than done. To this dilemma, Sills suggests that taking the time to pray and nurture the possibility of mission service, all the while building into one's marriage, is a more prudent approach than simply obliging the not-called spouse to submit and follow. In the end, a fruitful, contented partnership will do more good for the kingdom of God than a half-hearted partnership in a challenging ministry assignment.³²¹ But in this case, the perceived call is not considered to be absolute or may be so general as to be applicable to a number of possible career outcomes. In this case, the perceived sense of calling functions rather as a divine suggestion.

The Call of God—What if I Am Not Successful in Ministry?

If we understand calling to be a divine directive, then it follows that God will enable the individual to accomplish what he intends. God's plans are not just possible, they are guaranteed. This is the sentiment carried by the following verses.

- "But our God is in the heavens; he does whatever he pleases" (Ps 115:3).
- "Declaring the end from the beginning, and from ancient times things which have not been done, [he says,] 'My plan will be established, and I will accomplish all My good pleasure.'" (Isaiah 46:10).
- "I know that You can do all things, and that no plan is impossible for You" (Job 42:2).
- "And looking at them, Jesus said to them, 'With people this is impossible, but with God all things are possible'" (Matt 19:26).

And yet, the very notion of calling is lived out in the day-to-day performance of individuals who, though redeemed, are nonetheless imperfect, with limited skills and wisdom and subject to a host of factors outside their control. Furthermore, all of this takes place in a complex and dynamic world that is decaying under the weight of sin (Rom 8: 19–23). And so, inevitably, it seems, though God's plans prevail, man struggles to succeed. And sometimes, he does not.

And what can be said, therefore, of the individual who, though pursuing what he or she considers to be a clear call of God, does not succeed? What if the effort put forth does not yield the results that were intended? Was God's call insufficient for the task? Did the individual misunderstand and assume a call when there was none? Or is God's call in the end only a possibility of intended outcomes and not a guarantee?

Section 2: Biblical, Cultural, and Practical Challenges

Charles Simeon: Fifty-Four Years of Endurance

In his account of the life and ministry of Charles Simeon (1759–1836), John Piper recounts a unique story of endurance in the midst of what many would call ministry failure.

> Charles Simeon preached his first sermon at Trinity Church on November 10, 1782. But the parishioners did not want Simeon . . . . The first thing the congregation did in rebellion against Simeon was to refuse to let him be the Sunday afternoon lecturer. This second Sunday service was in their charge. For five years, they assigned the lecture to Mr. Hammond [the assistant curate]. Then when he left, instead of turning it over to their pastor of five years, they gave it to another independent man for seven more years! Finally, in 1794, Simeon was chosen lecturer. Thus for twelve years he served a church who was so resistant to his leadership they would not let him preach Sunday afternoons but hired an assistant to keep him out.
>
> Simeon tried to start a later Sunday evening service, and many townspeople came. But the churchwardens locked the doors while the people stood waiting in the street. Once Simeon had the doors opened by a locksmith, but when it happened again he relented and dropped the service. The second thing the church did was to lock the pew doors on Sunday mornings. The pewholders refused to come and refused to let others sit in their personal pews. Simeon set up chairs in the aisles and nooks and corners at his own expense. But the churchwardens took them and threw them into the churchyard. When he tried to visit from house to house, hardly a door would open to him. This situation lasted ten years.
>
> Finally in 1807, after twenty-five years of ministry, his health failed suddenly. His voice gave way so that preaching was very difficult and at times he could only speak in a whisper. After a sermon he would "feel more dead than alive." This broken condition lasted for thirteen years, till he was sixty years old.[322]

In 1819, Charles Simeon recovered his health just as suddenly as he had lost it and went on to preach for another seventeen years. No doubt Simeon is a model of perseverance. Others in his shoes would likely not have continued to put forth the effort that he did for fifty-four years, given the intense opposition from his congregation and the harsh health issues he endured later.

Piper takes pains to understand how Charles Simeon was able to endure such pointed opposition and harsh criticism for all those years. What he reveals is a man who was single-mindedly devoted to pleasing God, regardless of the opposition from the very people he had come to serve. And yet, despite the riveting account of Simeon's life and ministry, one cannot read the story and not wonder to what extent did Charles Simeon consider the relative emptiness of his first thirty-seven years of ministry to be a failure. At times, Simeon acknowledged as much. In an excerpt from his journal towards the end of the pew-locking era, he said,

> It was painful indeed to see the Church, with the exception of the aisles, almost forsaken; but I thought that if God would only give a double blessing to the congregation that did attend, there would on the whole be as much good done as if the congregation were doubled and the blessing limited to only half the amount. This comforted me many, many times, when, without such a reflection, I should have sunk under my burden.[323]

Piper does not consider Simeon's story in light of his supposed calling to the pastoral ministry. And, apparently, Simeon, does not openly ponder the dilemma of a divine calling in the midst of long-term and pointed opposition to his ministry. Despite the lack of evidence, the silence begs the question as to how Simeon must have reconciled the two. Nevertheless, if we assume that Simeon was indeed called to the ministry—as was the norm for those in pastoral ministry in his day—then it must be noted that calling is no guarantee of successful ministry.

David Brainerd: Four Years of Suffering

David Brainerd (1718–1747) was born in rural Connecticut.[324] The early death of his parents, coupled with his melancholy personality, plagued him throughout his short life with bouts of depression and sometimes morose introspection.[325] In 1739, after finding peace with God through Christ, he enrolled in Yale College to study for the ministry.[326] Two years later, in 1742, following an incident in which he was accused of criticizing the weak spirituality of one of the college tutors, Brainerd was expelled from the college,[327] ending his hoped-for career as a pastor. Though barred from official church pulpits, Brainerd took to itinerant preaching and became locally popular. One admirer, Jonathan Dickinson, a Presbyterian minister of New Jersey and commissioner of the Society in

Scotland for Propagating Christian Knowledge, invited him to become a missionary. To prepare for this new work, Brainerd came under the direction of John Sergeant, missionary to the Stockbridge Native Americans.[328] From 1743 to 1747, David Brainerd labored to preach the gospel to the Native Americans in western Massachusetts, eastern New York, the Lehigh region of Pennsylvania, and central New Jersey.

But all was not well. Brainerd had as a child developed symptoms that were later diagnosed as tuberculosis. Just four years into his Indian ministry, he collapsed and retired to the home of his friend Jonathan Edwards where he later died.

Brainerd's journals have become standard reading for missionary wannabees since the first edition was published posthumously by Jonathan Edwards in 1749.[329] Taken as a whole, they document the intense spirituality, courage, and faith of a young man who has since become a relative hero of the faith. But when one takes a closer look, Brainerd's life is hardly one to which many would aspire. His parents died when he was young, certainly leaving him in the care of others and apparently with little means. He was given to bouts of depression and introspection, likely related to the loss of his parents and the stability of a nuclear family. Though he made his way through the educational system of his day and on into divinity school at Yale, he was expelled and effectively barred from pastoral ministry as a result. Though he turned his attention to ministry among the Native American tribes, he only lasted about four years before tuberculosis claimed his life. In the end, his life was troubled and his ministry short. Though he realized some progress with the gospel among the Native Americans of the Northeast, he died a young man of twenty-nine, far from fulfilling his dreams.[330] A few excerpts from Brainerd's journals shed light on how he perceived his contribution to ministry.

> Thursday, April 7. Appeared to myself exceeding ignorant, weak, helpless, unworthy, and altogether unequal to my work. It seemed to me I should never do any service or have any success among the Indians. My soul was weary of my life; I longed for deaths beyond measure. When I thought of any godly soul departed, my soul was ready to envy him his privilege, thinking, "Oh, when will my turn come! must it be years first!"—But I know, these ardent desires, at this and other times, rose partly for want of resignation to God under all miseries; and so were but impatience. Towards night, I had the exercise of faith in prayer, and some assistance in writing. O that God would keep me near him![331]

> Saturday, April 16. Still in the depths of distress.—In the afternoon, preached to my people; but was more discouraged with them than before; feared that nothing would ever be done for them to any happy effect. I retired and poured out my soul to God for mercy; but without any sensible relief. Soon after came an Irishman and a Dutchman, with a design, as they said, to hear me preach the next day; but none can tell how I felt, to hear their profane talk. Oh, I longed that some dear Christian knew my distress. I got into a kind of hovel, and there groaned out my complaint to God; and withal felt more sensible gratitude and thankfulness to God, that he had made me to differ from these men, as I knew through grace he had.[332]
>
> Wednesday, May 18. My circumstances are such, that I have no comfort, of any kind, but what I have in God. I live in the most lonesome wilderness; have but one single person to converse with, that can speak English. Most of the talk I hear, is either Highland Scotch or Indian. I have no fellow-Christian to whom I might unbosom myself, or lay open my spiritual sorrows; with whom I might take sweet counsel in conversation about heavenly things, and join in social prayer. I live poorly with regard to the comforts of life: most of my diet consists of boiled corn, hasty pudding, &c. I lodge on a bundle of straw, my labor is hard and extremely difficult, and I have little appearance of success to comfort me. The Indians have no land to live on but what the Dutch people lay claim to; and these threaten to drive them off. They have no regard to the souls of the poor Indians; and, by what I can learn, they hate me, because I come to preach to them.—But that which makes all my difficulties grievous to be borne, is, that God hides his face from me.[333]

David Brainerd's years of ministry were short and marked with both mental and spiritual anguish as well as physical suffering. It is true that in the last couple of years of his life, he did see some response to his efforts among the Native Americans, but his declining health and relatively harsh living conditions sapped his strength and muted his joy.

His real influence came after his death with the publishing of his journals by his friend, Jonathan Edwards. Many found encouragement and hope in the honest, soul-baring accounts that Brainerd provided in his frequent journal entries. Though Brainerd does not seem to answer the question directly, one cannot help but ask if he would have considered himself to have fulfilled his calling. Additionally, was he even certain of that to which he had been called, since his first foray into ministry preparation ended in expulsion from Yale?

The examples of Simeon and Brainerd beg the question: if the call of God is indeed divine in origin, then whose failure is it if the individual is unable to see it through? The implication is that it must be the individual, for God cannot be held accountable for failure. And so, how does the individual who believes to have failed in the calling go on? Is one forever maligned to live the rest of one's days under the shadow of having failed the God who called? Does one rather, like Simeon, attribute the failure to a necessary instrument by which one learns humility and patience and dependence on the Lord? Or does one, like Brainerd, consider the consummation of one's life sufficient—regardless of the outcome of one's efforts?

The Call of God—What if I Am Dismissed for Moral Failure or Poor Performance?

It is one thing to fail in ministry due to poor health, obstinate parishioners, or inadequate ministry skills; it is quite another thing to disqualify oneself because of moral failure. The biblical record makes it clear that sinful behavior in the lives of ministry leaders is not a new phenomenon. In fact, many prominent actors from biblical history reveal blemished moral characters that negatively impacted their personal lives as well as the welfare of the people of God. Noah drank himself into a drunken stupor following the release of the animals from the ark (Gen 9:20–21). Abraham twice lied about his relationship to Sarah in order to save his own skin (Gen 12:14–20 and Gen 20: 1–13). Moses responded in anger, killing an Egyptian (Exod 2:11–14) and later angrily struck the rock in lieu of speaking to it as God had instructed (Num 20:10–13). David committed adultery with Bathsheba and had her husband killed in battle (2 Sam 11:1–27). In each case, the moral failure reaps consequences that linger personally and corporately for the people of God.

In the contemporary era, accounts of moral failure among those engaged in ministry have become all too commonplace. Though accounts of moral failure in the Catholic Church were acknowledged as largely rare, unusual occurrences in the 1980s and 1990s, they suddenly became the subject of widespread investigations amidst accusations of systemic cover-ups and denials in the early 2000s.[334]

Lack of a common governing body in Protestant Christianity makes comparing Protestant statistics to Catholic ones problematic. Furthermore, the means of investigation and disclosure vary from denomination to denomination, making comparisons all but impossible. Nevertheless, termination for cause of moral failure is common in Protestantism. Lifeway Christian Resources, which studies clergy within the Southern Baptist Convention, noted that nearly 1 percent of pastors leave the ministry each year (250 per month),[335] some of these for reasons of moral transgression. A joint study by the Barna Research Group, Fuller Seminary, and Pastoral Care Inc. reported that 33 percent of pastors confess to having been involved in inappropriate sexual behavior with someone in the church.[336] In addition to the statistics, the stories of high-profile leaders whose ministries are upended because of moral failure have become almost regular fare in recent years.[337]

But what does such moral failure do to one's call? Is the call then revoked? If so, by whom? Does God initiate another divine encounter to annul the initial call in a manner similar to the first call-experience, which had led the individual into ministry? Is the call revoked by the church or the ministry agency that employed the individual and provided ministry oversight? A recent survey by Lifeway Resources found that whereas the vast majority (upwards of 75 percent) of people feel that a minister who commits sexual assault should be barred permanently from ministry, only 27 percent feel that a permanent ban extends to those who commit adultery, and an additional 31 percent were not sure.[338] This suggests that the credentialing body who extended the secondary call to the initial candidate should, at some point, do so again to the individual, despite the moral failure.

The contemporary Catholic position on this takes a different approach. For Catholic theologians, God's call is considered to be an indelible, identifying mark on one's soul. And neither does failure to succeed nor, as in the case of King David, moral failure remove the mantle of the call from the life of the individual. As in David's case, though he was found guilty of sin, he was not removed from being king.[339] But this understanding of calling has moved the concept from "called to a task" to "called to be someone." And though David failed in the end to fulfill the task—he was disqualified from building the temple (see 1 Chron 17:4 and 1 Chron 28:2–3), and he gave the throne to a son born to someone whose husband he had killed—he remained the king. He fulfilled who he was called to be.

The moral character issue raises another set of questions with regard to calling. Is calling conditioned on the moral perfection of an individual? If so, then no one is qualified to be called, based on passages such as Romans 3:23 and 1 John 1:10 and the admission by Paul in Romans 7:7–24 where Paul laments over the ongoing nature of his struggle with sin. Additionally, accounts of men like Abraham, Moses, and Jonah all argue against the idea that calling is predicated on the perfection of the recipient. Like spiritual gifts, which are dispensed by the Holy Spirit as he wills (1 Cor 12:11)—to mature as well as immature believers—so, too, calling appears to not be conditioned on a particular moral condition. Though Noah and David were selected, in part, at least, because God saw in them some degree of exceptional character, God must have also known that they would go on to commit sin that would resonate publicly. In fact, it could be argued that God knew how and to what extent those whom he had called would go on to sin, even before he called them. And yet, this knowledge did not prevent his calling. But in that moral transgression demands consequences, should it be expected that an individual's call be retracted or set aside? Should this revocation be permanent?

Unfortunately, the biblical record apparently leaves the question unanswered. Noah, Abraham, Moses, and David went on to lead their people, albeit with consequences associated with their sin, but they were not entirely removed from their calling. Even Jonah, who turned his back (literally) on his divine assignment, was brought back by God through a series of extraordinary events to fulfill his mission to the people of Nineveh (Jonah 4).

Practical Challenges—A Summary

Practical issues related to the nature of calling are varied and complex. At the heart of the initial challenge is finding a coherent, commonly accepted definition of what exactly constitutes a calling. The fact that that notion operates in both the religious and secular domains only makes coming to agreement on a common meaning that much more difficult. Furthermore, the experience of individuals from the biblical era to the modern one makes defining the concept elusive. A related and perhaps even greater challenge is left to those in the position of seeking to validate the calling experience of a candidate. As noted, the tools and procedures designed to do so are ultimately unable to objectively verify that which is largely mystical. In addition to the challenges of defining and validating one's call are added the questions of specificity and whether the call, as it is understood today, has become a means of opting in (or out) of basic Christian discipleship.

The intersection of a divine call with the human condition inevitably leads to complex, even seemingly contradictory situations. For though God is sovereign and holy, humankind is subject to the weakness and imperfections of the human condition, which calling, apparently, does not always overcome. And so, failing health, obstinate parishioners, or an unconvinced spouse can effectively stand in the way of fulfilling one's call. And lest one imagine that calling is some kind of guarantee of ministry success, the examples of Simeon and Brainerd, together with the recent data from mission and pastoral research, indicate that large numbers of men and women who engaged in ministry as a result of the conviction of a divine call to do so do not realize extensive or trouble-free success. And many, in fact, leave the ministry every year, effectively abandoning or having to repurpose their calling.

Finally, from what can be discerned from the biblical accounts, calling is not necessarily conditioned on the moral integrity of the recipient per se but is rather, like spiritual gifts, dispensed by the God who is fully cognizant of the moral frailty of humankind. Surely, moral integrity is the preferred condition of the man or woman whom God calls, but no one (apart from Christ) is beyond the pale of sin. And so, calling seems to stand almost independent of the moral character of the individual; though biblical grounds for discipline may remove a person from continuing in public ministry, the verdict is still out as to whether moral failure permanently annuls one's call.

Calling, whatever it is and however it applies, must, it seems to me, take into consideration these practical challenges, as well as others that have not been articulated, if the notion of calling is to function widely beyond First World, Western contexts in the contemporary era. Failing to account for these practical challenges, I think, relegates calling to a highly personalized experience and interpretation, which, in lieu of addressing such issues, is forced into the background, leaving the individual frustrated, confused, and left with creating a new interpretation of events to explain a call that didn't work out. But is this really what the biblical conception of calling leaves us? Is the call of God really so fragile and potentially hazarded by humankind that, despite the reality of a divine encounter, the accomplishment of the task is truly open ended?

"Not *called*," did you say? "Not *heard* the call," I think you should say.... Put your ear down to the Bible, and hear Him bid you go and pull poor sinners out of the fire of sin.

—WILLIAM BOOTH

I believe that in each generation God has called enough men and women to evangelize all the yet unreached tribes of the earth. It is not God who does not call, it is man who will not respond.

—ISOBEL KUHN

The concern for world evangelization is not something tacked onto a man's personal Christianity which he may take or leave as he chooses. It is rooted in the character of the God who has come to us in Christ Jesus. Thus, it can never be the province of a few enthusiasts, a sideline, or a specialty of those who happen to have a bent that way. It is the distinctive mark of being a Christian.

—JAMES S. STEWART

Section 3

A Proposed Reimagining of What It Means to Be Called of God

7

The Call of God
A New Proposal

Introduction

IN THE CONTEMPORARY WESTERN context, ministry roles all but require the candidate to describe a call of God in order to be considered for the post. Due to the nature of the calling experience, which is often mystical and highly personal, agencies lack credible means/tools for verifying the call. Furthermore, the nature of calling is inevitably shaped by the community in which the candidate circulates and is therefore driven by experiences and vocabulary unique to the group. The number of possible elements considered to be part of calling is therefore so broad and varied that individual recipients of supposed calls as well as credentialing bodies are at a loss for understanding and validating a legitimate call primarily because there is no standard to which to appeal. To make matters even less certain, not only does the Bible not give a clear definition of what a call of God entails, descriptions of ministry candidacy, such as those found in 1 Timothy 3 and Titus 1, as well as the Great Commission passages such as Matthew 28, Mark 16 and Luke 24, all lack reference to calling as a prerequisite for ministry.

The contemporary understanding of calling is steeped in First World, twenty-first-century Western career choice theory. This is evidenced in how the call-experience is understood and utilized by individuals in the run-up to adulthood. As shown from surveys of Christian college students, the average age for perceiving a call-experience is just over sixteen years of age—conveniently at or near the age in which US high schoolers begin the process of sorting out career options, applying to colleges, and taking their first steps into paid jobs. Additionally, whereas more than 80 percent of Christian college students who were pursuing ministry-related degrees programs at Christian colleges indicated they had received a call of God that oriented their degree choice, almost 40 percent of students at secular universities indicated the same thing, and another 28 percent noted that they were seeking some kind of calling as an indicator for future direction. It seems to me that such high correlation between calling and career choice pursuits, as they relate to pursuit of degree programs in college, suggests correspondence (at least) of the notion of calling with career choice.

One final contribution to the relationship between calling and career choice comes from career counseling research. Duffy, in his review of spirituality, religion, and career development makes the claim that,

> for some clients, spirituality or religion may be a driving force in the career decision-making process, where choosing a career that they feel called to is a primary form of motivation. For others, spirituality and religion may be important sources of support that could prove valuable throughout the career development process, especially during times of career instability.[340]

Duffy and Sedlacek go on to argue in their article on the salience of career calling among college students at secular universities in the US that "students with a career calling report using this as a factor in their future career choices."[341] They note, due to the common presence of calling as part of the mix of elements that contribute to student choice, that career, high school, and university advisors should consider calling as part of career counseling. The unfortunate implication of the influence of Western, First World career-choice theory on calling is that those who have limited social mobility due to a range of factors are effectively unable to experience and/or exercise their call-experience. Again, Duffy argues,

> A key assumption in each of the theoretical models is that people have choices regarding the careers they pursue. This assumption may be valid in the case of most college students but in no way can be extended to the general population. Many workers may believe that they had little if any choice in selecting their current occupations because they did not have the opportunity to explore their options or receive training for more desirable careers. For this group of people, it is important to understand

how spirituality and religion affect their work lives, where religion and spirituality may be used more as a coping mechanism than as something that shapes career choices.[342]

As discussed in chapters 4 and 5, certain categories of people who are unduly influenced by cultural or practical challenges, such as those with physical or mental disabilities, the poor, or certain racial or ethnic groups, have historically been unable to participate in the free and unencumbered pursuit of career options, which, when put together with a sense of calling, implies an inability to pursue or even legitimately consider the possibility to receive such a calling. As a result, these groups are disproportionately absent from the ranks of those engaged in public ministry roles. One obvious example is the relative absence of men and women with physical and/or emotional disabilities from public ministry roles, despite the increased focus on ministry to these groups of people over the last several decades.

The functional reality is that calling—as it is understood in its contemporary context—really only applies to and therefore serves those who fit a largely First World, twenty-first-century, Western, able-bodied, socially mobile profile. Those who initially do not fit this profile are effectively unable to tether together the necessary education, skills, and resources to a conception of career options to be able to even consider the possibility of a call. And some who later encounter changes to their personal or social condition that move them into one of these challenged categories and remove them from active service in public ministry are faced with the need to reinterpret their calling in an effort to retain spiritual and emotional equilibrium.

In the end, the evidence leans in support of the conclusion that both cultural challenges, which are largely ignored, and practical challenges, which leave the individual to reinterpret their calling, are all but extemporaneous additions to the biblical concept of calling, which has evolved over time to largely accommodate this First World, twenty-first-century, Western (and in particular, American individualist) career-choice theory, which effectively eliminates many who do not fit this profile. This begs the question as to whether these individuals can in fact be called at all. The problem we have in responding to this simple question is that we really cannot say, because a common definition of calling and a robust means of validating a call-experience are lacking.

A Way Forward

The preceding discussion, which calls into question the biblical legitimacy and narrow applicability of the contemporary understanding of calling, leaves us with the question of how to move forward and wonders at the possibility of reimagining a notion of calling that is more firmly rooted in the biblical narrative and inclusive in nature. The difficulty of reimagining the concept of calling is duly noted, if for nothing else than the fact that the contemporary meaning is effectively tied to the understanding put forth by the likes of Martin Luther and John Calvin in the sixteenth century. Additionally, over the last five hundred years or so, the meaning of calling as described by the Reformers has become thoroughly embedded in the warp and woof of church denominations, religious NGOs, Christian colleges, and other ministry agencies. Furthermore, calling as a means of discerning career options has become a common element in the decision-making process for both Christian and secular students seeking to find their place in the world.

Because of the important role that calling continues to play in the orientation of men and women into public ministry, it is essential to take a fresh look at the biblical and contemporary context related to calling, despite the innate challenge to potentially and unnecessarily churning the waters over the meaning of this concept. The purpose in so doing is to attempt to re-root the concept in its biblical framework and provide a guide to its application in the contemporary context that removes cultural and practical barriers to inclusiveness.

In an effort to reimagine the notion of calling and suggest a revised application to the contemporary era, it seems essential first to circumscribe the biblical framework within which calling operates. Once we have determined the scope and purpose of biblical calling, we can move towards an applicational proposal for a reimagined definition.

Essential Truths Related to Calling

God May Still Call Today

For the Christian who ascribes to a biblical worldview, calling is a divine prerogative. This perhaps goes without saying, but for the Christian there can be no calling apart from that which emanates from God. Without the hand of God on a person's life to direct him or her to go, do, or say

The Call of God: A New Proposal

something on behalf of God and his purposes, calling has no sense. The biblical record gives us a number of examples of men and women who were ostensibly called to a particular task. Some of these callings, if we can refer to them as such, were of limited scope and duration. Like Jonah, whose mission is described and completed in just four chapters of the book that bears his name, calling seems to have been limited to a unique assignment that was accomplished in a relatively short period of time. Following the completion of the task, Jonah, for all intents and purposes, all but disappears from the biblical record. Others, whose missions are much more extensive not only in scope but also duration, find their calling to be a life-defining assignment that may last from birth (as in the case of Samuel and Jeremiah) or youth (as in the case of David) or the latter years of life (as in the case of Moses). Calling in these examples appears much more comprehensive and enduring.

That God calls in the accounts of the Old and New Testaments is without dispute. That God calls today is assumed, but can this be justified beyond an experiential basis that seeks to define and equate mystical call-like experiences with biblical examples and precedent? Though history has not recorded each and every encounter between God and humankind over the millennia, it is doubtful, nevertheless, that many are having call-experiences on the order of God-directed relocation orders (as for Abraham), burning bushes (as for Moses), or voices and flashes from heaven that result in blindness (as for Saul). And yet, we can be assured that God may still call today, even if history is not repeated in the same way, for the following reasons:

1. God has not changed. As noted in Hebrews 13:8, God is the same yesterday, today, and forever. His nature and intent to fulfill his salvific promise to the nations has not passed away. And so his capacity to call men and women in particular ways has also not dissipated. God may still call men and women to particular tasks today, because he is still able to do so.

2. God's plans have not changed. The argument for the *missio Dei* as the central theme of the Bible has been definitively made by others.[343] The biblical record clearly indicates that to accomplish this *missio Dei*, God calls upon men and women at particular times to serve a critical purpose to advance the agenda of the *missio Dei*. And so it is through this lens that the calling of men like Abraham who would become the father of the people of Israel is singled out for the task of

people taking up residency in Palestine, the future homeland of the Jews. Moses, likewise, was tapped at a particular moment in history from among all the other infant sons of Israelite mothers to become a prince in Pharaoh's household so that many years later he could serve as a shepherd of Israel for the forty years of desert wanderings. And on it goes. The Bible, as a record of God's intent for humankind and the working out of his plans in history, clearly does not record the story or the contributions to the advancement of the *missio Dei* in every person. However, those stories that have been recorded are clearly those God has deemed critical to our understanding of himself, his plans, and the role of humankind therein.

In that the *missio Dei* has not been fulfilled, God's plans have not been fully accomplished. Furthermore, the Bible seems to suggest that the means that he uses to accomplish his purposes also have not changed. This can be supported from the argument of the Great Commission passages that close each of the Gospels and which is hinted at in later epistles. One clear example comes from Matthew 28. In verses 19–20, Christ is recorded as saying,

> Go, therefore and make disciples of all the nations, baptizing them in the name of the Father and the Son and the Holy Spirit, teaching them to observe all that I have commanded you; and lo, I am with you always even to the end of the age.

The last part of verse 20 in which Jesus states his intent to be with the church until the end of the age, taken together with verse 19 and the first half of verse 20, suggests that this disciple-making charge is to continue until the end of the age. Matthew's Gospel ends with the expectation of continued mission and teaching. The five preceding sections in Matthew always conclude with a block of Jesus's teaching; but the passion and resurrection of Jesus end with a commission to his disciples to carry on the same ministry, in the light of the cross, the empty tomb, and the triumphant vindication and exultation of the risen Lord. In this sense, the Gospel of Matthew is not a closed book until the consummation. The final chapter is being written in the continuing mission and teaching of Jesus's disciples.[344] The means that are referred to here and that are essential to accomplishing this task are the church itself—in all its disciple-making impact—enabled by the command of Christ.[345] Later, as recorded in Acts 1:8, Jesus declares that the church is empowered to fulfill the proclamation aspect of disciple-making through the empowerment of the Holy Spirit.

3. God's promises are still valid. A fundamental aspect of the nature of God is that he does not lie. What he says is what he will do. The Bible reinforces this claim periodically as if to remind the people of God that God can be counted on to keep his word.

- "Not one of the good promises which the Lord had made to the house of Israel failed; all came to pass" (Josh 21:45).

- "The Lord has done what He purposed; He has accomplished His word which he commended from days of old" (Lam 2:17a).

- "For as many as are the promises of God, in Him they are yes; therefore, also through Him is our Amen to the glory of God through us" (2 Cor 1:20).

Nothing can nor will keep God from fulfilling his promises. In Genesis 12:1–3, God promised to Abraham that he would "bless those who bless you and whoever curses you I will curse, and all peoples on earth will be blessed through you." In Haggai 2:7, "God promised that He would 'shake all nations, and the desired of all nations shall come, and I will fill this house with glory.'" And finally, in John's record of the final revelation, God gives us a glimpse into the future. What strikes us is the picture of the fulfillment of the *missio Dei*. For in Revelation 5 and again in chapter 7 John records that people from every nation and tribe and tongue are present before the throne of God—in keeping with the promise to Abraham.

> After this I (John) looked and behold, a great multitude that no one could count, from every nation and all tribes and peoples and tongues, standing before the throne and before the Lamb, clothed in white robes, and palm branches were in their hands; and they cry out with a loud voice, 'Salvation to our God who sits on the throne and to the Lamb.'" (Rev 7:9–10).

Though God remains the sole arbiter of what he can and cannot do, the possibility of God intervening in human affairs to call men and women so as to set them aside for the accomplishment of his purposes is fully consistent with the biblical pattern. Though it goes beyond the evidence to conclude that God must call people today—after all, he may accomplish his purposes in ways not heretofore revealed—it is within a certain realm of solid possibility that he may still call today, because he remains the same, his plans have not changed, and his promises are still valid.

Calling Is Rare

The biblical accounts to which we attribute a call of God are relatively few in number and mark the contributions of men and women in particular moments in history in the fulfillment of the purposes of God. What is perhaps curious when perusing the Scriptures is the relative rarity of these incidents and the relatively few number of people who are involved. For example, among the Hebrew slaves of Egypt, apart from Moses and Aaron, we have no record of any other incidence of calling. For four hundred years, the people of Israel labored under the Egyptian task masters, but there is no recorded word of their experiences, intentions, or faith expression. Were they subject to calling and somehow missed it?

Or consider the case of the Jews in exile some eighteen hundred years after the beginning of their sojourn in Egypt. Whereas some ten to fourteen thousand Jews were deported from their homeland to Babylon, how many of these received a calling of God? And, because of their limited social mobility as captives in a foreign kingdom, if they had received such a calling, then what kind of calling had they received—for they would have been unable to pursue a free and unhindered role in ministry outside of their status and roles as Babylonian captives. In both the episode of slavery in Egypt and the exile in Babylon, there is no evidence that anything like a calling of God as understood in its contemporary sense was available to the people of God. Most (if not all) of God's people suffered through their time as captives without thought as to what God wants me to do with my life. Indeed, God did put his hand on a number of judges and prophets throughout the Old Testament record. But most of God's people remained in virtual obscurity, having accomplished little that was noteworthy.

With the advent of the New Testament era, the Jesus birth narrative brings together obscure shepherds, wisemen, and a young, as-yet unmarried couple who receive visions and directives related to the birth of the Messiah. It makes sense that God would intervene in dramatic and compelling ways to involve the handful of people he deemed essential to accomplish his purposes in this moment. For in addition to the timing of global events (the rise of Rome, together with the presence of Jews in the Roman Empire), God was also at work transforming the lives of individuals who would go on to become prominent figures in the story of the Christian faith. But what of the other faithful Jews who remain largely unnamed? Did they live in expectation of a call of God? Was this part of the common expectation of the faithful Jew?

In keeping with the pattern laid out in the Old Testament narrative, calling, for all intents and purposes in the New Testament, seems to be predicated upon a dramatic supernatural encounter with key individuals. This seems to be the pattern for several reasons. Firstly, so that it would be indelibly clear that the primary agent behind the calling experience was God himself, whether through an audible voice (as in his comments to Saul in Acts 9) or via fear-inspiring visitations of angels (as in the case of the shepherds in Luke 2:8–20; Mary in Luke 1:26–38; and Joseph in Matt 1:18–25). In these instances, God intervenes in the human story in such a way that it is clear that he is the author of the events. It is in this vein that Peter, in his sermon at Pentecost, argues that the incident of the miracle of the disciples' capacity to speak in other languages was not the result of too much wine, but rather, "this is what was spoken of through the prophet Joel: And it shall be in the last days, God says, that I will pour forth of My Spirit . . ." (Acts 2:16–17a). Later, in that same sermon, he argues that Jesus was not just some exceptional person with extraordinary wisdom and the capacity to do exceptional deeds but rather that he was "attested to you by God with miracles and wonders and signs which God performed through Him" (Acts 2:22b). Peter concludes that the crucifixion and resurrection episode of the end of Jesus's earthly life was not simply unique but supernatural evidence that "God has made Him both Lord and Christ—this Jesus whom you crucified" (Acts 2:36b). The intervention of God is evidenced in part by his indelible mark left on human history.

Secondly, God made use of supernatural encounters so that those involved would not forget. Forgetfulness of God and his commands clearly contribute to the decline of the nation of Israel across the Old Testament narrative and eventually lead them into exile (see Jer 3:21; 13:25 and 18:15; Hos 4:6). At one point, God offers an ironic lament through a metaphor of a nursing mother and asks rhetorically, "Can a woman forget her nursing child and have no compassion on the son of her womb? Even these may forget, but I will not forget you. Behold, I have inscribed you on the palms of My hands; your walls are continually before Me" (Isa 49:15–16)—the point being that, though Israel may forget God and all he has done in order to go after other gods, yet, like a nursing mother who could never forget her nursing child, so God would never forget his people.

The importance of remembering continues as a critical component of faith in the New Testament era. It is for this reason, among others, that Jesus instructs his disciples to celebrate the Last Supper in "remembrance of Me" (Luke 22:19). Elsewhere, in his instructions to the disciples about the Holy Spirit, Jesus notes one of the roles of the Spirit will be to remind them all that Jesus had said to them (John 14:26). And lastly, in an effort to comfort the believers under his care, Peter urges his readers to "remember the words beforehand spoken by the holy prophets and the commandment of the Lord and Savior spoken by your apostles" (2 Pet 3:2). The effort of remembering is essential to maintaining a robust faith for both Old Testament Jews and New Testament Christians. It is noteworthy that on two separate occasions in which he is on trial, Paul refers back to his encounter with God on the road to Damascus as the point of validation of his calling and authority as an apostle (Acts 22:6–11 and 26:13–19). His recollection of the supernatural encounter gives him confidence in the face of strident opposition.

Finally, God made use of dramatic supernatural encounters so that the call-experience would be duly marked as a divine occasion in the unfolding of human history. It is as if at these particular moments God is determined to show his hand, because the pieces of history at that moment require divine intervention so that they function in harmony with the overarching divine agenda. This is not to suggest that somehow these moments mark the only time that God works in the human story, for the Scriptures make it clear that God "works all things after the counsel of His will" (Eph 1:11), can do all things and no purpose of his can be thwarted (Job 42:2), and "does whatever He pleases" (Ps 115:3). John Piper sums up the doctrine of God's sovereignty nicely when he says, "God has the rightful authority, the freedom, the wisdom, and the power to bring about everything that he intends to happen. And therefore, everything he intends to come about does come about. Which means, God plans and governs all things."[346]

Calling that involves dramatic supernatural encounters of the kind typified in the Old and New Testament accounts is rare. The Bible records only a handful of such experiences over the course of the approximately four thousand years of its history. Those that are recorded are marked by divine supernatural encounters in which God is clearly understood as the agent, and the encounter is unforgettable and marks a critical moment in history for humankind in general or a targeted group of people in particular (such as the gentiles).

Calling Is Inclusive

The biblical record from which we understand not only the nature of God but also his revealed will for humankind is, as noted above, punctuated by a number of instances in which God intervened in human history in order to engage an individual for the express purpose of serving as his agent to accomplish a particular task for humanity in general or for a particular group of people. As the drama of redemption as recorded in the Old and New Testaments unfolds, it is clear that God is at the helm and steering history towards the accomplishment of his purposes. Despite humankind's disobedience in the garden (Gen 3) and ongoing rebellion (as noted especially in Gen 6:5–7 and also in Judg 21:25), God marks the human story by choosing or, in keeping with the language of this subject, by calling a variety of men and women, old and young, Jews and non-Jews to play a role in the unfolding of his divine purposes. Initially, of course, the conception of the people of God as the Jews had not yet been defined, and so early key figures were those who were marked out for God's purposes not because of their faith per se but because of the movement of divine grace. And so, Noah and Abraham and Sarah are called of God to fill their part of the story, not necessarily because their lives exhibited notable faithfulness, but because God saw in them men and women who could fulfill their part of his story.

As one reads through the genealogies as recorded either by Matthew (Matt 1) or Luke (Luke 3), one finds a rather inclusive array of individuals. One of the more interesting inclusions in this story comes during the time of the Judges following the Jews' entry into the promised land. At one particular *kairos* moment, God orchestrated a famine in Palestine, together with the death of a husband and two sons of a particular Moabitess, so as to provide an heir to an ancestor of David, the future king of Israel, and, in so doing, to preserve the lineage of Jesus's ancestry from Abraham through David to Joseph, husband of Mary, mother of Jesus. What is noteworthy about the inclusion of Naomi and Ruth in this story is the fact that Naomi is from Moab, a country whose pagan religion marked the inhabitants as detestable and suitable for extermination from the promised land. Furthermore, as Ruth begins to put herself in a position to be cared for by the local lord, Boaz, she refers to herself as a foreigner (Heb. *nakriya* [Ruth 2:10–12]), excluded by Old Testament laws from many benefits. However, as the unfolding reality of the kinsman-redeemer connection becomes clear, Boaz treats her as a resident-alien (Heb. *ger*), a status of foreigner to whom the Old Testament law afforded benefits, including protection and marriage.[347]

The New Testament record also gives evidence of an inclusive group called upon to serve as key individuals in the outworking of the redemptive plan of God. And so, Mary and Joseph, the twelve disciples, and Paul are tapped to serve. Others, perhaps of lesser importance but nevertheless critical to the story (hence the inclusion of their names in the written record of the first-century church), include Phoebe, Priscilla and Aquila, Titus, Timothy, and Luke. Here again the list of notable persons includes men and women, rich (Matthew) and poor (the fishermen), Jew and gentile (Luke) alike. In short, God's calling to service as exemplified by the range of identities of those engaged in his service across both Old and New Testament eras reflects a similar inclusiveness as that noted for the gospel. As Paul declares in Galatians 3:28, "There is neither Jew nor Greek, there is neither slave nor free man, there is neither male nor female, for you are all one in Christ Jesus." Though God may restrict certain roles in ministry to certain types of individuals (as the priesthood was reserved for male Jews), calling in general, like salvation, is inclusive. Upon reflection, it is evident that it must be so, and any rendering of divine calling that excludes any part of humankind because of culture or gender or social status does violence to the notion.

Calling Is Unconditional

The biblical examples of men and women whom God engaged for particular service in the outworking of his divine plan, those called of God, if you will, exhibit a number of compelling, common features that render calling unconditional.

Many, like Abraham, Moses, and Samuel, for example, were chosen by God for their particular service prior to any expression of faith or faithfulness on their part. Though Abraham seems to have been chosen as an adult, but arguably from a pagan context, Moses and Samuel were apparently chosen before or at the time of their births. This is also the case of Jacob and Esau whom Paul discusses in his argument concerning the prerogative of God's sovereignty in salvation that is by grace and not works. With regard to Jacob and Esau, Paul argues,

> And not only this, but there was Rebekah also, when she had conceived twins by one man, our father Isaac; for though the twins were not yet born, and had not done anything good or bad, so that God's purpose according to His choice would stand, not because of works, but because of Him who calls, it was said to her, "The elder (Esau) will serve the younger (Jacob)." Just as it is written, "Jacob I loved, but Esau I hated." (Rom 9:10–13)

Chosen as they were, prior to faith, for the part they were to play in the divine drama, these individuals clearly did not seek their particular calling; it was rather given to them or perhaps imposed upon them. In this sense, their calling was not conditioned upon on any expression of faith.

In other cases, calling additionally appears to preclude future faithfulness. Take the case of David. In the wake of the failure of King Saul, the prophet Samuel is instructed to select a successor from among the sons of Jesse. Having called to himself the sons of Jesse, he proceeds to examine them one by one, beginning with the eldest, in order to determine which of them God would choose to take the place of Saul as king. In response to Samuel's preference for Eliab, the oldest and, humanly speaking, best-suited son for the role, God says, "Do not look at his appearance or at the height of his stature, because I have rejected him; for God sees not as man sees, for man looks at the outward appearance, but the Lord looks at the heart" (1 Sam 16:7). In the end, the favor of God is revealed to fall upon David, the youngest of the sons of Jesse (1 Sam 16:12). What is of interest here is that if we assume the foreknowledge of God in this selection process, then surely God knew at the time of the anointing of David as king of Israel that he would later be involved in the heinous sin matrix surrounding Uriah and his wife Bathsheba, a set of sin-laden decisions that would erode his regal authority and invite a rebuke from the prophet Nathan (2 Sam 12:1–14). This presumption of foreknowledge is only heightened by the fact that in rejecting Eliab, God specifically states that his selection is based not on physical appearance but ostensibly on something more valuable, something that he alone can see—the heart. In the theology of the Old Testament, the heart of an individual refers to the "internal aspect of the soul ... the focus of the personal life: the reasoning, responding, deciding self."[348] And so, God looked at the very core of David and found it to be acceptable to him, and despite David's future transgressions, he called David to be king.

Similarly, the calling of Jonah who would take a detour through the belly of a fish or that of Peter who would deny Christ three times publicly were not withheld by God because of their moral failure that would be future to their being singled out by God for participation in his story. Apparently, God's calling is not conditioned upon the future moral perfection of the individual in this life.

Calling Is Effectual

If calling is understood as the means by which God enlists individuals[349] for roles in the outworking of his sovereign plan, then it follows that the success of one's call is not potential but rather effectual. This conclusion is based on the conviction that God's plans cannot be thwarted and that he is able to bring about the conditions necessary for his will to be accomplished, regardless of apparent political, social, or other human obstacles. The sovereignty of God, referenced earlier, speaks to this guarantee of God's accomplishments and the fulfillment of all that he has promised and set in motion from even before the creation of the world. This is not to say that the individual may see the result of the call realized regardless of the individual's participation in the task, for individuals are prone to disobedience. This is the point of Paul's argument in Romans 9–11 in which Paul seeks to explain and defend God's choice in temporarily setting aside Israel as an instrument of divine blessing. Had Israel fulfilled their calling by staying faithful to the law and embracing Jesus as Messiah so as to become the agent of the gospel to the nations, they would not have experienced what Paul describes as "a partial hardening . . . to Israel until the fullness of the Gentiles has come in" (Rom 11:25b).

Rather, the purpose for which God called the individual will be accomplished, regardless of the performance or moral integrity of the individual. And so, Paul notes that despite the failure of Israel to fulfill their calling, the fullness of the gentiles will be realized; additionally, Israel will be returned to a place of favor in keeping with God's promise to Abraham. In the end, God's calling is effectual; what he intends will come to pass. Our participation in the realization of the call is contingent on our cooperation with the Holy Spirit in obedience to the faith. This appears to be the plain implication of Paul's closing thought in 1 Corinthians

9:24–27 in which Paul intimates that failure to run the race appropriately could result in his being disqualified. Such a disqualification would not be from the faith but from the ongoing participation in that to which he had been called—an apostle to the gentiles (Rom 1:1,5; see also 1 Tim 1:18–20).[350]

This intimate union of calling with sovereignty ensures that what God intends he accomplishes. In that the calling is the means by which God engages humankind when possible to participate in a particular aspect of the outworking of his agenda, he enlists men and women whom he chooses. Whereas the individual's realization of the call is contingent on his or her continued obedience to the faith, the outcome of the call is sure, due to the sovereign oversight of God who, if necessary, can raise up someone else to carry the baton for the individual who has been disqualified.

Calling Accompanies Context

The contemporary world in which we live is complex and bound to become even more so in the years to come. Ministry roles, therefore, will demand men and women who are equipped and educated but also spiritually and relationally fit for the demands of the role they fill. It behooves an organization that is seeking to engage the very best candidates that they use the tools available to them to assess the capacity and potential resiliency of the candidate. Failure to do so is to flirt with expediency at the expense of responsibility. That God can and does still communicate with people on an individual, supernatural basis cannot be ignored nor relegated to a previous era, but this, as can be seen biblically, cannot serve as a primary criterion for candidate selection; it was not apparently so for either Jesus or Paul. Calling, therefore, should not be held up as the expectation of nor the gateway to effective, public ministry. Neither should a lack of a call-experience be used as an excuse not to engage in basic obligations of the Christian faith, namely, the proclamation of the gospel to the nations.

One considerable challenge with regard to calling in the contemporary Western church is the reality that the notion of calling is assumed as part of the normal Christian experience as the means whereby individuals sort out what they want to do with their lives. By using the interpretive universe of the community of faith to which they belong or aspire to join, individuals seek to interpret life experiences so as to satisfy the expectations of calling that they perceive as normative. But as shown over the course of the previous chapters, much of the language used to describe such experiences lacks clear biblical precedent. In this way, the concept of calling has become intertwined and at times used interchangeably with the notion of divine leading, which appeals to passages such as:

- "Trust in the Lord with all your heart and do not lean on your own understanding. In all your ways acknowledge Him and He will make your paths straight" (Prov 3:5–6).
- "For You are my Rock and my Fortress; For Your name's sake You will lead me and guide me" (Ps 31:3).
- "For all who are being led by the Spirit of God, these are the sons of God" (Rom 8:14).

To these and many others that could be added, the Scriptures, by virtue of example and exhortation, encourage men and women to seek God's mind through prayer when faced with decisions or obstacles. The idea from both Old and New Testaments is that God is more than just a deistic Creator who initiated the world and then sat back to watch it all wind down. Rather, God is intimately involved in the lives of men and women, for whom social status, gender, or ethnicity are not obstacles. And in his engagement in the world that is designed to ensure the accomplishment of his divine purposes, he invites men and women to participate through prayer and action. God does what he intends, and no one can stand in his way (Ps 115:3; Ps 135:6; Dan 4:35; Job 42:2; Isa 43:3), but he does so through the agency of men and women whom he leads.

One excellent example of this is found in the experience of Esther as recorded in the book of the same name. At the time of Esther (late fifth-century BC), the Jews were living in captivity under Xerxes who reigned as king of Persia from 486 to 464 BC. In the wake of a near-mortal scandal in which Queen Vashti refused to appear before the King, Esther (a Jew) replaces the deposed queen by winning a royal beauty pageant. Prior to her move to the palace, Esther is counseled by her Uncle Mordecai to not reveal her Jewish ethnicity and so perhaps avoid bringing shame on the kingdom of Xerxes as a result of Xerxes's union with a Jewish woman.

A short time later, Mordecai is able, with the help of Esther, to warn the king of a possible assassination plot. This salvific deed is recorded in the official registry in the name of Mordecai. Around the same time, an official named Haman is given authority over the princes of the kingdom,

The Call of God: A New Proposal 195

and when Mordecai refuses to bow to him in public, Haman sets things in motion to destroy both Mordecai and all the Jews of the kingdom. As part of that effort, Haman has an irrevocable decree drawn up and sealed with the king's signet ring, which authorized and ordered Persian princes in each of the towns and villages of Xerxes's kingdom to exterminate all Jews under their jurisdiction on a particular date. When Mordecai gets wind of the plot, he makes his way to Esther and implores her to appeal to the king on behalf of the Jews. Esther at first hesitates, noting,

> All the king's servants and the people of the king's provinces know that for any man or woman who comes to the king to the inner court who is not summoned, he has but one law, that he be put to death, unless the king holds out to him the golden scepter so that he may live. And I have not been summoned to come to the king for these thirty days. (Esth 4:11)

Mordecai's response to Esther captures both the impassioned anxiety of someone who senses the reality of a calamity steaming towards him (and his people) and someone who comprehends the possibility of a divine intervention. And so Mordecai replies,

> Do not imagine that you in the king's palace can escape any more than all the Jews. For if you remain silent at this time, relief and deliverance will arise for the Jews from another place and you and your father's house will perish. And who knows whether you have not attained royalty for such a time as this? (Esth 4:13–14)

In other words, Mordecai is suggesting that Esther is in a position to render deliverance for not just her family but all the Jews, because God has put her in such a position on purpose. In other words, God led Esther to this place so that she could intervene on behalf of his people. In contemporary parlance, one might refer to Esther's situation as her calling. She was effectively given a role to play in the divine drama for the survival of the Jewish people, and not just as a minor player but as the one who turned the king's favor towards the Jews. Neither Mordecai nor Esther make use of calling language, nor is the role of Esther later described in so many words. But it is clear from the record that God did indeed shape cultural, political, and ethnic realities in order to bring Esther—a Jewish woman who had no social, political, or ethnic standing in Persian society—into the royal palace in order to save the Jews and advance God's ultimate purposes. It is fair to say that Esther was led to this place and this role by God for the sake of his divine purposes for his people. This example of the divine hand of God played out in the lives of his people for greater or lesser purposes, is, I believe, what we have mistakenly ascribed to the concept of calling. Calling, which is particular and rare, has, as a result, become confused with and mistaken for the divine leading that is promised to all who put their trust in him (Prov 3:5–6).

Calling: A Proposed Definition

The contemporary understanding of calling when viewed through the lenses of historical, biblical, cultural, and practical elements seems to come up short. Its assimilation of First World, Western career-choice theory excludes groups of individuals who are unable to meet the conditions of assumed social mobility and individualistic decision-making in a context of potential multiplied career options. Furthermore, the contemporary understanding of the concept seems to have drifted far from the theological reality evidenced in the examples of calling from the Old and New Testament records. A reimagined understanding of the concept that seeks to reflect biblical and theological grounding and responds to transhistorical and transcultural realities follows:

A call of God is the unmistaken supernatural intervention of God whereby he enlists an individual for a divine purpose. Such a divine call is effectual in that its accomplishment is all but guaranteed by the will of God and critical to the advancement of the purposes of God in history for a particular people.

Based on this definition then, to say that God has called me to go somewhere, be someone, or do something—apart from clear, supernatural evidence—is to likely overstate the case. For though God leads all who call upon him in both large and small ways, his calling is reserved in his divine wisdom for extraordinary moments in history. Individuals should count on his leading, which the Scripture promises to those who seek him, but resign themselves that a divine call is not to be expected nor an essential prerequisite for ministry.

Implications for the Individual

Based on the proposed definition of calling, the idea that one should expect or seek such a calling falls away. Rather, believers should give themselves in obedience to the essentials of what it means to be a disciple of Christ instead of waiting for some kind of divine push to do so. Jesus exhorts his followers to "keep my word" (John 14:23), without condition. Later, in his near-final comments to the disciples that are now referred to as the Great Commission, he instructs his disciples to go and make disciples of all the nations, "teaching them to observe all that I commanded you" (Matt 28:20). This idea is echoed by John, when John makes reference to keeping all the commandments of Christ as proof of our love for him (1 John 5:3, 2 John 1:6). In none of these instances is obedience conditioned on a particular calling experience.

Likewise, with regard to the pursuit of a role in ministry-related occupations, the Bible is all but silent concerning the need for a particular calling as a prerequisite. As pointed out in chapter 4, none of Paul's companions on any of his missionary journeys were selected or passed over because of a call or lack thereof. Furthermore, neither in 1 Timothy 3 nor in Titus 1 where Paul reviews the qualifications for elders and deacons does Paul make reference to the evidence of a divine call as a condition for selection. Calling as a condition of ministry just does not seem to be a biblical notion.[351]

Though calling does not seem to factor commonly into the normal Christian life, that does not mean that God does not have his hand on his people. The Scriptures here are clear that God leads (Prov 3:5–6), he answers prayer (1 John 5:14–15), he provides (Phil 4:19), he protects (Ps 46:1), he delivers (Ps 34:17), and he fulfills his promises to his people (2 Cor 1:20). God oversees his creation and superintends the lives of men and women so that what he has purposed will come to pass. In so doing, the language that is more in line with how God works in the lives of his people is related to guiding and leading. Consider the following passages:

- "I will instruct you and teach you in the way which you should go; I will counsel you with my eye upon you" (Ps 32:8).
- "Your word is a lamp to my feet, and a light to my path" (Ps 119:105).
- "The steps of a man are established by the LORD, and He delights in his way. When he falls, he will not be hurled headlong, because the LORD is the One who holds his hand" (Ps 37:23–24).

- "Trust in the LORD with all your heart and do not lean on your own understanding; in all your ways acknowledge Him, and he will make your paths straight" (Prov 3:5–6).
- "Show me your ways, LORD, teach me your paths. Guide me in your truth and teach me, for you are God my Savior, and my hope is in you all day long" (Ps 25:4–5 NIV).
- "He guides the humble in what is right and teaches them his way. All the ways of the LORD are loving and faithful toward those who keep the demands of his covenant" (Ps 25:9–10).
- "In their hearts humans plan their course, but the LORD establishes their steps" (Prov 16:9).
- "The LORD will guide you always; he will satisfy your needs in a sun-scorched land and will strengthen your frame. You will be like a well-watered garden, like a spring whose waters never fail" (Isa 58:11).
- "But when he, the Spirit of truth, comes, he will guide you into all the truth. He will not speak on his own; he will speak only what he hears, and he will tell you what is yet to come" (John 16:13).

In these passages (and others that could no doubt be included) it is worth noting that God leads those who trust in him. The leading that God provides is related to his truth. This guidance is inclusive of gender, age, ethnicity, and physical/emotional capacity. The guidance that God promises with regard to living life, making decisions, and managing one's affairs could be equated with wisdom—the capacity to understand what is right and make good choices thereby. The Bible gives examples of many of those who sought guidance from the Lord. Two such examples come from the lives of David and Solomon.[352] In 2 Samuel 2:1, David seeks the mind of God as to whether he should go up to one of the cities of Judah where he would be anointed king over the house of Judah. Later, in 1 Kings 3:5–14, Solomon prays for wisdom to govern the people of Israel. In the New Testament, Jesus reminds his followers that they can ask anything from God their Father (John 14:13–14). Jesus himself seeks God's wisdom while in the garden of Gethsemane (Matt 26:38–42). Paul regularly prays for wisdom for the believers in the churches of Asia Minor (Eph 1:17; Col 1:9). Finally, believers are instructed to pray for wisdom (Jas 1:5). Friesen offers a helpful categorization of the various ways that

God guides, which, he notes, correspond to the particular need of the individual or community. The following table reflects these categories.[353]

Table 8: Types of Biblical Guidance

	Moral Guidance	Wisdom Guidance	Sovereign Guidance	Special Guidance
Sphere	Moral conduct	Nonmoral decisions	In all things	Unique cases
Nature	God directly guides believers	God mediately guides believers	God secretly guides believers	God supernaturally guides believers
Means	Through revealed commands and principles	Through acquired wisdom	Through sovereign control over all events	By divine voice, angel, dream, or miracle
Governing Principle	According to his moral will	According to spiritual expediency	According to his sovereign will	According to special revelation
Biblical Examples	Dan 1:8–23; Matt 5:33–37; 2 Cor 6:14–15	1 Kgs 3:5–27; Prov 3:5–6; Acts 6:1–6	Gen 45:4–8; Esth 4:12–14; 1 Cor 16:5–9	Exod 3:1–22; Matt 2:12, 13–23; Acts 16:6–10

The guidance that God provides brings satisfaction and fullness of life to those who follow it. One powerful illustration of this fullness comes from Proverbs 13:14, "The teaching of the wise is a fountain of life." In this metaphor, wisdom (ostensibly from God, the only source of true wisdom) is like a fountain of life that continues to bubble up with refreshment leading to satisfaction. In the Old Testament agricultural context in which water was essential to life, a fountain was a bonus, because it continually provided fresh, satisfying water that would not only be safe to drink but refreshing as well.

In contrast to calling, guidance, as promised by God throughout the Scriptures, is what the believer can and should expect. Guidance, which often is given as wisdom, is what the believer should pursue and follow once it has been given. But guidance differs fundamentally from calling, and not just in a semantic sense. Or, to say it more clearly, guidance is not just another word for calling. Calling, according to the definition proposed herein, is an unmistakable supernatural intervention. In giving such a call, God enlists an individual for a particular divine purpose whose outcome is all but guaranteed by the will of God. And finally, such a divine call serves a critical role in the advance of the purposes of God in history for a particular people. This kind of call is unmistakable. It has a "burning bush" kind of impact. Those who experience it have no doubt that this is of God. This kind of call is rare. The pages of Scripture attest to the fact that only a handful of men and women over the course of recorded biblical history give testimony to this kind of call-experience. And those who do receive such a call play pivotal roles in the accomplishment of God's purposes for a particular people in a particular time in history. Such a call is effectual in the sense that God enlists an individual to accomplish his purposes—which will be fulfilled. One prime example is that of Moses and his role in leading the Hebrews out of Egypt. At one point in the narrative, in response to God's instruction that he go to Pharaoh and demand that the Hebrews be freed, Moses mounts a multilevel argument as to why he should not be the instrument of deliverance (Exod 3:13—4:13). Moses's objections to God's plan are met with a personalized response in which God equips Moses not only with signs and symbols of the divine mandate but also with a spokesman, Aaron, so that the mission would not fail (Exod 4:1–31).

As for Collin, whose story was told at the outset, that which he refers to as calling is perhaps better understood as divine guidance. The inklings, the associations, the connections of one thing with another should not be freely cast aside as if they hold no meaning. God does speak and is able to communicate his divine will through a range of means (Heb 1:1–3). But these things in and of themselves, even though they may originate in God himself, do not equate to the biblical notion of calling. Rather, such divine markers are better aligned with the biblical notion of guidance that also is intended to direct, to clarify, and to lead us to wherever God wants us to go. Guidance, as noted above, is promised to all who "trust in the Lord" (Prov 3:5–6) and to those who are "humble" (Ps 25:9–10). But guidance, as it is associated with wisdom, considers the whole of one's journey and the whole of one's social and personal context. Guidance is how God "establishes their steps" (Prov 16:9) and "make(s) your paths straight (Prov 3:5–6) in the midst of the cultural, historical, and personal context in which we and Collin live. It may be that God does indeed wish

The Call of God: A New Proposal

for Collin to steer his career objective towards reaching Muslim youth. But if so, additional guidance would be necessary, guidance which could include additional training, ministry practicum and evaluation, and eventual alignment with a proven ministry affiliate. The process of exploring such a ministry assignment is itself a matter of trusting God, but it is just this trust that God says that he honors in the provision of guidance (Prov 3:5–6).

Implications for Credentialing Bodies

As discussed throughout, the challenge in discerning a call of God is not just for the recipient of the presumed calling experience but also for the credentialing body, whether a local church, mission agency, or some other NGO who insists on calling as a prerequisite of candidacy. Though credentialing bodies have added assessment tools and processes throughout history commensurate with the best practices of the day, the capacity for objective verification of someone else's supernatural call-experience is no better today than it was in the day of Joan of Arc. And even then, some forty theological specialists, after months of questioning and investigation, were still left divided over the question as to whether the maid was indeed called and sent by God or not.

This inability to verify a divine call, it seems to me, is an indication that the current understanding of calling has drifted far from its biblical moorings. Generally speaking, the contemporary call-experience remains personal and mystical. It is even commonly described as the secret or inward call. In this form, it generally lacks the supernatural elements that accompany the biblical examples held up as the pattern of those who are called, elements that make verification of the call-experience all but obvious. Lacking such evidence, how are others supposed to validate what has taken place in secret, perhaps even in the middle of the night? This is not to suggest that believers intend to not speak the truth or to verbalize something that they have not actually experienced. But as we have already seen, the conception of the call has evolved across history and even today is shaped differently by various faith communities who attach differing vocabulary, experiences, and expectations to the notion.

The biblical pattern, it seems to me, is different. God's call was so clear and often accompanied by such dramatic, supernatural elements that the verification of the call-experience was all but automatic. It is true that Moses presumed that the sons of Israel would not believe that God had sent him. To silence their supposed doubts, God gave to Moses three signs as evidence: a staff that could turn into a serpent, a gesture that made his hand leprous and then whole again in a moment, and the capacity to turn water from the Nile to blood (Exod 4:1–9). Later, Moses, accompanied by Aaron, met with the elders of Israel to announce that God had called and sent him to deliver Israel from Pharoah. After Aaron explained to the people all that God had said to Moses, Moses performed the signs that God had given him, and the people believed (Exod 4:31a). Calling in the biblical record is obvious and unambiguous. Those who were called knew it—even if all the details of the calling were not disclosed at once. God's calling, it seems, was regularly accompanied by signs that could not be missed. In contrast, biblical examples of calling that rely primarily on an inward or secret call are simply not prominent, if at all present. It is no wonder, then, that credentialing bodies struggle to validate an individual's call-experience, for they are faced with trying to verify a spiritual experience that lacks biblical precedent.

Lacking the means to confidently validate the inward or secret call of a candidate, credentialing bodies would do well to turn their attention to the assessment of the individual's qualifications relative to the particular ministry role, in part because the inability to confidently assess the validity of one's call leaves the question open ended at best. And even if they are convinced of such a call, they still need to do due diligence with regard to the technical aspects of ministry in an increasingly complex world. To this end, the imposition of a certain period of testing during which the candidate is given the opportunity to participate in various aspects of the ministry role would go a long way to assessing whether the individual possessed the interest, skills, and potential to satisfactorily perform on a long-term basis. In assessing candidates, care should be taken to ascertain that the candidates have a genuine faith in Christ, that they have an interest and experience in serving others, and that they have the requisite education and skills that correspond to the role that they seek to fill or that they can reasonably be expected to acquire such. To this end, the credentialing body serves to examine the means that God has used to guide the individual to the place of considering a particular ministry role. In so doing, the credentialing body is relieved of needing to verify a particular call-experience as a definitive indicator that an individual has been set apart by God. Rather, the credentialing body looks for a life pattern of divine guidance that considers the whole-person context and suitability for ministry.

This is not to say that God no longer calls people or that he no longer makes use of supernatural evidence to demonstrate his intervention in the life of someone. God, as noted earlier, has not changed. The God who called Moses from a burning bush and equipped him with signs to use to prove that God had sent him is able to act miraculously today. But these instances are rare, exceptional, and should not be held up as the norm or as a prerequisite for ministry candidacy. At no time did Jesus make participation in the *missio Dei* contingent upon a secondary call beyond the initial call to faith.

Calling—A Summary

The divine call to ministry has been a part of Christian experience and dogma since the emergence of the church in the first century. Origins of the call-experience harken back to divine encounters with men and women from the Old Testament era such as Abraham, Moses, Ruth, and Daniel.

Over the centuries, the development of the Roman Church in light of its own historical context yielded a clergy-laity division that fostered the notion of vocation—calling—which was all but restricted to religious work as part of the Church. The Protestant Reformation, in its efforts to restore the Scriptures as the central authority, also removed the clergy-laity distinction, thanks to the rediscovery of the doctrine of the priesthood of all believers by Martin Luther. This refocus on individual responsibility before God, among other things, broadened the notion of calling beyond religious vocations to all manner of work. Under John Calvin, calling to the ministry was considered a twofold process in which the individual would receive an inner or secret call and the church would extend an external call to a ministerial candidate who demonstrated both the spirit and the tools necessary for the role.

The notion of calling from its earliest revived use was nevertheless subject to the confines of the given cultural context in which it circulated, and so, from the era of the early church in the first century to the Reformation (and beyond), calling with regard to ministry roles was limited exclusively to male candidates. Even into the early 1900s, if a woman felt called to ministry, she was only able to pursue that calling if she was married to a husband who was also called to the same. It was not until the social context of women changed over the course of the nineteenth and twentieth centuries in the West that calling was granted to women as a legitimate expression of their Christian faith.

With the impact of the Industrial Revolution came the rise of occupational choice. As industry boomed and cities grew on the backs of manufacturing, labor became a commodity, and men and (increasingly) women left the farms and traditional roles for the new modern experience of labor as employees. Though most of the wealth was still held by a few aristocratic families at the top of the economic food chain, the expanse of manufacturing and the rise of inventiveness to support the ever-growing economic engine gave rise to increased education and the birth of the middle class. In the wake of these social changes, calling became a means of determining which career path one might follow, a spiritualized attempt to help answer the question "What should I be when I grow up?" In the end, the contemporary notion of calling is so heavily influenced by First World, Western, individualistic career-choice theory that it effectively excludes all who do not fit that profile.

The idea of a divine call as an indication of God's leading is in itself not something without precedent. The Bible describes such cases, and since the time of Calvin, calling has been associated with ministerial roles and candidacy. The contemporary importance of calling is not negligible. Virtually all church denominations, religious NGOs, and even secular organizations regard the notion of calling as all but essential for the preferred candidate. The problem with calling today is that it remains a highly subjective, individualized experience that is shaped in its vocabulary, experience, and expectations by the organization culture (religious or secular) in which the candidate circulates. As such, a common meaning of calling is lacking. Furthermore, credentialing bodies are all but unable to verify an individual's call-experience with any kind of objective certainty. As a result, some who think they are called may actually not be. And the lack of a perceived call has become a reason for some to not fulfill some aspects of Christian obedience.

Calling issues from God. In that he has not changed, his promises are sure, and his purposes have not yet been fulfilled, it follows that he is certainly able to call today as he has in the past. But in keeping with the biblical parameters, such calling is rare, is marked by unmistakable supernatural signs, and marks a critical moment in history for the advance of the gospel in a particular context and among a particular people. The vast majority of believers can and should rather expect God's leading, which he promises repeatedly to those who seek him. Such leading comes through wisdom as provided by the Holy Spirit in prayer, through the Scriptures, and the counsel of godly men and women. Such leading is personal, contextual, inclusive, and applicable in all walks and aspects of life.

As we stand at the cusp of the third millennium since the birth of Christ and the renewed command to make disciples of the nations, it behooves the church to remove whatever unnecessary barriers there are to help people engage with this central element of the Christian life. Calling, as it has evolved over time, has been a barrier for too long because of the cultural acculturation that has caused it to drift far from its biblical moorings. Does God call people to ministry today? Yes, most likely. But these will be dramatic, history-marking calls to men and women who will serve to change the spiritual trajectory of their people. For the rest of us, we need to seek God's leading as we seek to obey all that he has asked of us as his children. This is the nature of our faith and a sign of our love of him.

Endnotes

1. Collin, phone call with author, May 24, 2021.
2. Hale, *On Being a Missionary*, 16.
3. Hale, *On Being a Missionary*, 17.
4. Guinness, *Call*, 31.
5. See Smith, *Courage and Calling*; Sills, *Missionary Call*; or Packer, *God's Plans*, among others.
6. See Allen, *Discerning Your Call*, 19–21.
7. See Mohler et al., *Call to Ministry*, 5.
8. For Allen and Mohler, this final category of calling, because of its relationship to the ministry of the word, is limited to men.
9. Smith, *Courage and Calling*, 10.
10. Sills, *Missionary Call*, 51–52.
11. Secomb, "Hearing the Call," 42.
12. See Duffy, "Spirituality, Religion," 55.
13. See Ross, *Creation and Blessing*; Sailhamer, *Genesis*; and Cassuto, *Commentary*.
14. Burkhart, *Avodah*.
15. The Hebrew word *issabon* is translated in Genesis 3:17 as "toil" (NASB). But it also occurs in Genesis 3:16 where God says to Eve, "I will greatly multiply your pain (*issabon*) in childbirth" and again in 5:29 where Lamech names his son Noah, saying, "This one shall give us rest from our work and from the toil (*issabon*) of our hands."
16. Crouch, *Culture Making*, 23.
17. Crouch, *Culture Making*, 35–36.
18. Bacote, "Beyond 'Faithful Presence,'" 202.
19. Ellul, "Work and Calling," 8.

20. The book of Proverbs is a collection of writings principally authored and edited by Solomon. Despite the possible contributions by others such as Agur (Prov 30) and Lemuel (Prov 31), little is known of them. The final compilation of the book as we have it now dates to around 700 B.C. (See Buzzell, "Proverbs," 901.)

21. Ellul argues that the influence of Greek thought on this issue of calling is most perceptible from the third to fifth centuries after Christ ("Work and Calling," 9).

22. Ellul, "Work and Calling," 9.

23. Ellul, "Work and Calling," 9.

24. Ellul, "Work and Calling," 9.

25. Esler, *Early Christian World*, 267, 283.

26. Froehlich, "Luther on Vocation," 197–98.

27. Froehlich, "Luther on Vocation," 197–98.

28. Froehlich, "Luther on Vocation," 198.

29. Zentner, "Black Death," 1–2.

30. The flagellation movement arose in the midst of the Black Death as an effort on the part of laymen (and women) to seek atonement for their sins and hence bring about an end to the plague through physical self-punishment. Flagellant groups travelled from village to village dressed particularly and following certain rituals that involved singing, preaching, and self-inflicted beatings. According to Gottfried, "Most people in the Rhineland (region of Germany) were well-disposed to the flagellants and turned out in great numbers to watch them. Even neutral observers agreed that the effects of the processions were overwhelming. Spectators sobbed, cried, howled, and tore at their hair. The flagellants were seen as martyrs who atoned for the sins of the world and, hence, helped avert further suffering from the plague and future visitations. Most villagers and townspeople regarded a visit by the flagellants as a privilege and an honor, and turned out to welcome them. Church bells were rung, usually without the sanction of the clergy, who saw their own positions undermined, and local people opened their homes, fed the flagellants, and gave them candles for their rites. In some German towns, municipal councils even drew on public funds to help them. Much of this reflected the general dissatisfaction with the clergy, who were seen as corrupt and incapable of assuaging the pain of the Black Death in any way" (Gottfried, *Black Death*, 71).

31. Much of the worldview of the medieval person assumed a spiritual cause-effect reality. If the world was suffering because of the plague, it had to be due to some sort of divine judgment for sins. As distress mounted with the increasing devastation of the plague and incompetence of the church to provide a coherent response, it didn't take long for certain groups to become the focus of blame. Despite their widespread and heretofore functional assimilation into European communities, the Jews were different enough socially and religiously to quickly become a preferred scapegoat. Gottfried offers this explanation: "Many Christians believed that the Jews brought on the Black Death by poisoning supplies of drinking water. This was an old idea. For example, in 1321 in Languedoc, a number of lepers had been accused of fouling the drinking supplies; as they were

being executed, several cried out that they had been encouraged in their deed by the Jews. This idea became current again in 1348. In the German town of Neustadt, after being broken on the rack, a Jewish physician named Balovignus confessed that a Jewish boy had been sent to him by the chief rabbi of Toledo, Spain. The boy had carried a powder which, on pain of ex-communication, Balovignus was to use to contaminate the wells. This he did, after warning his co-religionists. Word spread from Germany, and pogroms erupted wherever there were Jews" (Gottfried, *Black Death*, 52).

32. Historians note that the plague returned to various parts of Europe repeatedly, sometimes as often as every five to seven years, until the eighteenth century and medical science had developed scalable responses to the plague that, though they did not prevent its recurrence, at least contained the spread and all but eliminated uncontrolled outbreaks and mass mortality. See Gottfried, *Black Death*, and McNeill, *Plagues and Peoples*.

33. By 1514, just seven years after his ordination as a priest, Luther had been named the preacher in the Castle Church in Wittenberg, in addition to his duties as the vicar of the Wittenberg monastery and vicar-general of eleven regional monasteries over which he had oversight. See Metaxas, *Martin Luther*, 42, 76.

34. Luther, *Against the Spiritual State of the Pope*, in *Church and Ministry I*, 259.

35. Luther, "Open Letter."

36. See Luther, *Church and Ministry I and III*.

37. See Weber, *Protestant Ethic*, 85. Here he notes that, "The individual should remain once and for all in the station and calling in which God had placed him and should restrain his worldly activity within the limits imposed by his established station in life. While this economic traditionalism was originally the result of Pauline indifference, it later became that of a more and more intense belief in divine providence, which identified absolute obedience to God's will, with absolute acceptance of things as they were."

38. See Metaxas, *Martin Luther*, 328. In his tract "Admonition to Peace: Reply to the Twelve Articles of the Peasants of Swabia," Luther severely admonished both sides. He took the nobles to task for their unchristian behavior in oppressing the peasants, and he took the peasants to task for wanting to proceed impatiently with violence. Luther always had respect for authority, even when it was wrong, and he believed that going to war with the powers that be would be far more destructive than constructive.

39. Weber, *Protestant Ethic*, 85.

40. For more on the story of Martin Luther, see Metaxas, *Martin Luther*.

41. Froelich, "Luther on Vocation," 201.

42. Luther, *Church and Ministry III*, 130. Froelich also discusses this notion of the "both/and" necessity of calling. For whereas God calls one to the ministry of the word and another to the keeping of sheep, there is the necessity that someone be given the primary responsibility of administering the sacred rituals. And so, the church, "must call a suitable person to do this central work of God for and among them [the people] so that it may be done for all people everywhere" (Froelich, "Luther on Vocation," 203).

43. See Weber, *Protestant Ethic*, 83.
44. Weber, *Protestant Ethic*, 160.
45. Weber, *Protestant Ethic*, 162.
46. Weber, *Protestant Ethic*, 36. For a very helpful discussion of Weber's often complex treatment of the subject see Collins, "Weber's Last Theory."
47. See Ellul, "Work and Calling," 11.
48. Ellul, "Work and Calling," 11.
49. Ellul, "Work and Calling," 13.
50. See Brewer, "Vocational Souljourn Paradigm."
51. Brewer, "Vocational Souljourn Paradigm," 86.
52. Brewer, "Vocational Souljourn Paradigm," 87.
53. Father Rey Pineda Avellaneda, phone call with author, Apr. 27, 2021.
54. John Paul II, "Pastores Dabo Vobis," §11.
55. This notion of a primary relationship with Christ is reminiscent of the monastic orders, both past and present. However, contemporary Catholic praxis allows for the calling to consecrated singleness without the necessity of membership in a monastic order (Father Rey Pineda Avellaneda, phone call with author, Apr. 27, 2021).
56. Father Rey Pineda Avellaneda, phone call with author, Apr. 27, 2021. This is further described in the *Program of Priestly Formation*, which notes that "all applicants should give witness to their conviction that God has brought them to the seminary to discern whether or not they are really called to the priesthood, and they should commit themselves wholeheartedly to carrying out that discernment" (Committee on Spiritual Formation, *Program of Priestly Formation*, 22).
57. Committee on Spiritual Formation, *Program of Priestly Formation*, 17–18.
58. See 2 Sam 11–19 for the extended account of King David's sin with Bathsheba and its consequences on David and the kingdom of Israel.
59. Metaxes, *Martin Luther*, 101–2.
60. Metaxes, *Martin Luther*, 103.
61. Metaxes is not the only one to reveal the corruption surrounding the motivations associated with the priesthood. Historian Alexander Flick provides a similar assessment. "The Papal financial policy [constructed over the previous centuries] caused general embitterment in Europe from the King to the peasant and nourished dissatisfaction and hostility everywhere. Clever men were not slow to perceive that the easiest road to an assured income and a fat living was to seek service and office in the Church. Pope Hadrian VI complained that in Rome cooks and mule-drivers became priests and prelates" (Flick, *Decline of Medieval Church*, 2:377).
62. Metaxes, *Martin Luther*, 436.
63. Flick, *Decline of Medieval Church*, 2:408.

64. Helmer, "Common Priesthood," 211–12.
65. Helmer, "Common Priesthood," 212.
66. Helmer, "Common Priesthood," 225.
67. Luther, "Concerning the Ministry," in *Church and Ministry II*, 22.
68. Luther, "Treatise," in *Word and Sacrament I*, 101.
69. Luther, "Concerning the Ministry," in *Church and Ministry II*, 21.
70. Luther, "Concerning the Ministry," in *Church and Ministry II*, 35.
71. Eastwood, *Priesthood of All Believers*, 44.
72. Montover, *Luther's Revolution*, 64.
73. Sermon at the dedication, *LW* 13:331.
74. Luther, "Concerning the Ministry," in *Church and Ministry II*, 21, 36–37.
75. That a Christian Assembly, *LW* 39:305.
76. Montover, *Luther's Revolution*, 51.
77. Luther, "Concerning the Ministry," in *Church and Ministry II*, 21.
78. Luther does not appeal to Paul's description of spiritual gifts and the unique equipping of the members of the body of Christ in this discussion, but one must assume that Paul's teaching on the subject from 1 Corinthians would not have been far from his mind.
79. Eastwood, *Priesthood of All Believers*, 45.
80. For Luther, spiritual ministry was relegated to the local congregation. Mobilization and preparation of Christians for mission-related gospel ministry does not really become a normative part of the Protestant Church until the nineteenth century for a number of reasons: 1) the emergent Protestant Church was struggling to survive under the opposition of the Roman Catholic Church, 2) the Protestant Church lacked ministry-focused modalities such as the Catholic orders (Jesuits and other fraternal societies) given to ministry to those outside the Church, 3) the Protestant Church was localized and lacked centralized resources or administrative structures to be able to articulate a common strategy/training. For these reasons and others, the notion of a call of God to what we would refer to today as "missions" is also absent from Luther's thoughts.

    An exception to this is the experience of the Moravian Church, which emerges in Bohemia (modern-day Czech Republic) in the fifteenth century. The Moravians owe their origins to another Catholic priest, Jon Hus, who opposed the Roman Catholic Church over issues that predated Luther by some fifty years. Hus, who was burned at the stake for his opposition to the Roman Catholic Church in 1415, left a following referred to as the Hussites, who merged with other pietistic groups to become the *Unitas Fratrum* (United Brethren) in the second half of the fifteenth century. By the early seventeenth century, due to additional mergers and theological adjustments, this group became known as the Moravian Church. The Moravian Church underwent revival in the early eighteenth century under Count Von Zinzendorf and became the first large scale Protestant missionary movement—but this was nearly two hundred years after Luther's initial protest! See Vogt, "Everywhere at Home."

81. Montover, *Luther's Revolution*, 12.
82. Calvin, *Commentary upon Acts*.
83. Calvin, *Commentaries on Epistle of Paul*.
84. Calvin, *Commentaries on Book of Prophet*.
85. Calvin, *Commentaries on Book of Prophet*.
86. Calvin, *Calvin: Institutes*, 4.3.15.
87. Calvin, *Commentaries on Epistles to Timothy*.
88. Calvin, *Commentary on Gospel*.
89. Calvin, *Commentaries on Epistle of Paul*.
90. Zachman, *John Calvin as Teacher*, 21.
91. Zachman, *John Calvin as Teacher*, 22.
92. A copy of the survey instrument is included in appendix A.
93. Student participants represent several Christian colleges or college training programs and several major denominations from Baptist to Methodist, Pentecostal to Catholic.
94. See www.studentresearchfoundation.org/blog/how-do-high-school-students-consider-their-future-careers/.
95. For a fuller discussion of this supposed correlation, see Super, "Life-Span, Life-Space Approach."
96. Typical ministry-related college majors include pastoral ministries, youth ministries, counseling, biblical languages, church music ministry. Non-ministry related college majors include sports management, education, biology/chemistry (pre-med), accounting, etc.
97. Duffy and Sedlacek, "Presence," 597.
98. Rambo, *Understanding Religious Conversion*, 137.
99. Rambo, *Understanding Religious Conversion*, 138.
100. Calvin, *Commentary on Gospel* and *Commentaries on Epistle of Paul*.
101. Pitt, *Divine Callings*, 9.
102. Pitt, *Divine Callings*, 9.
103. Piper and Grudem, *Recovering*, 77.
104. Ahlstrom, *Religious History*, 4.
105. Hymowitz and Weissman, *History of Women*, 4–5.
106. Hymowitz and Weissman, *History of Women*, 15.
107. An exception to this would be in Catholicism, where women were allowed in ministry as part of the monastic orders. These sisters, as they were commonly called, served as a practical extension of the Church in feeding the poor and caring for orphans and unwed mothers.

108. Robert, *American Women in Mission*, 18. See also Tucker, "Female Mission Strategists."

109. Kraft and Crossman, "Women in Mission," 296.

110. Though the first version of an Equal Rights Amendment was written by Alice Paul and Crystal Eastman and introduced in Congress in Dec. 1923, it was not until Mar. 22, 1972, that the ERA was placed before the state legislatures, with a seven-year deadline to acquire ratification by three-fourths (thirty-eight) of the states. As of Jan. 2020, the requisite thirty-eight states needed to ratify the amendment have done so. All that remains is for the final steps to amend the Constitution to be completed, and the ERA will become the Twenty-Eighth Amendment to the US Constitution.

111. Hunt, "Evolution and Revolution," 77–78.

112. Bowler, *Preacher's Wife*, 19.

113. Clouse and Clouse, *Women in Ministry*, 17.

114. One early exception to the practice of excluding women from active roles in ministry was the Methodist Church. John Wesley made a point of elevating women to an all but equal status—a conclusion he derived from his understanding that both men and women were to be considered as full members of the church, since both have access to grace and the gift of entire sanctification. As a result, under Wesley, women led class meetings and prayer meetings, influenced denominational decisions, and spoke at public meetings (though this "speaking" was not referred to as "preaching"). See English, "Dear Sister," 27.

115. See Bowler, *Preacher's Wife*, 19.

116. Hunt, "Evolution and Revolution," 77–78.

117. See Clous and Clouse, *Women in Ministry*, 19.

118. Zikmund et al., *Clergy Women*, 7–12.

119. Zikmund et al., *Clergy Women*, 13.

120. See Weber, *Protestant Ethic*, 162.

121. Elizabeth Brewer, in her article concerning the concept of a vocational souljourn paradigm, disagrees with this conclusion by Hall and Chandler that calling is no longer spiritual in origin and argues rather that, "One does not experience calls without collaboration with a supernatural Source. [However,] the definition of Source depends on a personal belief system: it could be God, Divine, Transcendent, Eternal, or Infinite. The concept of vocations recognizes something greater than humanity, beyond, larger" (Brewer, "Vocational Souljourn Paradigm," 87).

122. Hall and Chandler, "Psychological Success," 161.

123. Novak, *Business as a Calling*, 37.

124. For instance, calling must somehow relate to what is possible. An individual who is deprived of access to certain professional careers because of religious, social, or economic conditions can hardly expect to receive a calling to such.

125. Novak, *Business as a Calling*, 39.

126. Novak, *Business as a Calling*, 37.

127. Dik and Duffy, "Calling and Vocation," 430. As Dik and Duffy note further, the reference to "legitimate work" refers to the notion that calling and vocation are related to the idea of contributing to the common good. Some areas of work cannot be considered callings because they are not helpful to overall society (i.e., manufacture of cigarettes) or are fundamentally dehumanizing (e.g., slavery, prostitution).

128. Brantley, *Calling*, 12.

129. Brantley, *Calling*, 55.

130. See Isa 61:1.

131. Brewer, "Vocational Souljourn Paradigm," 86.

132. Brewer, "Vocational Souljourn Paradigm," 84. Note: Brewer's fourfold distinction differs from the seminal work by Bellah et al, *Habits of the Heart* (1985), in which is posited that people relate to work in one of three distinct categories: jobs, careers, and callings. Brewer's addition of "occupation" as a fourth category is not distinct in kind as much as distinct in degree from that posited by Bellah et al. Despite this distinction, Bellah et al. and Brewer agree that jobs are primarily taken for their financial (extrinsic) benefits, whereas careers, at the other end of the spectrum, are pursued for their capacity to render fulfillment to the individual and thus provide intrinsic benefits.

133. Duffy, "Spirituality, Religion," 55.

134. Dik and Duffy, "Calling and Vocation," 427.

135. Dik and Duffy, "Calling and Vocation," 428.

136. Dik and Duffy, "Calling and Vocation," 428

137. Wrzesniewski et al., "Jobs, Careers, and Callings," 29.

138. See Duffy and Sedlacek, "Salience of Career Calling."

139. Other research has suggested that calling and religiousness are correlated. See Davidson and Caddell, "Religion and Meaning." Note also the work of Luther, Calvin, and others such as Niebuhr, as well as documentation from the Catholic Church and virtually every Protestant denomination for whom calling and religiousness are highly correlated.

140. Niebuhr, *Purpose of the Church*, 64.

141. Dik and Duffy, "Calling and Vocation."

142. Ellul, "Work and Calling," 8.

143. In all, there were forty-two kings (and one queen). Saul, David, and Solomon ruled over Israel before the kingdom divided under Solomon. Once divided, nineteen kings ruled the northern tribes (ten) of Israel and twenty kings ruled the southern tribes (two) of Judah.

144. After the fall of Babylon to the Persian king Cyrus the Great in 538 BC, exiled Jews began to return to the land of Judah. Cyrus the Great ended the exile of the Jewish people in 537 BC, the year after he conquered Babylon, granting

permission to return to Israel and rebuild the temple (Second Temple, 521–16 BC) under Zerubbabel. The return of the exiles was a gradual process rather than a single event, and many of the deportees and their descendants did not return.

145. I count the prominent individuals as Adam, Eve, Noah, Abraham, Isaac, Jacob, Joseph, Moses, Joshua, Samuel, David, Elijah, Elisha, Solomon, Ezra, and Nehemiah (sixteen total). In addition, one can add the sixteen prophets—though they are more spokesmen than actors in the unfolding of the historical narrative.

146. Ross suggests, with Cassuto, that these could be proselytes from Haran who have been "converted" in a way and agree to leave their pagan context to settle with Abram in this new promised land (Ross, *Creation and Blessing*, 265).

147. Ross, *Creation and Blessing*, 262.

148. In addition to the staff that God enabled to turn into a serpent, Moses was also able to demonstrate a leprous hand and then healing of the hand and have Nile River water turn into blood. Behind all of these demonstrations of God's power, God also revealed to Moses an intimate reference: "I am who I am." This, God said, was to be the indication that God-himself had sent Moses (see Exod 3:11—4:9).

149. Habel, "Form and Significance," 298.

150. According to the call narrative motif, the account of Isaiah's call does not include that which could be referred to as a sign. It is possible that the entire dream/vision event (Isa 1:1-13) could serve that purpose, though Habel does not draw that conclusion.

151. However, Matthew the tax collector, is enlisted some time before this incident on the mountain (see Mark 3:13-17).

152. In addition to Matt 28:18-20, see Mark 16:15-18, Luke 24:45-49, John 20:21-23, and Acts 1:8. Nowhere in these passages does Jesus make any connection between participation in the task and calling to do so.

153. Carey, "Enquiry into the Obligation," 314.

154. Robert, *American Women in Mission*, 274.

155. Beach, "Evangelism," 16.

156. Beach, "Evangelism," 16.

157. Kinnaman et al., "Almost Half."

158. Sills, *Missionary Call*, 103.

159. See Acts 22:6-21, in which Paul addresses the crowd to explain himself following his arrest in Jerusalem. See Acts 26:12-18, in which Paul is defending himself before King Agrippa. Paul makes other less-comprehensive references to his conversion in 1 Cor 15:3-8, in which he is defending his true apostleship because of his encounter with Christ. Lastly, Paul makes a brief reference to his conversion in Gal 1:11-16 to validate the legitimacy of his ministry among the gentiles.

160. Possible exceptions to this can be found in 1 Cor 7:15 where Paul says, "But God hath called us to peace." This could mean that the realm of the calling is to peace between believers and this only in a temporal, horizontal relational context. In

this case, the verse could read, "But God has asked us to act in peace towards each other." The calling here could also refer to the call to salvation so that, or by which, peace should result between believers. In this case, the text could read, "But God has called us to salvation through which he requires and enables us to act in peace towards each other."

Another example can be found in 1 Thess 4:7 where Paul says, "For God has not called us for impurity, but in sanctification." Here the calling could refer to the domain of impurity in a temporal, human context alone. In this case, the passage could read, "For God has not asked us to act impurely." The calling here could also refer to salvation, a salvation that is incompatible with impure behavior. In this case, the passage could read, "For God has not called us to salvation so that we could act in impure ways." In neither case, however, is the use of calling so distinct from the realm of salvation that to read it that way would misrepresent the text.

161. Klein, "Paul's Use of Kalein," 57.

162. The Old Testament in both its didactic and narrative sections makes it clear that suffering is most often the result of sin/disobedience, and blessing, a result of obedience. The exceptions to this pattern are Job and Joseph, who endure suffering despite their obedience. That Paul would suffer as a result of obedience would have been a difficult concept for many Jews of Paul's day to grasp despite the fact that Jesus discusses this paradigm shift in his Sermon on the Mount in Matt 5:10–12 and again in his upper room discourse in John 15:18–25.

163. Klein, "Paul's Use of Kalein," 63.

164. Vogt, "Everywhere at Home," 16–17.

165. Winter, "Three Missionary Eras," 264.

166. Zeze, "John Calvin," 605.

167. Calvin, *Commentary upon Acts*.

168. Calvin, *Commentaries on Epistle of Paul*.

169. In Acts 20:4, at the beginning of Paul's third missionary journey, Luke lists the names of eight individuals who accompany Paul on at least part of the journey. Nothing in the run up to this journey gives us any hint that these people were joining Paul because of some particular calling to do so.

170. Friesen and Maxson, *Decision Making*, 327.

171. Penney, *Overcoming*, 270.

172. Friesen and Maxson, *Decision Making*, 313–14.

173. Hussey, "Soteriological Use of Call," 141.

174. This is not intended to be a veiled argument for universalism. The notion that God would make the benefits of the gospel available to all is derived from passages such as John 3:16, "For God so loved the world that whosoever believes in Him has everlasting life"; Heb 2:9, "But we do see Him who was made for a little while lower than the angels, namely, Jesus, because of His suffering death crowned with glory and honor, so that by the grace of God He might taste death for everyone"; and 1 John 2:2, "And He Himself is the propitiation for our sins;

and not for ours only, but also for the sins of the whole world." One way to read the inclusive ideas in these passages is to equate "all" with "both Jew and gentile" as opposed to a strictly individual sense. In this way, God's provision has been made available to all—though the response by grace through faith is the condition of personally benefitting from it.

175. Calvin, *Calvin: Institutes*, 3.11.1.
176. Ho, "Filial Piety," 350.
177. Sun et al., "Relations," 2.
178. Bedford and Yeh, "Evolution of Conceptualization," 5.
179. Jujing, "Number Eight: Taking on Menial Labor to Support His Mother: Jiang Ge," in *Twenty-Four Paragons*.
180. Bedford and Yeh, "Evolution of Conceptualization," 10.
181. Brown, "Role of Work," 48.
182. Brown, "Role of Work," 49.
183. Bedford and Yeh, "Evolution of Conceptualization," 12.
184. Hung, "Filial Piety and Missionary Calling."
185. Hay et al., *Worth Keeping*, 78.
186. Hay et al., *Worth Keeping*, 78.
187. Meharia, "History of Indian Caste," 520.
188. Raj, "Origins of Caste System," 10.
189. Encyclopedic references to caste and *jatis* note that there may be as many as 250 castes and more than 3000 subcastes or *jatis*. See Madan and Editors, "Caste."
190. Deshpande, "History," 16.
191. Meharia, "History of Indian Caste," 519.
192. Lower caste members were not allowed to share the same water source, eat at the same restaurants, or even share common space at public events such as movies, concerts, or festivals.
193. Martin, "Suraj's Shadow."
194. Meharia, "History of Indian Caste," 523.
195. "Refugee Review Tribunal," §3.
196. One can point to people like Mary, Priscilla, and perhaps Lydia or Dorcas, among others, who are identified as important women in the New Testament story, but nowhere does the text refer to calling as part of their story.
197. Hymowitz and Weissman, *History of Women*, 313.
198. Piper and Grudem, *Recovering*, 77. The text by Piper and Grudem describes and defends complementarianism as espoused by the Danvers Statement that summarizes the need for the Council on Biblical Manhood and Womanhood (CBMW) and serves as an overview of the core beliefs. This statement was prepared by several evangelical leaders at a CBMW meeting in Danvers, Massachusetts, in

Dec. 1987. It was first published in final form by the CBMW in Wheaton, Illinois, in Nov. 1988. See https://cbmw.org/about/danvers-statement/.

199. For example, complementarianism is now better represented by "broad complementarianism" vs. "narrow complementarianism," two slightly differing views of women's roles and responsibilities in the church, home, and society.

200. See, for example, the conferences organized by Christian Feminism Today (formerly known as The Evangelical and Ecumenical Women's Caucus).

201. See Grudem, *Evangelical Feminism*; Köstenberger and Schreiner, *Women in the Church*; Miller, *Beyond Authority and Submission*; and Byrd, *Recovering*.

202. Fraioli, *Joan of Arc*, 164.

203. Fraioli, *Joan of Arc*, 166.

204. Pitt, *Divine Callings*, 30.

205. Pitt, *Divine Callings*, 9.

206. Pitt, *Divine Callings*, 10.

207. Pitt, *Divine Callings*, 222.

208. See Rambo, *Understanding Religious Conversion*, and Snow and Machalek, "Sociology of Conversion."

209. Pitt, *Divine Callings*, 222.

210. Pitt, *Divine Callings*, 225.

211. Pitt, *Divine Callings*, 31.

212. Pitt, *Divine Callings*, 227.

213. Niebuhr, *Purpose of the Church*, 64.

214. Fraioli, *Joan of Arc*, 193.

215. Scholars of the medieval church cite Meister Eckhart (1260–1327/28), Johann Tauler (ca. 1300–1361), and Heinrich Suso (1295–1366) as Dominicans whose writings and teaching, spurred by mysticism, resulted in theological treatises in the vernacular that helped foster spiritual life among the laity who were unable to comprehend the Latin text of the Mass. Other women mystics of this era include Catherine of Siena (1347–1380), Margery Kempe (ca. 1373–after 1439), and Julian of Norwich (1342–after 1416).

216. Corbett and Fikkert, *When Helping Hurts*, 51.

217. Ekins, "What Americans Think," 6.

218. Oriakhi et al., "Influence of Poverty," 152.

219. Oriakhi et al., "Influence of Poverty," 152–53.

220. Oriakhi et al., "Influence of Poverty," 153–54.

221. Thernstrom, *Poverty and Progress*, 18.

222. Thernstrom, *Poverty and Progress*, 18.

223. Thernstrom, *Poverty and Progress*, 25.

Endnotes

224. Thernstrom, *Poverty and Progress*, 23.
225. Thernstrom, *Poverty and Progress*, 24.
226. Thernstrom, *Poverty and Progress*, 38.
227. Rogin, *Fathers and Children*, 6–7.
228. Rogin, *Fathers and Children*, 9.
229. Of note here is that some of the Cherokee had become lawyers, businessmen, and educators. Some were plantation owners and even owned slaves. They had made great strides already in assimilating to the White Man. Despite their efforts to defend themselves from inclusion in the Act, they were shocked to learn what their progress to adapt meant little in real terms. In the late 1830s, several thousand Cherokee were forcibly removed from their tribal lands in the Carolinas, Georgia, Tennessee, and Alabama and forced to relocate to territory that today is located in Oklahoma. Along the 700-plus-mile journey, which took nearly ten months, between 4000 and 8000 Cherokee out of the nearly 20,000 who made the trip lost their lives (Sturgis, *Trail of Tears*, 2).
230. Britannica, "Indian Removal Act," lines 16–30.
231. Perdue, "Legacy of Indian Removal," 11.
232. Perdue, "Legacy of Indian Removal," 12.
233. Perdue, "Legacy of Indian Removal," 3.
234. Churchill, *Kill the Indian*, 12.
235. A similar system of residential schools was established in Canada as a means of reeducating children of the First Nation peoples at approximately the same time.
236. Churchill, *Kill the Indian*, 13–14.
237. Churchill, *Kill the Indian*, 68.
238. Churchill, *Kill the Indian*, 70.
239. Muhammed et al., "Racial Wealth Snapshot," 2–3.
240. Muhammed et al., "Racial Wealth Snapshot," 3.
241. Churchill, *Kill the Indian*, 73.
242. Churchill, *Kill the Indian*, 73.
243. Tisby, *Color of Compromise*, 32–33.
244. Tisby, *Color of Compromise*, 33–34.
245. Tisby, *Color of Compromise*, 34–35.
246. Tisby, *Color of Compromise*, 35.
247. Tisby, *Color of Compromise*, 59.
248. Jones et al., "Fifty Years," 4.
249. Muhammad et al., "Racial Wealth Snapshot," 2–3.
250. Jones et al., "Fifty Years," 3.
251. Jones et al., "Fifty Years," 3–4.

252. Schermerhorn, "Why Racial Wealth Gap," lines 84–86.

253. Schermerhorn, "Why Racial Wealth Gap," lines 84–86.

254. Jones et al., "Fifty Years," 5.

255. "Connections among Poverty."

256. Nellis, "Color of Justice," 11.

257. Nellis, "Color of Justice," 11.

258. Roach, "Southern Baptists," lines 23–24.

259. David Cornelius identifies at least three factors that hindered what he refers to as "full participation of African Americans in international missions." These include slavery, which kept blacks from pursuing any sort of independent career interest; the disapproval by some white Christians of blacks serving alongside them in missions; and governmental actions, which hindered the visa process for blacks (Cornelius, "Historical Survey").

260. Roach, "Southern Baptists," lines 83–84.

261. See ch. 2, where survey data concerning calling and college students was presented and discussed.

262. Gugushvili, "Intergenerational Social Mobility," 422.

263. Gugushvili, "Intergenerational Social Mobility," 422.

264. Okoro et al., "Prevalence of Disabilities," 882.

265. Okoro et al., "Prevalence of Disabilities," 884–85.

266. "Information and Technical Assistance."

267. Deuel and John, *Disability in Mission*, 10.

268. Deuel and John, *Disability in Mission*, 21.

269. Whitehead, "Religion and Disability," 379–80.

270. Whitehead, "Religion and Disability," 379.

271. Hardwick, *Disability and the Church*, 53, 57.

272. Hardwick, *Disability and the Church*, 58.

273. Deuel and John, *Disability in Mission*, 3.

274. Lewis, "Clarifying," 155–56.

275. Deuel and John, *Disability in Mission*, 134–35.

276. Deuel and John, *Disability in Mission*, 135.

277. Deuel and John, *Disability in Mission*, 154.

278. Deuel and John, *Disability in Mission*, 154–55.

279. Deuel and John, *Disability in Mission*, 157.

280. Robert, *American Women in Mission*, 18.

281. Zikmund et al., *Clergy Women*, 96.

282. Niebuhr, *Purpose of the Church*, 64.

283. Dik and Duffy, "Calling and Vocation," 434.

284. Dik and Duffy, "Calling and Vocation," 427.

285. Legitimate work would exclude any type of slavery or servitude in which the worker was exploited or work that was deleterious to life in general (e.g., sale of illicit drugs).

286. Bellah et al., *Habits of the Heart*, 66.

287. Pitt, *Divine Callings*, 225.

288. Rambo, *Understanding Religious Conversion*, 138.

289. Castor, *Joan of Arc*, 64–65.

290. Castor, *Joan of Arc*, 4.

291. Castor, *Joan of Arc*, 91.

292. Castor, *Joan of Arc*, 92.

293. Castor, *Joan of Arc*, 96.

294. Castor, *Joan of Arc*, 118.

295. Castor, *Joan of Arc*, 126.

296. Castor, *Joan of Arc*, 179.

297. Fraioli, *Joan of Arc*, 50.

298. Fraioli, *Joan of Arc*, 34.

299. Fraioli, *Joan of Arc*, 56.

300. Fraioli, *Joan of Arc*, 96.

301. Kennedy, "Why Was Joan," 3.

302. Pitt, *Divine Callings*, 10.

303. Pitt, *Divine Callings*, 103.

304. Pitt, *Divine Callings*, 101.

305. Calvin, *Commentary on Gospel*, 268.

306. Niebuhr, *Purpose of the Church*, 64.

307. The New Testament actually identifies thirty-one reasons Christ came. See Beeke and Boekenstein, *Thirty-One Reasons*.

308. The following brief citations are taken from the student surveys on calling from those attending Christian colleges in the US.

309. One example of a cognitive issue of faith is the Great Commission. Christ's words in Matt 28:18–20 have been argued to apply to all believers (with the exception of some Hyper-Calvinists), regardless of a sense of calling. However, it is not uncommon to consider direct involvement in Great Commission activities conditional upon a call-experience. Those who hold to this conditional involvement argue that the cognitive issue of faith—that obedience to Christ means involvement in the Great Commission—does not apply to them unless they have an express calling experience that directs them to do so.

310. Kane, *Understanding Christian Mission*, 41.

311. Hay et al., *Worth Keeping*, 102.

312. Hay et al., *Worth Keeping*, 101.

313. Hay et al., *Worth Keeping*, 14.

314. Hay et al., *Worth Keeping*, 14. For OSC, attrition for preventable reasons is nearly two-thirds of the total per annum. For NSC, preventable attrition is nearly 90 peercent of the total.

315. Pitt, *Divine Callings*, 101.

316. Father Rey Pineda Avellaneda, phone call with author, Apr. 27, 2021.

317. Thompson, *A. B. Simpson*, 120–21.

318. Nienkirchen, *Man, Movement, and Mission*, 90.

319. Henry, *A. B. Simpson*, 136.

320. Nienkirchen, *Man, Movement, and Mission*, 91–95.

321. Sills, *Missionary Call*, 123.

322. Piper, *Roots of Endurance*, 92–93, 95.

323. Moule, *Charles Simeon*, 38.

324. Edwards, *Life and Diary*, 35.

325. Edwards, *Life and Diary*, 36.

326. Edwards, *Life and Diary*, 48.

327. Edwards, *Life and Diary*, 53.

328. Edwards, *Life and Diary*, 303.

329. According to Conforti, through the 1749 publication of *An Account of the Life of the Late Reverend Mr. David Brainerd* by Jonathan Edwards, "Edwards initiated the historical process that resulted, by the nineteenth century, in the canonization of Brainerd" (Conforti, "David Brainerd," 310.

330. Conforti notes several times that Brainerd's missionary success was at best limited (Conforti, "David Brainerd," 310–311, 312, 321). His status as a missionary hero really came following his death through the publication of his journals and its relationship to the ideal of disinterested benevolence towards the uncivilized Native Americans who were the focus of his ministry.

331. Edwards, *Life and Diary*, 85.

332. Edwards, *Life and Diary*, 87.

333. Edwards, *Life and Diary*, 91.

334. Burton, "Decades-Long Catholic Priest," lines 48–49, 78–84.

335. Dance, "Pastors Are Not," lines 15–16.

336. Maxwell, "Why Pastors Leave," line 19.

337. In the last several years, Bill Hybels, John Ortberg, Carl Lentz, Ravi Zacharias,

Bill Gothard, and Jerry Falwell Jr. have all been implicated in sexual scandal to the detriment of their ministry and legacy.

338. Earls, "Most Pastors Say," lines 16–18, 80–83.
339. Rey, Personal Communication, Apr. 27, 2021.
340. Duffy, "Spirituality," 52.
341. Duffy and Sedlacek, "Salience of Career Calling," 37.
342. Duffy, "Spirituality," 59.
343. See Piper, *Let the Nations Be Glad*, and Wright, *Mission of God*.
344. Carson, "Matthew," 599.
345. The church in this sense is not the institutional religious structure but the local collection of believers who, saved by faith and endowed with spiritual gifts, bear witness by their lives and words of the saving grace of Christ to "Jerusalem, Judea and to the uttermost parts of the earth" (Acts 1:8b).
346. Piper, "Sovereignty of God," lines 51–54.
347. Gowan, "Alien," in *Westminster Theological Wordbook*, 5–6.
348. Dyrness, "Heart," in *Themes*, 89–90.
349. Though the argument here is focused on individual men and women who are called, both the Jews as a people and the church are sometimes referred to as called. See Isa 19:25; 41:8; Hos 4:16; Acts 9:31; 12:15, among others, in which Israel or the church is referred to in the singular and assumed to act as or on behalf of the people of God.
350. It could be argued that Paul's repeated urgings to Timothy to fight the good fight (1 Tim 1:18), to conduct himself worthy (3:15), to not neglect the spiritual gift (4:14), to maintain these principles (5:21), and to guard what has been entrusted to him (6:20) were more than just pastoral advice from a well-intentioned father-figure but rather pointed exhortations to help Timothy avoid being disqualified from his calling. Whereas the effectual outcome of his calling would be the pastoral care of the church under persecution, Timothy's continued participation in this ministry was contingent on his faithful obedience and heed given to Paul's affectionate warnings.
351. Calling as referred to here is not the calling to salvation that is a biblical essential for a ministry role. The calling referred to here is some sort of supplemental divine encounter that endows an individual with a special directive or empowerment for ministry.
352. The Old Testament records nine different times in which David specifically prays for God's direction and wisdom: 1 Sam 23:1–3; 23:4–5; 23:10–11; 23:12–14; 30:8–9; 2 Sam 2:1–2; 5:17–21; 5:22–25; 21:1).
353. Adapted from Friesen and Maxson, *Decision Making*, 230.

Bibliography

Ahlstrom, Sydney E. *A Religious History of the American People*. New Haven, CT: Yale University Press, 1972.
Allen, Jason K. *Discerning Your Call to Ministry: How to Know for Sure and What to Do about It*. Chicago: Moody, 2016.
Andrews, Edward E. *Native Apostles: Black and Indian Missionaries in the British Atlantic World*. Cambridge, MA: Harvard University Press, 2013.
Armstrong, Karen, ed. *The English Mystics of the Fourteenth Century*. Translated by Karen Armstrong. London: Kyle Cathie, 1991.
Arthur, Michael B. "The Boundaryless Career: A New Perspective for Organizational Inquiry." *Journal of Organizational Behavior* 15 (1994) 295–306.
Ault, Melinda Jones, et al. "Congregational Participation and Supports for Children and Adults with Disabilities: Parent Perceptions." *Intellectual and Developmental Disabilities* 51, no. 1 (Feb. 1, 2013) 48–61.
Bacote, Vincent. "Beyond 'Faithful Presence': Abraham Kuyper's Legacy for Common Grace and Cultural Development." *Journal of Markets and Morality* 16, no. 1 (Spring 2013) 195–205.
Beach, Bert B. "Evangelism and the Ecumenical Movement." *Ministry: International Journal for Clergy* 65, no. 4 (Apr. 1992) 15–18.
Bedford, Olwen, and Kuang-Hui Yeh. "Evolution of the Conceptualization of Filial Piety in the Global Context: From Skin to Skeleton." *Frontiers in Psychology* 12 (Mar. 2021) 1–14.
Beeke, Joel R., and William Boekestein. *Thirty-One Reasons Why Christ Came: Meditations on the Incarnation*, Kentwood, MI: Reformation Heritage, 2020.
Bellah, Robert N., et al. *Habits of the Heart: Individualism and Commitment in American Life*. Los Angeles: University of California Press, 1985.
Bishop, David W. "Plessy v. Ferguson: A Reinterpretation." *Journal of Negro History* 62, no. 2 (Apr. 1977) 125–33.
Blackaby, Henry T., and Henry Brandt. *The Power of the Call*. Nashville: Broadman and Holman, 1997.
Bledstein, Burton J. *The Culture of Professionalism: The Middle Class and the Development of Higher Education in America*. New York: W. W. Norton, 1976.
Booth, William. "Go!" Salvation Factory, Nov. 1884. http://www.salvationfactory.org/wp-content/uploads/2015/12/Go.pdf.

Bowler, Kate. *The Preacher's Wife: The Precarious Power of Evangelical Women Celebrities.* Princeton, NJ: Princeton University Press, 2019.

Brantley, Pierce. *Calling: Awaken to the Purpose of Your Work.* Colorado Springs, CO: Cook, 2020.

Brewer, Elizabeth W. "Vocational Souljourn Paradigm: A Model of Adult Development to Express Spiritual Wellness as Meaning, Being, and Doing in Work and Life." *Counseling and Values* 45, no. 2 (2001) 83–93.

Bridges, Charles. *The Christian Ministry: With an Inquiry into the Causes of Its Inefficiency.* London: Banner of Truth Trust, 1967.

Britannica, Editors of Encyclopedia. "Indian Removal Act." *Encyclopedia Britannica*, Nov. 13, 2019. https://www.britannica.com/topic/Indian-Removal-Act.

Brown, Duane. "The Role of Work and Cultural Values in Occupational Choice, Satisfaction, and Success: A Theoretical Statement." *Journal of Counseling & Development* 80 (Winter 2002) 48–56.

Bulkely, Kelly, et al., eds. *Dreaming in Christianity and Islam: Culture, Conflict and Creativity.* New Brunswick, NJ: Rutgers University Press, 2009.

Bunderson, J. Stuart, and Jeffrey A. Thompson. "The Call of the Wild: Zookeepers, Callings and the Double-Edged Sword of Deeply Meaningful Work." *Administrative Science Quarterly* 54 (2009): 32–57.

Burkhart, Austin. "'*Avodah*': What It Means to Live a Seamless Life of Work, Worship, and Service." Institute for Faith, Work & Economics, Mar. 31, 2015. https://tifwe.org/avodah-a-life-of-work-worship-and-service/.

Burton, Tara Isabella. "The Decades-Long Catholic Priest Child Sex Abuse Crisis, Explained." Vox, Sept. 4, 2018. https://www.vox.com/2018/9/4/17767744/catholic-child-clerical-sex-abuse-priest-pope-francis-crisis-explained.

Buzzell, Sid S. "Proverbs." In *The Bible Knowledge Commentary: Old Testament*, edited by John F. Walvoord and Roy B. Zuck, 901–74. Wheaton, IL: Victor, 1989.

Byrd, Aimee. *Recovering from Biblical Manhood and Womanhood: How the Church Needs to Rediscover Her Purpose.* Grand Rapids: Zondervan, 2020.

Calvin, John. *Calvin: Institutes of the Christian Religion.* Edited by John T. McNeill. Vol. 1. Philadelphia: Westminster, 1960.

———. *Commentaries on the Book of the Prophet Jeremiah and the Lamentations.* Translated by John Owen. Vol. 3. Grand Rapids: Christian Ethereal Library, 1999. https://ccel.org/ccel/calvin/calcom19/calcom19.i.html.

———. *Commentaries on the Epistle of Paul to the Galatians and Ephesians.* Translated by William Pringle. Grand Rapids: Christian Ethereal Library, 1999. https://ccel.org/ccel/calvin/calcom41/calcom41.i.html.

———. *Commentaries on the Epistles to Timothy, Titus, and Philemon.* Translated by William Pringle. Grand Rapids: Christian Ethereal Library, 1999. https://ccel.org/ccel/calvin/calcom43/calcom43.i.html.

———. *Commentary on the Book of Psalms.* Translated by James Anderson. Vol. 1. Grand Rapids: Christian Classics Ethereal Library, 1999. https://ccel.org/ccel/calvin/calcom08/calcom08.i.html.

———. *Commentary on the Gospel According to John.* Translated by William Pringle. Vol. 2. Grand Rapids: Christian Ethereal Library, 1999. https://ccel.org/ccel/calvin/calcom35/calcom35.i.html.

———. *Commentary upon the Acts of the Apostles.* Translated by Henry Beveridge. Vol. 1. Grand Rapids: Christian Ethereal Library, 1999. https://ccel.org/ccel/calvin/calcom36/calcom36.i.html.

Cameron, J. E. M., ed. *The Cape Town Commitment: A Confession of Faith and a Call to Action*. Cambridge, UK: Tyndale, 2011.

Carey, William. "An Enquiry into the Obligation of Christians to Use Means for the Conversion of the Heathens." In *Perspectives on the World Christian Movement: A Reader*, edited by Ralph W. Winter and Steven C. Hawthorne, 312–18. 4th ed. Pasadena, CA: William Carey, 2009.

Carson, D. A. "Matthew." In Vol. 8 of *The Expositor's Bible Commentary*, edited by Tremper Longman III and David E. Garland, 23–670. Rev. ed. Grand Rapids: Zondervan, 1984.

Cassuto, Umberto. *A Commentary on the Book of Genesis: Part 1: From Adam to Noah*. Jerusalem: Magnes, 1989.

Castor, Helen. *Joan of Arc: A History*. New York: HarperCollins Publishers, 2015.

Christopherson, Richard W. "Calling and Career in Christian Ministry." *Review of Religious Research* 35, no. 3 (Mar. 1994) 219–37.

Churchill, Ward. *Kill the Indian, Save the Man: The Genocidal Impact of American Indian Residential Schools*. San Francisco: City Lights, 2004.

Clouse, Bonnidell, and Robert G. Clouse, eds. *Women in Ministry: Four Views*. Downers Grove, IL: InterVarsity, 1989.

Clowney, Edmund P. *Called to the Ministry*. Phillipsburg, NJ: Presbyterian and Reformed, 1976.

Collins, Randall. "Weber's Last Theory of Capitalism: A Systemization." *American Sociological Review* 45, no. 6 (Dec. 1980) 925–42.

Committee on Spiritual Formation of the United States Conference of Catholic Bishops. *Program of Priestly Formation*. 5th ed. Washington, DC: United States Conference of Catholic Bishops, 2006. https://www.usccb.org/upload/program-priestly-formation-fifth-edition.pdf.

Conforti, Joseph A. "David Brainerd and the Nineteenth Century Missionary Movement." *Journal of the Early Republic* 5, no. 3 (Autumn 1985) 309–29.

"Connections among Poverty, Incarceration and Inequality." Institute for Research on Poverty, May 2020. https://www.irp.wisc.edu/resource/connections-among-poverty-incarceration-and-inequality/.

Corbett, Steve, and Brian Fickert. *When Helping Hurts: How to Alleviate Poverty Without Hurting the Poor . . . and Yourself*. Chicago: Moody, 2012.

Cornelius, David. "A Historical Survey of African Americans in World Missions." In *Perspectives on the World Christian Movement: A Reader*, edited by Ralph W. Winter and Steven C. Hawthorne, 299–304. 4th ed. Pasadena, CA: William Carey, 2009.

Crouch, Andy. *Culture Making: Recovering Our Creative Calling*. Downers Grove, IL: InterVarsity, 2008.

Dalton, Jon C. "Career and Calling: Finding a Place for the Spirit in Work and Community." *New Directions for Student Services* 95 (Fall 2001) 17–25.

Dance, Mark. "Pastors Are Not Quitting in Droves." Lifeway Research, July 10, 2019. https://lifewayresearch.com/2019/07/10/pastors-are-not-quitting-in-droves-2/.

Davidson, James C., and David P. Caddell. "Religion and the Meaning of Work." *Journal for the Scientific Study of Religion* 33, no. 2 (1994) 135–47.

Deshpande, Manali S. "History of the Indian Caste System and Its Impact on India Today." Senior project, California Polytechnic State University, San Luis Obispo, 2010. https://digitalcommons.calpoly.edu/cgi/viewcontent.cgi?article=1043&context=socssp.

Deuel, David C., and Nathan G. John. *Disability in Mission: The Church's Hidden Treasure*. Peabody, MA: Hendrickson, 2019.

Dewar, Francis. *Called or Collared? An Alternative Approach to Vocation*. London: SPCK, 1991.

Dik, Bryan J., and Ryan D. Duffy. "Calling and Vocation at Work: Definitions and Prospects for Research and Practice." *Counseling Psychologist* 37 (2009) 424–50.

Donovan, Keith, and Ruth Myors. "Reflections on Attrition in Career Missionaries: A Generational Perspective into the Future." In *Too Valuable to Lose: Exploring the Causes and Cures of Missionary Attrition*, edited by William D. Taylor, 41–74. Pasadena, CA: William Carey, 1997.

Duffy, Ryan D. "Spirituality, Religion, and Career Development: Current Status and Future Directions." *Career Development Quarterly* 55 (Sept. 2006) 52–63.

Duffy, Ryan D., and William E. Sedlacek. "The Presence of and Search for a Calling: Connections to Career Development." *Journal of Vocational Behavior* 70 (2007) 590–601.

———. "The Salience of a Career Calling among College Students: Exploring Group Differences and Links to Religiousness, Life Meaning, and Life Satisfaction." *Career Development Quarterly* 59 (Sept. 2010) 27–41.

Dyrness, William. *Themes in Old Testament Theology*. Downer's Grove: IVP Academic, 1977.

Earls, Aaron. "Most Pastors Say Sexually Abusive Ministers Should Step Down Permanently." Lifeway Research, June 22, 2021. https://lifewayresearch.com/2021/06/22/most-pastors-say-sexually-abusive-ministers-should-step-down-permanently/.

Eastwood, Cyril. *The Priesthood of All Believers: An Examination of the Doctrine from the Reformation to the Present Day*. London: Epworth, 1960.

Edwards, Jonathon. *The Life and Diary of David Brainerd: With Notes and Reflections*. N.p.: Readaclassic, 2010.

Ekins, Emily. "What Americans Think About Poverty, Wealth and Work: Findings from the Cato Institute 2019 Welfare, Work, and Wealth National Survey." Cato Institute, Sept. 24, 2019. https://www.cato.org/publications/survey-reports/what-americans-think-about-poverty-wealth-work#downloads.

Ellul, Jacques. "Work and Calling." *Katallagete* 4 (Fall/Winter 1972) 8–16.

English, John C. "'Dear Sister': John Wesley and the Women of Early Methodism." *Methodist History* 33, no. 1 (Oct. 1994) 26–33.

Erum, Humaira, et al. "The Calling of Employees and Work Engagement: The Role of Flourishing at Work." *Business, Management and Education* 18 (2020) 14–32.

Esler, Philip F., ed. *The Early Christian World*. 2 vols. London: Routledge, 2000.

Farnham, Suzanne G., et al. *Listening Hearts: Discerning God's Call in Community*. Harrisburg, PA: Morehouse, 1991.

Flick, Alexander Clarence. *The Decline of the Medieval Church*. 2 vols. New York: Burt Franklin, 1967.

Fraioli, Deborah A. *Joan of Arc: The Early Debate*. Woodbridge, UK: Boydell, 2000.

Friesen, Garry, and J. Robin Maxson. *Decision Making and the Will of God: A Biblical Alternative to the Traditional View*. Portland: Multnomah, 1980.

Froehlich, Karlfried. "Luther on Vocation." *Lutheran Quarterly* 13 (1999) 195–207.

Goffman, Erving. *The Presentation of Self in Everyday Life*. Garden City, NY: Doubleday, 1959.

Gottfried, Robert S. *The Black Death: Natural and Human Disaster in Medieval Europe*. New York: Free Press, 1983.

Gowan, Donald E., ed. *The Westminster Theological Wordbook of the Bible*. Louisville: Westminster John Knox, 2003.

Grudem, Wayne. *Evangelical Feminism and Biblical Truth: An Analysis of More Than One Hundred Disputed Questions*. Wheaton, IL: Crossway, 2012.

Gugushvili, Alexi. "Intergenerational Social Mobility and Popular Explanations of Poverty: A Comparative Perspective." *Social Justice Research* 29 (2016) 402–28.

Guinness, Os. *The Call: Finding and Fulfilling the Central Purpose of Your Life*. Nashville: Word, 1998.

Habel, Norman. "The Form and Significance of the Call Narratives." *Zeitschrift für die Alttestamentliche Wissenschaft* 77, no. 3 (1965) 297–323.

Hale, Thomas. *On Being a Missionary*. Pasadena, CA: William Carey Library, 1995.

Hall, Douglas T., and Dawn E. Chandler. "Psychological Success: When the Career Is a Calling." *Journal of Organizational Behavior* 26 (2005) 155–76.

Hardwick, Lamar. *Disability and the Church: A Vision for Diversity and Inclusion*. Downers Grove, IL: InterVarsity, 2021.

Hardy, Lee. *The Fabric of This World: Inquiries into Calling, Career Choice, and the Design of Human Work*. Grand Rapids: Eerdmans, 1999.

Harvey, Dave. *Am I Called? The Summons to Pastoral Ministry*. Wheaton, IL: CrossWay, 2012.

Hassey, Janette. "A Brief History of Christian Feminism." *Transformation* 6, no. 2 (1989) 1–5.

Hay, Rob, et al., eds. *Worth Keeping: Global Perspectives on Best Practices in Missionary Retention*. Pasadena, CA: William Carey, 2007.

Heilbroner, Robert. *The Making of Economic Society*. 11th ed. Englewood Cliffs, NJ: Prentice Hall, 2001.

Helmer, Christine. "The Common Priesthood: Luther's Enduring Challenge." In *Remembering the Reformation: Martin Luther and Catholic Theology*, edited by Declan Marmion et al., 211–33. Minneapolis: Augsburg Fortress, 2017.

Henry, Daryn. *A. B. Simpson and the Making of Modern Evangelicalism*. Montreal: McGill-Queen's University Press, 2019.

Hernandez, Esperanza F., et al. "Hearing the Call: A Phenomenological Study of Religion in Career Choice." *Journal of Career Development* 38, no. 1 (2011) 62–88.

Ho, David Yau-Fai. "Filial Piety, Authoritarian Moralism and Cognitive Conservatism in Chinese Societies." *Genetic, Social and General Psychology Monographs* 120, no. 3 (1994) 349–65.

Hoge, Dean R., and Jacqueline E. Wenger. *Pastors in Transition: Why Clergy Leave Local Church Ministry*. Grand Rapids: Eerdmans, 2005.

Hung, Vanessa. "Filial Piety and Missionary Calling." In *Worth Keeping: Global Perspectives on Best Practices in Missionary Retention*, edited by Rob Hay et al., 82–83. Pasadena, CA: William Carey, 2007.

Hunt, Mary E. "The Evolution and Revolution of Feminist Ministry: A U.S. Catholic Perspective." *Journal for the Study of Religion* 26, no. 2 (2013) 75–87.

Hussey, Ian. "The Soteriological Use of 'Call' in the New Testament: An Undervalued Category?" *Biblical Theology Journal* 46, no. 3 (2016) 133–43.

Hymowitz, Carol, and Michaele Weissman. *A History of Women in America; From Founding Mothers to Feminists—How Women Shaped the Life and Culture of America*. New York: Bantam, 1978.

"Information and Technical Assistance on the Americans with Disabilities Act." ADA, n.d. https://www.ada.gov/ada_title_I.htm.

Jensen, Eric. *Teaching with Poverty in Mind: What Being Poor Does to Kids' Brains and What Can Be Done About It*. Alexandria, VA: Association for Supervision and Curriculum Development, 2009.

John Paul II, Pope. "Pastores Dabo Vobis." Vatican, Mar. 25, 1992. https://www.vatican.va/content/john-paul-ii/en/apost_exhortations/documents/hf_jp-ii_exh_25031992_pastores-dabo-vobis.html.

Johnston, Jerome Richard. "An Exploration of Rates and Causes of Attrition among Protestant Evangelical Clergy in the United States." DMin diss., Acadia University, 2012.

Jones, Janelle, et al. "Fifty Years after the Kerner Commission." Economic Policy Institute, February 26, 2018. https://www.epi.org/publication/50-years-after-the-kerner-commission/.

Jujing, Gu. *The Twenty-Four Paragons of Filial Piety*. Rice University. https://www.ruf.rice.edu/~asia/24ParagonsFilialPiety.html.

Kane, J. Herbert. *Understanding Christian Mission*. Grand Rapids: Baker, 1974.

Kennedy, Lesley. "Why Was Joan of Arc Burned at the Stake?" History, April 16, 2019, updated May 30, 2019. https://www.history.com/news/joan-arc-burned-stake.

Kinnaman, David, et al. "Almost Half of Practicing Christian Millennials Say Evangelism Is Wrong." Barna, Feb. 5, 2019. https://www.barna.com/research/millennials-oppose-evangelism/.

Klein, William W. "Paul's Use of Kalein: A Proposal." *Journal of the Evangelical Theological Society* 27, no. 1 (Mar. 1984) 53–64.

Kolmer, Elizabeth. "Catholic Women Religious and Women's History: A Survey of the Literature." *American Quarterly*, 30, no. 5 (Winter 1978) 639–51.

Köstenberger, Andreas J., and Thomas R. Schreiner, eds. *Women in the Church: An Interpretation and Application of 1 Timothy 2:9–15*. 3rd ed. Wheaton, IL: Crossway, 2016.

Kraft, Marguerite, and Meg Crossman. "Women in Mission." In *Perspectives on the World Christian Movement: A Reader*, edited by Ralph W. Winter and Steven C. Hawthorne, 294–98. 4th ed. Pasadena, CA: William Carey, 2009.

Kroll, Woodrow. *The Vanishing Ministry in the Twenty-First Century: Calling a New Generation to Lifetime Service*. Grand Rapids: Kregel, 2002.

Laughlin, Tabor. *China's Ambassadors of Christ to the Nations: A Groundbreaking Survey*. Evangelical Missionary Society 6. Eugene, OR: Wipf & Stock, 2020.

Lewis, R. W. "Clarifying the Remaining Frontier Mission Task." *International Journal of Frontier Missiology* 35, no. 4 (Winter 2018) 154–68.

Luther, Martin. *The Babylonian Captivity of the Church 1520*. Edited by Erik H. Herrmann. Minneapolis: Fortress, 2016.

———. *Church and Ministry I*. Edited by Ed Gritsch. Vol. 39 of *Luther's Works*. Philadelphia: Fortress, 1970.

———. *Church and Ministry II*. Edited by Conrad Bergendoff and Helmut T. Lehmann. Vol. 40 of *Luther's Works*. Philadelphia: Fortress, 1975.

———. *Church and Ministry III*. Edited by Ed Gritsch. Vol. 41 of *Luther's Works*. Philadelphia: Fortress, 1966.

———. "An Open Letter to the Christian Nobility Concerning the Reform of the Christian Estate, 1520." Translated by C. M. Jacobs. Project Wittenberg. http://www.projectwittenberg.org/pub/resources/text/wittenberg/luther/web/nblty-01.html.

———. *Word and Sacrament I*. Edited by E. Theodore Bachmann and Helmut T. Lehmann. Vol. 35 of *Luther's Works*. Philadelphia: Fortress, 1976.
Madan, T. N., and Editors of Encyclopedia Britannica. "Caste." *Encyclopedia Britannica*, Feb. 14, 2019. https://www.britannica.com/topic/caste-social-differentiation.
Martin, Phillip. "Suraj's Shadow: Wherever He Goes, His Caste Follows—Even in America." *WGBH*, Feb. 25, 2019. https://www.wgbh.org/news/international-news/2019/02/25/surajs-shadow-wherever-he-goes-his-caste-follows-even-in-america.
Massey, Douglas S. "The Legacy of the 1968 Fair Housing Act." *Sociological Forum* 30, S1 (June 2015), 571–88.
Maxwell, Julie. "Why Pastors Leave the Ministry." Shepherds Watchmen, Aug. 11, 2019. https://shepherdswatchmen.com/browse-all-posts/why-pastors-leave-the-ministry/.
McKnight, Scot. *One Life: Jesus Calls, We Follow*. Grand Rapids: Zondervan, 2010.
McNeill, William H. *Plagues and Peoples*. Garden City, NY: Doubleday, 1976.
Meagher, Gerard. "The Prophetic Call Narrative." *Irish Theological Quarterly* 39, no. 2 (Apr. 1972) 162–77.
Meharia, Akshat. "History of Indian Caste System and Its Prevalence Post-Independence." *International Journal of Research and Analytical Reviews* 7, no. 2 (Apr. 2020) 519–25.
Metaxas, Eric. *Martin Luther: The Man Who Rediscovered God and Changed the World*. New York: Viking Penguin, 2017.
Miller, Rachel Green. *Beyond Authority and Submission: Women and Men in Marriage, Church, and Society*. Phillipsburg, NJ: P & R, 2019.
Mohler, R. Albert, Jr., et al. *The Call to Ministry*. Louisville: SBTS, 2013.
Mokyr, Joel. "Progress, Useful Knowledge and the Origins of the Industrial Revolution." In *Institutions, Innovations and Industrialization: Essays in Economic History and Development*, edited by Avner Greif et al., 33–67. Princeton, NJ: Princeton University Press, 2015.
Montover, Nathan. *Luther's Revolution: The Political Dimensions of Martin Luther's Universal Priesthood*. Princeton Theological 161. Eugene, OR: Pickwick, 2011.
Mott, Stephen Charles. *Biblical Ethics and Social Change*. Oxford, UK: Oxford University Press, 1982.
Moule, H. C . G. *Charles Simeon*. London: Metheun & Co., 1892.
Muhammad, Dedrick Asante, et al. "Racial Wealth Snapshot: American Indians/Native Americans." National Community Reinvestment Coalition, Nov. 18, 2019. https://ncrc.org/racial-wealth-snapshot-american-indians-native-americans/.
Myers, Bryant L. *Walking with the Poor: Principles and Practices of Transformational Development*. Maryknoll, NY: Orbis, 1999.
Naidu, Maheshvari, and Nokwanda Nzuza. "When God Beckons: Stories of the 'Call' in a Pentecostal Church." *Journal of Social Sciences* 36, no. 2 (2013) 153–63.
Nel, Malan, and Eric Scholtz. "Calling, Is There Anything Special about It?" *Theological Studies* 72, no. 4 (2016) 1–7.
Nellis, Ashley. "The Color of Justice: Racial and Ethnic Disparity in State Prisons." Sentencing Project, Oct. 13, 2021. https://www.sentencingproject.org/publications/color-of-justice-racial-and-ethnic-disparity-in-state-prisons/.
Niebuhr, H. Richard. *The Purpose of the Church and Its Ministry*. New York: Harper & Row, 1956.

Nienkirchen, Charles, ed. *The Man, the Movement, and the Mission: A Documentary History of the Christian & Missionary Alliance.* Vol. 1. Calgary: Canadian Theological Seminary, 1987.

Novak, Michael. *Business as a Calling: Work and the Examined Life.* New York: Free Press, 1996.

Okoro, Catherine A., et al. "Prevalence of Disabilities and Health Care Access by Disability Status and Type Among Adults—United States, 2016." Centers for Disease Control and Prevention, Aug. 17, 2018. https://www.cdc.gov/mmwr/volumes/67/wr/mm6732a3.htm.

Oriakhi, Unity, et al. "The Influence of Poverty on Students' Behavior and Academic Achievement." *Educational Research International* 2, no. 1 (Aug. 2013) 151–60.

Ott, Craig, et al. *Encountering Theology of Mission: Biblical Foundations, Historical Developments, and Contemporary Issues.* Grand Rapids: Baker, 2010.

Packer, J. I. *God's Plans for You.* Wheaton, IL: Crossway, 2001.

Pantel, Pauline Schmitt, ed. *From Ancient Goddesses to Christian Saints.* Vol. 1 of *A History of Women in the West.* Translated by Arthur Goldhammer. Cambridge, MA: Belknap, 1992.

Park, Jiyoung, et al. "Having a Calling on Board: Effects of Calling on Job Satisfaction and Job Performance among South Korean Newcomers." *Frontiers in Psychology* 10 (July 17, 2019) 1–12.

Pekerti, Andre A. "The Interdependent Family-Centric Career: Career Perspective of the Overseas Chinese in Indonesia." *Career Development Quarterly* 56 (June 2008) 362–77.

Penney, Russell L., ed. *Overcoming the World Missions Crisis: Thinking Strategically to Reach the World.* Grand Rapids: Kregel, 2001.

Perdue, Theda. "The Legacy of Indian Removal." *Journal of Southern History* 78, no. 1 (Feb. 2012) 3–36.

Peters, George W. *A Biblical Theology of Missions.* Chicago: Moody, 1972.

Pierce, Ronald W., and Rebecca Merrill Groothuis, eds. *Discovering Biblical Equality: Complementarity without Hierarchy.* Downers Grove, IL: IVP, 2012.

Piper, John. *Let the Nations Be Glad: The Supremacy of God in Missions.* 3rd ed. Grand Rapids: Baker, 2010.

———. *The Roots of Endurance: Invincible Perseverance in the Lives of John Newton, Charles Simeon, and William Wilberforce.* Wheaton, IL: Good News, 2002.

———. "The Sovereignty of God: 'I Will Accomplish All My Purpose.'" Desiring God, Nov. 3, 2012. https://www.desiringgod.org/messages/the-sovereignty-of-god-my-counsel-shall-stand-and-i-will-accomplish-all-my-purpose.

Piper, John, and Wayne Grudem, eds. *Recovering Biblical Manhood and Womanhood: A Response to Evangelical Feminism.* Wheaton, IL: Crossway, 2006.

Pitt, Richard N. *Divine Callings: Understanding the Call to Ministry in Black Pentecostalism.* New York: New York University Press, 2012.

Raj, Ebenezer Sunder. "The Origins of the Caste System." *Transformation* 2, no. 2 (1985) 10–14. http://www.jstor.org/stable/43052102.

Rambo, Lewis. *Understanding Religious Conversion.* New Haven, CT: Yale University Press, 1993.

Ramelli, Ilaria L. E. "Constantine: The Legal Recognition of Christianity and Its Antecedents." *Anuario de Historia de La Iglesia* 22 (2013) 65–82.

"Refugee Review Tribunal." Refworld, Oct. 27, 2006. https://www.refworld.org/cgi-bin/texis/vtx/rwmain?page=search&docid=4b6fe221d&skip=0&query=ind30815.

Roach, David. "Southern Baptists Have Only Thirteen African American Career Missionaries. What Will It Take to Mobilize More?" *Christianity Today*, Feb. 28, 2020. https://www.christianitytoday.com/news/2020/february/southern-baptist-imb-african-american-missionaries.html.

Robert, Dana Lee. *American Women in Mission: A Social History of Their Thought and Practice*. 4th ed. Macon: Mercer University Press, 2005.

Robertson, George W. *Am I Called?* Phillipsburg, NJ: P & R, 2013.

Rogin, Michael Paul. *Fathers and Children: Andrew Jackson and the Subjugation of the American Indian*. New Brunswick, NJ: Transaction, 2009.

Ross, Allen P. *Creation and Blessing: A Guide to the Study and Exposition of Genesis*. Grand Rapids: Baker, 1988.

Sailhamer, John. *Genesis*. Expositor's Bible Commentary. Grand Rapids: Zondervan, 2017.

Saunders, Linda. "A Feasibility Study to Develop a Missions Training Center to Recruit African-American Young Adults for Global Missions through Education and Training." Master's thesis, Liberty University School of Divinity, 2015.

Schermerhorn, Calvin. "Why the Racial Wealth Gap Persists, More Than 150 Years after Emancipation." *Washington Post*, June 19, 2019.

Secomb, Meredith Ann. "Hearing the Call of God: Toward a Theological Phenomenology of Vocation." PhD diss., Australian Catholic University, 2010.

Sills, M. David. *The Missionary Call: Finding Your Place in God's Plan for the World*. Chicago: Moody Publishers, 2008.

Singh, Indervir. "Social Norms and Occupational Choice: The Case of Caste System in India." *Indian Journal of Economics and Business* 11, no. 2 (2012) 431–54.

Smith, Gordon T. *Courage and Calling: Embracing Your God-given Potential*. Downer's Grove, IL: InterVarsity, 2011.

Snow, David A., and Richard Machalek. "The Sociology of Conversion." *Annual Review of Sociology* 10 (1984) 167–90.

Stohry, Hannah. "An Ethnographic Approach to Understanding Filial Piety's Influence on Korean Families Living in Thailand." Master's thesis, Miami University, 2013.

Stott, John R. W. *Christian Mission in the Modern World*. Downers Grove, IL: InterVarsity, 1975.

Sturgis, Amy H. *The Trail of Tears and Indian Removal*. Westport, CT: Greenwood, 2007.

Sun, Peizhen, et al. "Relations between Dual Filial Piety and Life Satisfaction: The Mediating Roles of Individuating Autonomy and Relating Autonomy." *Frontiers in Psychology* 10 (Nov. 29, 2019) 1–9.

Super, D. E. "A Life-Span, Life-Space Approach to Career Development." In *Career Choice and Development; Applying Contemporary Theories to Practice*, edited by Duane Brown and Linda Brooks, 197–261. 2nd ed. San Francisco: Jossey-Bass, 1990.

Sy, Jann Adriel, et al. "A Review of Decision-Making Models on End-of-Life Care in Singapore." *Clinical Case Reports and Reviews* 1, no. 8 (2015) 169–72.

Taylor, William D., ed. *Too Valuable to Lose: Exploring the Causes and Cures of Missionary Attrition*. Pasadena, CA: William Carey, 1997.

Teelucksingh, Jerome. *The Lost Gospel: Christianity and Blacks in North America*. Newcastle upon Tyne, UK: Cambridge Scholars, 2010.

Thernstrom, Stephan. *Poverty and Progress: Social Mobility in a Nineteenth Century City*. Boston: Joint Center for Urban Studies of the Massachusetts Institute of Technology and Harvard University, 1964.

Third Lausanne Congress. *The Cape Town Commitment: A Confession of Faith and a Call to Action*. Lausanne Movement, n.d. https://lausanne.org/wp-content/uploads/2021/10/The-Cape-Town-Commitment---Pages-20-09-2021.pdf.

Thompson, A. E. *A. B. Simpson: His Life and Work*. Harrisburg, PA: Christian, 1960.

Tisby, Jemar. *The Color of Compromise: The Truth about the American Church's Complicity in Racism*. Grand Rapids: Zondervan, 2019.

Tucker, Ruth. "Female Mission Strategists: A Historical and Contemporary Perspective." *Missiology: An International Review* 15, no. 1 (Jan. 1987) 73–89.

"Twenty-Twenty Ministry Report." SBC, 2020. https://www.sbc.net/resource-library/ministry-reports/2020-ministry-report/.

Van Engen, Charles E. *The State of Missiology Today: Global Innovations in Christian Witness*. Downer's Grove, IL: IVP, 2016.

Vogt, Peter. "'Everywhere at Home': The Eighteenth-Century Moravian Movement as a Transatlantic Religious Community." *Journal of Moravian History* 1 (2006) 7–29.

Weber, Max. *The Protestant Ethic and the Spirit of Capitalism*. Translated by Talcott Parsons. New York: Charles Scribner's Sons, 1958.

Weinrich, William. "Women in the History of the Church: Learned and Holy, but Not Pastors." In *Recovering Biblical Manhood and Womanhood: A Response to Evangelical Feminism*, edited by John Piper and Wayne Grudem, 263–79. Wheaton, IL: Crossway, 2006.

Whitehead, Andrew L. "Religion and Disability: Variation in Religious Service Attendance Rates for Children with Chronic Health Conditions." *Journal for the Scientific Study of Religion* 57, no. 2 (June 2018) 377–95.

Winter, Ralph W. "Three Missionary Eras and the Loss and Recovery of Kingdom Mission, 1800–2000." In *Perspectives on the World Christian Movement: A Reader*, edited by Ralph W. Winter and Steven C. Hawthorne, 263–78. 4th ed. Pasadena, CA: William Carey, 2009.

Wright, Christopher J. *The Mission of God: Unlocking the Bible's Grand Narrative*. Downer's Grove, IL: IVP, 2006.

Wrzesniewski, Amy, et al. "Jobs, Careers, and Callings: People's Relations to Their Work." *Journal of Research in Personality* 31 (1997) 21–33.

Yeagley, Rebekah May. "Why Native American Reservations Are the Most Poverty-Stricken Lands in America." FEE Stories, Nov. 9, 2020. https://fee.org/articles/why-native-american-reservations-are-the-most-poverty-stricken-lands-in-america/.

Yeago, David S. "'A Christian, Holy People': Martin Luther on Salvation and the Church." *Modern Theology* 13, no. 1 (Jan. 1997) 101–20.

Zachman, Randall C. *John Calvin as Teacher, Pastor and Theologian: The Shape of His Writings and Thought*. Grand Rapids: Baker, 2006.

Zentner, McLaurine H. "The Black Death and Its Impact on the Church and Popular Religion." Honors thesis, University of Mississippi, 2015.

Zeze, Willie S. D. "John Calvin on God's Calling: Service in the Church and the World." *Stellenbosch Theological Journal* 5, no. 3 (2019) 595–619.

Zikmund, Barbara Brown, et al. *Clergy Women: An Uphill Calling*. Louisville: Westminster John Knox, 1998.